First World War
and Army of Occupation
War Diary
France, Belgium and Germany

4 DIVISION
10 Infantry Brigade
Duke of Wellington's (West Riding Regiment)
2nd Battalion
1 January 1918 - 6 June 1919

WO95/1481/3

The Naval & Military Press Ltd
www.nmarchive.com
Published in association with The National Archives

Published by

The Naval & Military Press Ltd

Unit 10 Ridgewood Industrial Park,

Uckfield, East Sussex,

TN22 5QE England

Tel: +44 (0) 1825 749494

www.naval-military-press.com

www.nmarchive.com

This diary has been reprinted in facsimile from the original. Any imperfections are inevitably reproduced and the quality may fall short of modern type and cartographic standards.

© **Crown Copyright**
Images reproduced by permission of The National Archives, London, England, 2015.

Contents

Document type	Place/Title	Date From	Date To
Heading	4 Division 10 Inf Bde 2Bn Duke of Wellington Regt 1918 Jan-1919 Jun From 12 Bde 4 Div		
Heading	4th Division 2nd Battn Duke of Wellington Reg. Come From 12 Bde Feb. 1918 Jan To August 1918 June 1919		
War Diary	In The Line	01/01/1918	04/01/1918
War Diary	In Support	04/01/1918	07/01/1918
War Diary	In The Line	08/01/1918	11/01/1918
War Diary	Schrammbks	12/01/1918	14/01/1918
War Diary	Bois Des Boeufs	15/01/1918	19/01/1918
War Diary	Brown Line	20/01/1918	23/01/1918
War Diary	In The Line	24/01/1918	27/01/1918
War Diary	Bde Set (Fosse Cave)	28/01/1918	31/01/1918
Operation(al) Order(s)	2nd Bn Duke of Wellington's Regt Operation Order No. Z.49	02/01/1918	02/01/1918
Operation(al) Order(s)	2nd. Bn. Duke of Wellington's Regt. Operation Order No. Z.50	06/01/1918	06/01/1918
Operation(al) Order(s)	2nd. Bn. Duke of Wellington's Regt. Operation Order No. Z.51	10/01/1918	10/01/1918
Operation(al) Order(s)	2nd Bn Duke of Wellington's Regt. Operation Order No. 53.Z	14/01/1918	14/01/1918
Operation(al) Order(s)	2nd. Bn. Duke of Wellington's Regt. Operation Order No. Z.54	18/01/1918	18/01/1918
Miscellaneous	Mons Star	08/01/1918	08/01/1918
Operation(al) Order(s)	2nd. Bn Duke of Wellington's Regt. Operation Order No. Z.55	22/01/1918	22/01/1918
Operation(al) Order(s)	2nd. Bn Duke of Wellington's Regt. Operation Order No. Z.56	24/01/1918	24/01/1918
Operation(al) Order(s)	2nd. Bn Duke of Wellington's Regt. Operation Order No. Z.57	26/01/1918	26/01/1918
Heading	War Diary of 2nd Bn. Duke of Wellington's Regt. From 1st February 1918 To 28th February 1918 Volume IV		
War Diary	Bde Support Fosse Cave	01/02/1918	01/02/1918
War Diary	Left Sub Sector	02/02/1918	05/02/1918
War Diary	Schramm Barracks	06/02/1918	06/02/1918
War Diary	Arras	06/02/1918	06/02/1918
War Diary	Berneville	07/02/1918	10/02/1918
War Diary	Ecole Communale Arras	11/02/1918	28/02/1918
Operation(al) Order(s)	2nd Bn. Duke of Wellington's Regt. Operation Order No. Z. 58	31/01/1918	31/01/1918
Operation(al) Order(s)	2nd Bn. Duke of Wellington's Regt. Operation Order No. Z. 59	01/02/1918	01/02/1918
Operation(al) Order(s)	2nd Bn. Duke of Wellington's Regt. Operation Order No. Z. 60	01/02/1918	01/02/1918
Operation(al) Order(s)	2nd Bn. Duke of Wellington's Regt. Operation Order No. Z. 61	02/02/1918	02/02/1918
Operation(al) Order(s)	2nd Bn. Duke of Wellington's Regt. Operation Order No. Z. 62	04/02/1918	04/02/1918
Operation(al) Order(s)	2nd Bn. Duke of Wellington's Regt. Operation Order No. Z. 63	05/02/1918	05/02/1918

Type	Description	From	To
Operation(al) Order(s)	2nd Bn. Duke of Wellington's Regt. Operation Order No. Z. 64	09/02/1918	09/02/1918
Miscellaneous	12th Infantry Brigade No. C. 39/18	09/02/1918	09/02/1918
Miscellaneous	Preliminary Examination Of 5 Prisoners Of 139th I.R 24th Division (Saxon) Captured In A Raid On Strap Trench Between Bat And Badger Trenches, 2nd February 1918		
Heading	10th Inf. Bde. 4th Div. War Diary 2nd Battn. The Duke of Wellington's (West Riding Regiment) March 1918		
Heading	War Diary of 2nd Bn. Duke of Wellington's Regt. From 1st March 1918 To 31st March 1918 Volume		
War Diary	Ecole Communale Arras	01/03/1918	19/03/1918
War Diary	Trenches Rouex Sector	20/03/1918	25/03/1918
War Diary	Gordon Camp	26/03/1918	28/03/1918
War Diary	Army Line	28/03/1918	28/03/1918
War Diary	East of Battery Valley	29/03/1918	29/03/1918
War Diary	Army Line	30/03/1918	31/03/1918
Miscellaneous	2nd Duke of Wellingtons Regt.	29/03/1918	29/03/1918
Heading	10th Brigade 4th Division 2nd Battalion Duke of Wellington's (West Riding) Regt. April 1918		
Heading	War Diary of 2nd Bn. Duke of Wellington's Regt. From 1st April 1918 To 30th April 1918 Volume IV		
War Diary	Army Line (Pelves Lane to Arras-Douai Run)	01/04/1918	03/04/1918
War Diary	Intermediate Line	04/04/1918	05/04/1918
War Diary	Left Batt Sector	06/04/1918	08/04/1918
War Diary	Agnez Le Duisans	09/04/1918	10/04/1918
Miscellaneous	Under Heading 17	15/08/1930	15/08/1930
War Diary	Agnez Le Duisans	11/04/1918	12/04/1918
War Diary	l'Ecleme	13/04/1918	13/04/1918
War Diary	Lannoy	14/04/1918	14/04/1918
War Diary	Le Vertannoy	15/04/1918	15/04/1918
War Diary	Trenches in Vicinity of Pacout Wood	16/04/1918	16/04/1918
War Diary	Trenches On Canal Bank Near Hinges	17/04/1918	19/04/1918
War Diary	Cense La Valley	20/04/1918	20/04/1918
War Diary	Connehem	21/04/1918	24/04/1918
War Diary	Right Batt Sub. Sector Left Bde Sector	25/04/1918	30/04/1918
Operation(al) Order(s)	2nd Duke of Wellington's Regt Operation Order No.76	05/04/1918	05/04/1918
Operation(al) Order(s)	2nd Duke of Wellington's Regt Operation Order No.2	03/04/1918	03/04/1918
Operation(al) Order(s)	Operation Orders No.78 2nd Duke of Wellington's Regt	08/04/1918	08/04/1918
Miscellaneous	A.T.4	13/04/1918	13/04/1918
Miscellaneous	G.O.C 4th Division No.937 (G.O.)	18/04/1918	18/04/1918
Miscellaneous	4th Division No.G.S.208		
Miscellaneous	4th Division No.G.A.156		
Operation(al) Order(s)	2nd Duke of Wellington's Regt Operation Order No.76	05/04/1918	05/04/1918
Miscellaneous	Operation Order No 2nd Duke of Wellington's Regt	07/04/1918	07/04/1918
Operation(al) Order(s)	Operation Orders No.78 2nd Duke of Wellington's Regt	08/04/1918	08/04/1918
Operation(al) Order(s)	2nd Bn Duke of Wellington's Reg Warning Order No.1	23/04/1918	23/04/1918
Miscellaneous	A Form Messages And Signals		
Miscellaneous	Operation Order No.79 2nd Bn Duke of Wellington's Regt	19/04/1918	19/04/1918
Miscellaneous	Supplementary Press Communique	22/04/1918	22/04/1918
Operation(al) Order(s)	2nd Bn Duke of Wellington's Regt Operation Order No. 80	29/04/1918	29/04/1918
Heading	War Diary of 2nd Bn. The Duke of Wellingtons Regt. From 1st May 1918 To 31st May 1918 Volume		
War Diary	Left Bde Sector Right Battn Sub Sector	01/05/1918	02/05/1918

Type	Description	Start	End
War Diary	L'Ecleme	03/05/1918	06/05/1918
War Diary	Bellerive Bde Support	07/05/1918	08/05/1918
War Diary	Pacout Wood	09/05/1918	15/05/1918
War Diary	L'Ecleme Bde In Reserve	16/05/1918	18/05/1918
War Diary	Riez Du Vinage Area	20/05/1918	27/05/1918
War Diary	L'Ecleme	28/05/1918	31/05/1918
Operation(al) Order(s)	2nd Bn Duke of Wellingtons Regt Operation Order No. 83		
Operation(al) Order(s)	2nd Bn Duke of Wellingtons Regt Operation Order No. 81	02/05/1918	02/05/1918
Operation(al) Order(s)	2nd Bn Duke of Wellingtons Regt Operation Order No. 82	06/05/1918	06/05/1918
Operation(al) Order(s)	2nd Bn Duke of Wellingtons Regt Operation Order No. 84	15/05/1918	15/05/1918
Operation(al) Order(s)	2nd Bn Duke of Wellingtons Regt Operation Order No. 85	19/05/1918	19/05/1918
Miscellaneous	2nd Bn. Duke of Wellington's Regiment After Order To Operation Order No. 85	19/05/1918	19/05/1918
Operation(al) Order(s)	2nd Bn Duke of Wellington's Regt Operation Order No. 86	26/05/1918	26/05/1918
Heading	War Diary of 2nd Bn. The Duke of Wellingtons Regt. From 1st June 1918 To 30th June 1918 Volume		
War Diary	Bde In Reserve Eclene	01/06/1918	02/06/1918
War Diary	Centre Bn in Line Pacaut Wood	02/06/1918	13/06/1918
War Diary	Bde In Reserve Eclene	14/06/1918	18/06/1918
War Diary	In The Line Centre Battn Left Bde (Riez Du Vinage Sector)	20/06/1918	30/06/1918
Map	Map		
Operation(al) Order(s)	2nd Bn Duke of Wellington's Regiment Operation Order No. 87	03/02/1918	03/02/1918
Operation(al) Order(s)	2nd Bn Duke of Wellington's Regiment Operation Order No. 88	08/06/1918	08/06/1918
Operation(al) Order(s)	2nd Bn Duke of Wellington's Regiment Operation Order No. 88	13/06/1918	13/06/1918
Operation(al) Order(s)	2nd Bn Duke of Wellington's Regiment (Operation) Order No. 90	16/06/1918	16/06/1918
Operation(al) Order(s)	2nd Bn Duke of Wellington's Regiment (Operation) Order No. 91	19/06/1918	19/06/1918
Operation(al) Order(s)	2nd Bn Duke of Wellington's Regiment Operation Order No. 92	25/06/1918	25/06/1918
Heading	War Diary of 2nd Bn. The Duke of Wellingtons Regt. From 1st July 1918 To 31st July 1918		
War Diary	Centre Sub Sector Riez Du Vinage	01/07/1918	01/07/1918
War Diary	Rest Billets In L'Ecleme	02/07/1918	07/07/1918
War Diary	Centre Sub-Sector Pacaut Wood Sector	08/07/1918	19/07/1918
War Diary	Rest Billets In L'Ecleme	20/07/1918	27/07/1918
War Diary	Centre Sub-Sector Riez Du Vinage Sector	28/07/1918	31/07/1918
Operation(al) Order(s)	2nd Bn. Duke of Wellington's Regt. Operation Order No. 93	01/07/1918	01/07/1918
Operation(al) Order(s)	2nd Bn. Duke of Wellington's Regt. Operation Order No. 94	07/07/1918	07/07/1918
Operation(al) Order(s)	2nd Bn. Duke of Wellington's Regt. Operation Order No. 95	12/07/1918	12/07/1918
Operation(al) Order(s)	2nd Bn. Duke of Wellington's Regt. (Operation) Order No. 96	17/07/1918	17/07/1918
Miscellaneous	Report On Raid By 2nd Bn. Duke of Wellington's Regt.	18/07/1918	18/07/1918

Type	Description	Date From	Date To
Operation(al) Order(s)	2nd Bn. Duke of Wellington's Regt. (Operation) Order No.97	20/07/1918	20/07/1918
Operation(al) Order(s)	2nd Bn. Duke of Wellington's Regt. (Operation) Order No.98	27/07/1918	27/07/1918
Heading	War Diary of 2nd Bn. The Duke of Wellingtons Regt. From 1st Aug 1918 To 31st Aug. 1918		
War Diary	Centre Sub-Sector Riez Du Vinage Sector	01/08/1918	09/08/1918
War Diary	Chateau Du Quesnoy	10/08/1918	14/08/1918
War Diary	Right Support Position Pacaut Sector	15/08/1918	23/08/1918
War Diary	Lozinghem	24/08/1918	24/08/1918
War Diary	Maisnil St Pol.	25/08/1918	26/08/1918
War Diary	Villers Au Bois	27/08/1918	29/08/1918
War Diary	Haucourt	30/08/1918	31/08/1918
Miscellaneous	2nd Bn. Duke of Wellington's Regt. (Operation) Order No.	27/08/1918	27/08/1918
Operation(al) Order(s)	2nd Bn. Duke of Wellington's Regt. (Operation) Order No.100	09/08/1918	09/08/1918
Operation(al) Order(s)	2nd Bn. Duke of Wellington's Regt. (Operation) Order No.101	11/08/1918	11/08/1918
Operation(al) Order(s)	2nd Bn. Duke of Wellington's Regt. (Operation) Order No.102	14/08/1918	14/08/1918
Operation(al) Order(s)	2nd Bn. Duke of Wellington's Regt. Operation Order No. 103	10/08/1918	10/08/1918
Operation(al) Order(s)	2nd Bn. Duke of Wellington's Regt. Operation Order No. 104	22/08/1918	22/08/1918
Operation(al) Order(s)	2nd Bn. Duke of Wellington's Regt. (Operation) Order No. 105	23/08/1918	23/08/1918
Operation(al) Order(s)	2nd Bn. Duke of Wellington's Regt. (Operation) Order No. 106	24/08/1918	24/08/1918
Operation(al) Order(s)	2nd Bn. Duke of Wellington's Regiment Operation Order No. 107	26/08/1918	26/08/1918
Operation(al) Order(s)	2nd Bn. Duke of Wellington's Regt. Warning Order	27/08/1918	27/08/1918
Operation(al) Order(s)	2nd Bn. Duke of Wellington's Regiment Operation Order No. 108	28/08/1918	28/08/1918
Operation(al) Order(s)	2nd Bn. Duke of Wellington's Regt. Warning Order No. 1	20/08/1918	20/08/1918
Operation(al) Order(s)	2nd Bn. Duke of Wellington's Regiment Operation Order No. 109	30/08/1918	30/08/1918
Heading	War Diary of 2nd Bn. Duke of Wellington's Regt. From Sept 1st 1918 To Sept. 30th 1918 Volume		
Heading	4th Division 2nd Battn Duke of Wellington's Reg. Came From 12th Bde Feb 1918 Sep-1919 Jun		
War Diary	Haucourt	01/09/1918	03/09/1918
War Diary	Averdoingt	04/09/1918	17/09/1918
War Diary	Lecluse	18/09/1918	18/09/1918
Operation(al) Order(s)	2nd Bn. Duke of Wellington's Regiment (Operation) Order No. 111	01/09/1918	01/09/1918
War Diary	Lecluse	19/09/1918	25/09/1918
War Diary	St. Servins Fm.	26/09/1918	29/09/1918
War Diary	Orange Hill	30/09/1918	30/09/1918
Miscellaneous	2nd Bn. Duke of Wellington's Regt. (Operation) Order No.	01/09/1918	01/09/1918
Miscellaneous	2nd Bn. Duke of Wellington's Regt. Congratulatory Messages	02/09/1918	02/09/1918
Miscellaneous	2nd Bn. Duke of Wellington's Regt. (Operation) Order No.	02/09/1918	02/09/1918

Type	Description	Start	End
Miscellaneous	2nd Bn. Duke of Wellington's Regt. (Operation) Order No.	03/09/1918	03/09/1918
Miscellaneous	2nd Bn. Duke of Wellington's Regt. (Operation) Order No.	04/09/1918	04/09/1918
Operation(al) Order(s)	2nd Bn. Duke of Wellington's Regt. (Operation) Order No. 116	18/09/1918	18/09/1918
Operation(al) Order(s)	2nd Bn. Duke of Wellington's Regt. (Operation) Order No. 117	23/09/1918	23/09/1918
Operation(al) Order(s)	2nd Bn. Duke of Wellington's Regt. (Operation) Order No. 118	29/09/1918	29/09/1918
Operation(al) Order(s)	2nd Bn. Duke of Wellington's Regt. (Operation) Order No. 119	30/09/1918	30/09/1918
War Diary	Orange Hill	01/10/1918	05/10/1918
War Diary	Wanquentin	06/10/1918	10/10/1918
War Diary	Cambrai	11/10/1918	11/10/1918
War Diary	St Olle	12/10/1918	12/10/1918
War Diary	Naves	13/10/1918	17/10/1918
War Diary	Saultzoir	18/10/1918	25/10/1918
War Diary	Verchain	20/10/1918	24/10/1918
War Diary	Mur Copse	24/10/1918	24/10/1918
War Diary	Verchain-Querenaing	24/10/1918	25/10/1918
War Diary	Verchain	26/10/1918	31/10/1918
Operation(al) Order(s)	2nd Bn. Duke of Wellington's Regt. Warning Order No. 1	04/10/1918	04/10/1918
Operation(al) Order(s)	2nd Bn. Duke of Wellington's Regt. (Operation) Order No. 120	04/10/1918	04/10/1918
Operation(al) Order(s)	2nd Bn. Duke of Wellington's Regiment Operation Order No. 121	11/10/1918	11/10/1918
Operation(al) Order(s)	2nd Bn. Duke of Wellington's Regiment Warning Order No. 1	10/10/1918	10/10/1918
Operation(al) Order(s)	2nd Bn. Duke of Wellington's Regiment. Operation Order No. 122	12/10/1918	12/10/1918
Operation(al) Order(s)	2nd Bn. Duke of Wellington's Regiment. Operation Order No. 123	17/10/1918	17/10/1918
Miscellaneous	2nd Bn. Duke of Wellington's Regiment Amendment To O.O. 123		
Operation(al) Order(s)	2nd Bn. Duke of Wellington's Regiment Operation Order No. 184	10/10/1918	10/10/1918
Operation(al) Order(s)	2nd Bn. Duke of Wellington's Regiment Operation Order No. 185	21/10/1918	21/10/1918
Operation(al) Order(s)	2nd Bn. Duke of Wellington's Regiment Operation Order No. 186	23/10/1918	23/10/1918
Map	Identification Trace For Use With Artillery Maps		
Map	Map		
Map	Air Reconnaissance Of Enemy Trenches		
Heading	War Diary of 2nd Bn. Duke of Wellington's Regt. From 1st Nov 1918 To 30th Nov 1918		
War Diary	Verchain	01/11/1918	02/11/1918
War Diary	Saulzoir	03/11/1918	06/11/1918
War Diary	Preseau	07/11/1918	18/11/1918
War Diary	Valenciennes	19/11/1918	30/11/1918
Operation(al) Order(s)	2nd Bn. Duke of Wellington's Regiment (Provisional) Order No. 1	01/11/1918	01/11/1918
Miscellaneous	2nd Bn. Duke of Wellington's Regiment (Warning) Order No. 1	18/11/1918	18/11/1918

Miscellaneous	2nd Bn. Duke of Wellington's Regiment (Warning) Order No. 1	01/11/1918	01/11/1918
Miscellaneous	2nd Bn. Duke of Wellington's Regt. K. 432	01/11/1918	01/11/1918
Operation(al) Order(s)	2nd Bn. Duke of Wellington's Regiment (Operation) Order No. 128	02/11/1918	02/11/1918
Operation(al) Order(s)	2nd Bn. Duke of Wellington's Regiment (Operation) Order No. 129	02/11/1918	02/11/1918
Operation(al) Order(s)	2nd Bn. Duke of Wellington's Regiment (Operation) Order No. 130	06/11/1918	06/11/1918
Operation(al) Order(s)	2nd Bn. Duke of Wellington's Regiment (Operation) Order No. 131	18/11/1918	18/11/1918
Heading	War Diary of 2nd Bn. Duke of Wellington's Regt. From December 1st 1918 To December 31st 1918 Volume		
War Diary	Valenciennes	01/12/1918	05/01/1919
War Diary	Binche	06/01/1919	31/01/1919
Operation(al) Order(s)	2nd Bn. Duke of Wellington's Regiment (Operation) Order No. 1	04/01/1919	04/01/1919
Heading	War Diary of 2nd Bn. Duke of Wellington's Regt. From February 1st 1919 To February 28th 1919 Volume		
War Diary	Binche	01/02/1919	28/02/1919
Miscellaneous	No 2 Sub Sect Record Office British Troops in France & Flanders Wimereux	16/06/1919	16/06/1919
War Diary	Binche (Belgium)	01/06/1919	06/06/1919

4 DIVISION

10 INF BDE

2 BN DUKE OF WELLINGTON REGT

1918 JAN — 1919 JAN

FROM 12 BDE 4 DIV

4th Division

2nd Battn Duke of Wellington Reg.

came from 12 Bde Feb.

1916 JAN ~~Feb~~. To August

1918

June 1919

WAR DIARY or INTELLIGENCE SUMMARY.

Army Form C. 2118.

2 W Riding

(Erase heading not required.)

Place	Date	Hour	Summary of Events and Information	Remarks and references to Appendices
IN THE LINE	JANUARY 1918 1st		Batn holding the line. The trench quietly quiet. Nothing to Report	
	2		" "	
	3		Bn relieved from the front by the 9/ESSEX REGT. and immediately afterwards relieved the 2/RAME FUS who were temporarily in dugouts in ORCHARD PGT. (see O.O. 7 app) "I"	
			OURS SWITCH & MUSKET T.R. inclusive STRONG POINTS	
	4		MAT P.R.2 MARKER Taking over the command of the Battalion	
To Dugouts			Nothing to report	
	5		CAPT. A. GRIMIE R.A.M.C	
	6		" "	
	7		Bn relieved the 9/ESSEX REGT in the line. The relief carried out successfully without casualties. 2/LT P.G. HENDERSON + 2/LT W. HKOY join Battn from 2/Bn B.M.M	A1
In the Line	8		Bn holding the line.	
	9		Nothing to report	
	10		Capt. A. Grimie proceeds to ETAPLES to take over the duties of Medical Officer at C. Camp at ETAPLES. Having been M.O. to this Bn	
			since 21-2-17	11/30

Army Form C. 2118.

WAR DIARY
or
INTELLIGENCE SUMMARY.
(Erase heading not required.)

Instructions regarding War Diaries and Intelligence Summaries are contained in F. S. Regs., Part II. and the Staff Manual respectively. Title pages will be prepared in manuscript.

Place	Date	Hour	Summary of Events and Information	Remarks and references to Appendices
	JAN 1918			
THE LINE	11TH		Bn relieved in the line by the 1st EAST LANCS REGT. Relief carried out successfully, on relief Bn moved into Billets at PUHIAMM BKS. The casualties throughout the tour: O.R. 1 killed 3 wounded. Officer Lieut. EDWARDS slightly wounded (on A warrenten)	'B' Coy
PUHIAMM BKS	12TH		Battalion resting: nothing to report.	
	13TH		Battalion on Full Firing Range at WAILLY. Maj. BERKELEY takes over duties of Commanding Officer. Major P.L.E. WALKER detailed to 10th Field AmB. 2/LT A. KING joins Battalion.	
	14TH			
BOIS-JES	15TH		Battalion relieves 2nd ESSEX REGT at BOIS DES BOEUFS camp. (Brigade Reserve)	C.1
BOEUFS	16TH		45 O.R. join from 4th Gen. Dept. Batt. Nothing to report.	
	17TH			
	18TH			

Army Form C. 2118.

WAR DIARY
or
INTELLIGENCE SUMMARY.
(Erase heading not required.)

Instructions regarding War Diaries and Intelligence Summaries are contained in F. S. Regs., Part II. and the Staff Manual respectively. Title pages will be prepared in manuscript.

Place	Date	Hour	Summary of Events and Information	Remarks and references to Appendices
BOIS DES ISOELFS	Jan 1918 19th		The Battⁿ relieved the HOUSEHOLD BATTⁿ at the BROWN LINE (Bois Rogevin) (Right Sector) The Battⁿ provided Working Parties for the C.R.E. at night	C. W
				W
			provided Working Parties for the C.R.E.	W
BROWN LINE	20		The Battⁿ provided Working Parties for C.R.E. during day & night	W
"	21		List of Officers, N.C.O.s & men eligible for the award of the 1914 Star	D. W
			Congratulatory message from B.G.C. for good work done. Working parties	W
			provided for C.R.E. as on previous days.	W
"	22		Working parties for C.R.E. Nothing to report	W
"	23		The Battⁿ relieved the 2nd ESSEX REGT in the LEFT BATTⁿ SECTOR Successful Relief Right Brigade	E
In the	24		Holding the line. Very quiet	W
LINE	25		Nothing to Report (Nos 3 & 4 Coys relieved Nos 1 & 2 Coys in FRONT LINE)	E
	26		Holding the line. A prisoner captured at 10am belongs to 149 Regt	F
	27		The Battⁿ relieved by the 2nd ESSEX REGT and proceeded to Bois Sutport (FOSSE COVE) Relief carried out successfully	G
BDE SPT (FOSSE COVE)	28		The Battⁿ provides working parties for C.R.E.	
"	29		"	Major HAINES returned from Gunnery Course
"	30		"	
"	31		"	Nothing to report

Maurice Worthington
Major Comdg

SECRET

2nd. Bn. Duke of Wellington's Regt. OPERATION ORDER. No. Z49.   Copy No. 1

1. INTENTION.

In the Field 2nd. January 1918.

The Battalion will be relieved in the line by The 2nd. Essex Regt. to-morrow, 3rd. inst. and will then relieve the 2nd. Lancashire Fusiliers in Support.

2. ORDER OF RELIEF.

```
A Coy. 2nd. Essex Regt. will relieve No. 1 Coy. Dukes in RIGHT FRONT.
B  "       "     "     "      "       "   "  2  "      "     "  LEFT FRONT.
C  "       "     "     "      "       "   "  3  "      "     "  RIGHT SUPPORT
D  "       "     "     "      "       "   "  4  "      "     "  LEFT     "
```

On completion of above relief, Companies will take over from the 2nd. Lanc. Fus. the Battalion in Support as follows :-

```
No. 4 Company  F.G. and H. STRONG POSTS.
No. 3    "     MUSKET TRENCH.
No. 2    "     CURB SWITCH RESERVE.
No. 1    "     ORCHARD RESERVE.
```

3. GUIDES.

O.C. No. 2 and 3 Companies will arrange to guide themselves.
Guides for No. 1 Company will be at the Junction of CURB SWITCH & MONCHY TRENCH.
Guides for No. 4 Company will report to Company Hd.Qrs. at 5 pm.

4. ADVANCE PARTY.

An advance party consisting of :-
2nd. Lieut. H.R.Moody and 1 N.C.O. 1 Signaller and 1 Guide per Company and Battalion Hd. Qrs. will report to Bn. HD. Qrs. 2nd. Lanc. Fus. at 1p.m.
The above party will report to 2nd. Lieut. H.R.Moody at Bn. Hd. Qrs. at 1p.m.
O.C. No.4 Coy. will detail 1 Officer to reconnoitre F.G. and H. Posts early to-morrow morning.
O.C.Companies will arrange to have 1 Guide per Platoon at the entrance of HAPPY VALLEY by 5 p.m. and guide in Platoons of the 2nd. Essex Regt.

5. LEWIS GUNS.

The Lewis Gun personnel and Observers will move off to their new positions in Support immediately their relief is complete.
O.C.Companies will detail 1 Lewis Gunner to be at Bn. Hd. Qrs. at ~~12p.m.~~ 12-45 p.m. to guide the Lewis Gun personnel of the 2nd. Essex Regt. in.

6. RELIEF COMPLETE.

Relief Complete will be reported by any sentence containing the word "Socks."

(Sd) W.S.Newroth Captain.
Adjt. 2nd. Bn. Duke of Wellington's Regt.

SECRET.

A1   Copy No.

2nd. Bn. Duke of Wellington's Regt. OPERATION ORDER. No. Z.50.
In the Field January 6th. 1918.

1. INTENTION.

The Battalion will relieve the 2nd. Essex Regt. in the LEFT SUB-SECTOR to-morrow. 7th. inst.

2. ORDER OF RELIEF.

No. 3 Company will relieve A Company Essex Regt. in the RIGHT FRONT.
" 4 " " " B " " " " " LEFT " .
" 1 " " " C " " " " " RIGHT SUPPORT.
" 2 " " " D " " " " " LEFT " .

SRONG POSTS F.G.and H. will not be vacated until the garrisons have been relieved by the incoming unit. They will be relieved by C.Coy. Essex Regt. No. 1 Company will move off at 8 a.m. less Lewis Gunners.

3. GUIDES.

Guides of the 2nd. Essex Regt. for No. 4 Company will report to the O.C. of each Strong Post at 9 a.m. Two guides for No. 1 Company will report to the Company Hd. Qrs. at 7 a.m.Two guides each for Nos. 2 & 3 Companies will report to Company Hd. Qrs. at 9 a.m.
Guides for Lewis Gunners (excepting No. 1 Company) will be at the Junction of LONE and MUSKET. at 9a.m.

4. LEWIS GUNS.

Lewis Gun personnel and Observers under J. Ward(Sgt.) will move off in time to meet guides from the 2nd. Essex Regt. at the Junction of LONE and MUSKET by 9 a.m. less Lewis Gunners and Observers of No. 1 Company.
The Lewis Gunners of No. 1 Company will report to the O.C. Company 2nd. Essex Regt.in MUSKET Trench. by 9 a.m.
The Lewis Gun Sergt. will arrange to hand over 32 magazines per gun and take over same No. on arrival in the line.

5. ROUTE and TIME.

No. 1 Company via CURB SWITCH at 8 a.m. to RIFLE SUPPORT.
" 3 " " " " " 10 a.m. " RIGHT FRONT.
" 4 " " MUSKET, LONE and SCABBARD after relieved to LEFT FRONT.
O.C. No. 2 Company will make his own arrangements,and move last in order to avoid congestion; moving not later than 10- 45a .m.

6. DOCUMENTS.

All documents and trench store lists will be handed over to incoming unit.

7. ADVANCE PARTY.

An advance party consisting of :-
2nd. Lieut. H.R.Moody, 1 N.C.O. 1 Signaller and 1 Runner per Company and Bn. Hd. Qrs. (less No. 1 Coy.) willreport to Hd. Qrs. 2nd. Essex Regt. at 9 a.m.
The above party to report to 2nd. Lieut. H.R.Moody at Bn. Hd. Qrs.8-30a.m.
No. 1 Company Advance Party reporting to No. 3 Company Hd.Qrs. Essex Regt. at 7-30 a.m. in MUSKET TRENCH.

8. INSPECTION.

O.C.Companies will detail 1 Officer per Company to inspect all latrines. O.C.Nos. 1&4 Coys. will detail 1 Officer per Coy. to inspect their cook-houses and render a certificate to Orderly Room on completion of relief that the latrines and cook-houses are left clann and in a sanitary condition.

9. RELIEF COMPLETE.

Relief complete will be reported by any sentence containing the word "LEAVE".

(Sd) W.S.Newroth. Capt.

2nd. Bn. Duke of Wellington's Regt. OPERATION ORDER. No. Z51.

SECRET.
In the Field. January 10th. 1918.

1. **INTENTION.**
The Battalion will be relieved in the line to-morrow, 11th. inst. by the 1st. E. Lancs. Regt.
On completion of relief the Battalion will proceed to ARRAS to be billeted there.

2. **ORDER OF RELIEF.**
Companies will be relieved in the order named:-
    C. Coy. E.Lancs. will relief No.3 Coy. RIGHT FRONT.
    D. "   "   "   "   " 1 "   RIFLE SUPPORT.
    A. "   "   "   "   " 4 "   LEFT FRONT.
    B. "   "   "   "   " 2 "   RESERVE.

On completion of relief Companies will move out as follows:-
Nos. 3 & 1 Coys. via CURB SWITCH N. CURB SWITCH RESERVE and ORANGE AVENUE.
 "   4 " 2 "   " LONE AVENUE.
Hd. Qrs. will follow in rear of No. 2 Company.
Out going Companies will give way to in-coming Companies in LONE AVENUE.
A distance of 200 yards between Platoons will be maintained.

3. **GUIDES.**
O.C.Coys. will detail 2 guides per company to be at Bn. Hd. Qrs. at 3-45 p.m. 2nd. Lieut. T.D.Stocks will be in charge of the guides and will be at the Junction of Sword Lane and CROMARTY TRENCH by 5 p.m.

4. **DOCUMENTS.**
All Documents, Maps etc., will be handed over also all information with regard to the enemy and detail of work in hand will be handed over, so that there may be no break in the continuty.

5. **SANITATION.**
O.C.Companies will each detail one Officer per Coy. to inspect all Latrines, Dug-Outs and Cubby-holes and render a certificate to Orderly Room by 4-30 p.m. that they are thoroughly clean and in a sanitary condition.

6. **TRANSPORT.**
The Transport Officer will arrange to have two Limbers in Happy Valley for the conveyance of Lewis Guns, etc., by 5 p.m. and the Mess Cart by 6 p.m.

7. **OFFICERS SERVANTS.**
All Officers servants who are being sent in advance will be at Bn. Hd. Qrs. and will be marched down by Sergt. W.Wild at 5-30 p.m.

8. **CHARGERS**
Chargers for Bn. Hd. Qrs. and No. 4&2 Coys. will come to Happy Valley if it is a clean night, otherwise they will remain near Bn. Hd. Qrs.
Chargers for Nos. 1 & 3 Coys. will remain at Bn. Hd. Qrs.

9. **RELIEF.**
Relief will be reported by any sentence containing the word "COLD".

10. **LEWIS GUNS.**
Lewis Gun Personnel will move off immediately on relief via LONE AVENUE under the senior Lewis Gun N.C.O. in each Coy. Sergt. Ward will, when the Lewis Guns have been loaded on the limbers, march the party to ARRAS.

(Sgd) W.S.Hewroth Capt.
Adjt. 2nd. Bn. Duke of Wellington's. Regt.

SECRET.   Copy No. 11
   2nd Bn. Duke of Wellington's Regt. OPERATION ORDER No. 53.Z.
   @@@

                                            In the Field, 14th January, 1918.

1. INTENTION.
       The Battalion will relieve the 2nd Essex Regt. at BOIS DES BOEUFS
   Camp tomorrow, 15th inst.

2. HOUR OF START.
       The Battalion will parade on the Battalion Parade Ground ready to
   move off at 10-15 a.m.

3. ORDER OF MARCH.
       Headquarters, Nos. 1. 2. 3. & 4. Companies.
       Intervals between Companies, 200 Yards.

4. DRESS.
       Marching Order.

5. ROUTE.
       ARRAS-CAMBRAI Road.

6. BILLETING PARTY.
       A Billeting Party consisting of :-
   2Lieut. G.W.Hanna, 4 C.Q.M.Sergts, and Sgt. J.Ward will report to the
   Orderly Room of the 2nd Essex Regt. at 8.30 a.m.
       Officers Commanding Companies will hand a certificate to the
   Adjutant on the Parade Ground that the Billets vacated by the Companies
   have been left clean and tidy.

7. TRANSPORT.
       The Transport Officer will arrange with the Q.M. for the conveyance
   of Stores and Blankets.
       Officers Kits will be stacked at the Q.M. Stores at 9 a.m.

8. WORK.
       2Lieut. J.W.Hughes will report to an R.E. Representative at the
   Junction of PICK AVENUE and FORK RESERVE at 12 noon tomorrow, to be shown
   tasks for night of 16/17th and following nights.

                                                    Captain & Adjt.
                                              2nd Bn Duke of Wellington's Regt.

         D I S T R I B U T I O N.

No. 1 C.O.   No. 2 Bn. H.Q.   Nos. 3 - 6 All Coys.   No. 7 Q.M.   No. 8 T.O.
No. 9 R.S.M.   Nos. 10 - 11 War Diary.   No. 12 File.   No. 13 Essex Regt.

SECRET.   Copy No. 4
         2nd Bn. Duke of Wellington's Regt. OPERATION ORDER No. Z.54
         @@
                                             In the Field, 18th January, 1918.

1. INTENTION.
         The Battalion will relieve the Household Battalion in the BROWN
    LINE tomorrow, 19th inst.

2. ORDER OF RELIEF.
         No. 1 Coy. Dukes will relieve No. 1 Coy. Household Battalion.
          " 2 ----------------do--------- 2 -------------------------------
          " 3 ----------------do--------- 3 -------------------------------
          " 4 ----------------do--------- 4 -------------------------------
         H.Q. ----------------do--------- H.Q.------------------------------

3. HOUR OF START.
         The leading Platoon of No. 1 Coy. will pass the Starting Point at
    10.45 a.m., remainder of Battalion by Platoons at not less than 200 Yards
    distance.

         STARTING POINT. Battalion Guard Room.
         DRESS.   Marching Order.

4. ADVANCE PARTY.
         An Advance Party consisting of :-
    2Lieut. T.D.Stocks, 4 C.Q.M.Sergts, Sgt. J.Ward, One Signaller and One
    Orderly per Company and H.Q., will report to the Orderly Room, Household
    Battalion at 9 a.m., 19th inst.

5. TRANSPORT.
         The Transport Officer will arrange for the conveyance of Blankets,etc

6. RATIONS.
         The Q.M. will arrange with the Transport Officer for the conveyance
    of Rations.
         Blankets and Stores will be stacked on to wagons, etc, by 9 a.m.
    Officers Mess Cart will be at the H.Q.Mess at 9.30 a.m.
         The Drums and N.C.O's Class will return to SCHRAMM BARRACKS
    immediately after the Battalion has marched off, under Sgt. Wilkinson.

7. RELIEF COMPLETE.
         Relief to be Completed by 12 noon, and to be reported by the word
    "DONE".

8. CERTIFICATES.
         The usual certificate will be handed to the Adjutant prior to
    Companies moving off, that All Huts and Latrines were left thoroughly
    clean and tidy.
         The Q.M. will arrange for handing over of Camp to Area Commandant.

                                    W.S. Newton
                                                              Captain.
                                    Adjt. 2nd Duke of Wellington's Regt.

                           D I S T R I B U T I O N.

No. 1 C.O. No. 2 Bn. H.Q. No. 3 Household Battn. Nos. 4 - 7. All Coys.

No. 8 Q.M. No. 9 T.O. No. 10 R.S.M. Nos. 11 - 12 War Diary. No. 13 File.

MONS STAR.

The under-mentioned Officers, W.O's., N.C.O's.,and Men are eligible for the award of the 1914 Star, the Ribbon for which will be issued as soon as possible.

OFFICERS.
2nd. Lieut. F.H.Hill, 2nd. Lieut. H.R.Moody, 2nd. Lieut. J.P.Colson.
2nd. Lieut. G.W.Hanna, Lieut. & Q.M., C.Shepherd.

No. 1 Company.

7528 C.Q.M.S. Brown A.J.	9488 Sgt. Ogden J.R.	9568 Sgt. Spriggs. W.
10475 C.S.M. McClelland. G.	9171 " Wild. W.	1041 A.S.Sgt. Copsey, S.
8278 L/Cpl. Stead J.	8287. L/Cpl. Whitbread, L.	8357 Pt. Aldham, F.
8300 Pte. Bloomfield, C.	8200 Pte. Colbran, C.	7705 " Gundry, C.
10131 " Owen C.	9223 " Saxton, L.	7963 " Saunders, A.
8939 " Wright, G.	7231 " Watt A.	8642 " Russell, T.
10519 " Baines, J.A.	6923 " Miller, W.	

No. 2 Company.

9827 R.S.M. Metcalfe, C.	10597. C.S.M. Ramsbottom,C.	7885 Sgt. Harvey, A.
7675 Sgt. Shaw, F.	8713 Sgt. Postlewaite, T.	6895 " Bird W.
10624 " Senior, A.	9382 " Mote, J.	9846 Cpl. Sargent, A.
9213 Cpl. Dennett, T.	10281 Cpl. Stopps, J.	10261 L/Cpl. Walker, H.
7898 " Foster L.	6887 Pte. Ramsden, J.	6559 Pte. Cooper, J.
9896 Pte. Sugden, W.	7722 " Billing J.	9083 " Glynn, T.
10282 " Anderson J.	10381 " Binns, C.	6755 Pte. Moorhouse, W.
9350 " Pike W.	8615 " Whitear, A.	8333 Pte. Southgate, A.

No. 3 Comapny.

8593 A/C.S.M. McHugh, D.	8784 Sgt. Halfacre, A.	9266 Sgt. Ward, J.
7851 Sgt. Pogson, E.	8402 A/Sgt. Parker, F.	7807 " Burns, F.
6489 Cpl. Gilgallon, J.	8619 Cpl. Short, F.	10237 L/Cpl. McCarthy, J.
8216 Pte. Bailey, S.	10151 Pte. Comber, T.	10253 Pte. Caton, J.
8455 " Charman, H.	9360 Fitzgerald, A.	9874 " Hucklesby, A.
8962 " Mee, F.	7662 O'Kelly, F.	7956 " Ramsey, E.
8614 " Ruffell, F.	9430 " Waddingham, R.	8270 " Walsh, J.
9856 " Thomas, W.	26021" Somers, W.E.	8893 " Clark, F.
9556 " Heggarty, J.	9338 L/Cpl. Shepherd, W.	10428 " Mitchell, W.
10308 " Mazurke, A.		

No. 4 Company.

9886 R.Q.M.S. Moseley, E.	9617 C.S.M. Smith, E.	6826 Sgt. Whittaker, G.
8183 Sgt. Black, A.	9512 Cpl. Fowler, W.	9597 L/Cpl. Turner, F.
9615 L/Cpl. Gower, W.	10254 Pte. Bennett, H.	8139 Pte. Griggs, G.
8951 Pte. Hopkins, A.	9339 " Nicholson, W.	10589 " Hawe, G.
3953 " Harte, F.	10383 " Chaplin, F.	9533 " Butterworth, A.A.
8842 " McCormick, J.	8346 " Holland, A.	9501 " Woodcock, B.

Extract from Battalion Orders No. 8 dated January 20th. 1918.

SECRET.   Copy No. 13

2nd. Bn. Duke of Wellington's Regt. OPERATION ORDER No. L.35.
══

                                        In the Field, 22nd. January, 1918.

1. INTENTION.
    The Battalion will relieve the 2nd. Essex Regt. in the LEFT
SUB-SECTOR to-morrow the 23rd. inst.

2. ORDER OF RELIEF.
    No. 1 Coy. Duke's will relieve R. Coy. Essex Regt.   LEFT FRONT.
    "   2 "   "   "   "   A. "   "   "   RIGHT   "
    "   3 "   "   "   "   D. "   "   "   LEFT SUPPORT.
    "   4 "   "   "   "   C. "   "   "   RIGHT   "
        Hd. Qrs.   "   "   Hd. Qrs. "   "   PICK CAVE.
    Nos 3 & 4 Coys. will each supply two sections under an Officer for
close support. They should be attached to Nos. 1 & 2 Coys. respectively
for tactical purposes.

3. HOUR OF START.
    The leading Platoon of No. 1 Coy. will be ready to pass the Starting
Point at 5 p.m., remainder of the Battalion by Platoons at not less than
200 Yards distance.

    STARTING POINT. ARRAS-CAMBRAI Road, North of the Battalion present LEFT
                     FLANK.
    ROUTE. ARRAS-CAMBRAI Road and No. 1 & 2 Coy. to MONCHY DUMP.
              "   "   "   " Nos. 3 & 4 Coys. and Bn. H.Q. to LES FOSSES
                                                                        FARM.
    DRESS. Battle Order. Jerkins to be worn and Gum Boots carried.

4. GUIDES.
    One Guide per Platoon will meet the Platoons of the RIGHT Coys. and
Bn. H.Q. at LES FOSSES FARM at 5.30 p.m. and One Guide per Platoon for
the LEFT Coys. at MONCHY DUMP at 5.15 p.m.

5. ADVANCE PARTY.
    An Advance Party consisting of :-
2Lieut. J.Cooke, One Senior N.C.O., One Runner, One Signaller per Coy.,
and Sgt. W.Will, One Runner, and One Signaller for Bn. H.Q., will report
to the Bn. H.Q., 2nd Essex Regt., at 1 p.m.

6. LEWIS GUNS AND OBSERVERS.
    The Lewis Gun personnel and Observers will relieve with the Battn.

7. DOCUMENTS.
    All Documents, Trench Stores, etc., will be taken over.

8. RATIONS.
    By Limber to LA BERGERE FARM and then by truck to PICK CAVE.

9. WATER POINT.
    PICK CAVE. The M.O. will arrange that One R.A.M.C. Orderly and
two water duty men take charge of the Water Point in PICK CAVE.

10. AID POST.
    PICK CAVE.

11. GUM BOOT STORE AND DRYING ROOM.
    PICK AVENUE near Battalion H.Q.

                                                                    P.T.O.

11. **GUM BOOT STORE AND DRYING ROOM.** (Continued.)

In addition to the Gum Boots issued to the Battalion a reserve of dry boots are kept in the Drying Room, PICK AVENUE, where any wet or damaged boots can be exchanged pair for pair.

12. **ANTI-TRENCH FEET PRECAUTIONS.**

Officers Commanding Companies will carefully take over all existing arrangements regarding Sock Changing and Drying Rooms.

13. **TRANSPORT.**

The T.O. will arrange with the Q.M. for the removal of Officers Kits, Blankets and Stores.

Blankets should be stacked by the Main ANZAC-DIEPPE Road by 10.30 a.m.

14. **RELIEF COMPLETE.**

Relief Complete will be reported by any sentence containing the word "YEAR".

Captain.
Adjt, 2nd Duke of Wellington's Regt.

DISTRIBUTION.

No. 1 G.O.
2 Bn. H.Q.
3 Essex Regt.
4 No. 1 Coy.
5 No. 2 Coy.
6 No. 3 Coy.

No. 7 No. 4 Coy.
8 Q.M.
9 T.O.
10 R.S.M.
11 War Diary.
12 " "
13 File.

SECRET

E1

Copy No. 10

2nd Bn. Duke of Wellington's Regt. OPERATION ORDER No. Z.56.

In the Field, 24th January, 1918.

1. **INTENTION.**

    Nos. 3 & 4. Companies will relieve Nos. 1 & 2 Companies in the FRONT LINE tomorrow, 25th inst., commencing at 2 p.m. On being relieved No. 1 Company will proceed and occupy the position vacated by No. 3 Company. No. 2 Company will occupy the position vacated by No. 4 Company.

    No. 1 Company will furnish 2 Sections under an Officer as CLOSE SUPPORT to No. 3 Company.

    No. 2 Company will furnish 2 Sections under an Officer as CLOSE SUPPORT to No. 4 Company.

2. **ROUTE.**

    No. 3 Company will move to the LEFT FRONT via VINE AVENUE.
    No. 4 Company will move to the RIGHT FRONT via PICK AVENUE.
    Particular attention must be paid to the fact that only small parties should move at any one time.
    All other instructions issued in Operation Order No. Z.55 will remain as stated therein.

3. **RELIEF COMPLETE.**

    Relief complete will be reported by any sentence containing the word "OIL".

(Sgd) W.S.Newroth, Captain.
Adjt. 2nd Duke of Wellington's Regt.

DISTRIBUTION.

No. 1	C.O.	No. 7	R.S.M.
2	Bn. H.Q.	8	Q.M.
3	No. 1 Coy.	9	T.O.
4	No. 2 Coy.	10 - 11	War Diary.
5	No. 3 Coy.	12	File.
6	No. 4 Coy.		

SECRET   Copy No 1

2nd Bn Duke of Wellington's Regt. Operation Order No 259
                                    In the Field 26th Jan.

1. INTENTION.

The Battalion will be relieved in the LEFT SUB-SECTOR by the 2nd Bn Essex Regt., tomorrow, 27th inst.

2. ORDER of RELIEF

    D. Coy, Essex Regt. will relieve No 3 Coy Duke's, in LEFT FRONT.
    B "   "   "   "   "   "   1   "   "   "   "   SUPPORT.
    C "   "   "   "   "   "   4   "   "   "   " RIGHT FRONT
    A "   "   "   "   "   "   2   "   "   "   "   PICK CAVES.

On completion of relief the Bn will relieve the LANC FUS, in SUPPORT as follows:-

No 1 Coy. C, D, & E. Strong Points, via VINE AVENUE
No 2 Coy to SPADE.   Coy. H.Q in FORK TRENCH.
No 3 Coy to EAST and FORK TRENCH via VINE AVENUE.
No 4 Coy (less TWO Officers + 48 O.Ranks) to LES FOSSES FARM.
TWO Officer and 48 O.Ranks of No 4 Coy. to B. STRONG POINT via PICK, SPADE, Trench and GORDON AVENUE.

3. GUIDES.

Officers Commanding No 1 & 3 Coys will each detail:-
3 Guides to meet B and D. Coys, 2nd Essex Regt at MONCHY DUMP at 5-30 p.m.

Officers Commanding No 2 & 4 Coys. will each detail:-
3 Guides to meet A and C Coys, 2nd Essex Regt at LES FOSSES FARM at 5-30 p.m.

Guides for Companies moving to B. C. D & E STRONG POINTS will report to the Coy. H.Q. concerned at 4-30 p.m.

Officers Commanding No 2. 3 & 4 Coys will each send One Officer and One Guide per Company to reconnoitre their new positions, no other Guides will be provided.

Lewis Gun Personnel & Observers will relieve with the Battalion.

4. ADVANCE PARTY

An Advance Party consisting of:-
2Lt. J. Cooke, Sgt. W. Wild, One Signaller and One Guide will report to the Orderly Room, Support Bn, LES FOSSES FARM. at 4 p.m. tomorrow.

P.T.O

5. DOCUMENTS.
   Lists of all Documents, Trench Stores, etc, should be handed over.

6. CERTIFICATES.
   Officers Commanding Companies will render to the Adjutant a certificate stating that all Cubby-Holes, Dug-outs & Latrines have been handed over in a clean & sanitary condition.

7. GUM BOOTS.
   Officers Commanding Companies will ensure that every N.C.O. & Man who was issued with a pair of Gum Boots prior to moving into the Line, takes a pair out.
   A careful check should be made and any deficiencies reported to Orderly Room immediately after relief is complete.

8. RELIEF COMPLETE
   - Relief Complete will be reported by any sentence containing the word "BOOT."

   W.S. Newton
   Capt
   Adjt 2nd Duke of Wellington's Regt

DISTRIBUTION.

No 1 C.O
" 2 Bn H.Q.
" 3-6 All Coys
" 7 R.S.M.
" 8 T.O
" 9 Q.M.
" 10-11 WAR DIARY
" 12 Essex Regt
" 13 Lanc Fus
" 14 FILE.

S E C R E T.

W A R   D I A R Y.

of

2nd Bn. Duke of Wellington's Regt.

From...1st February...1918.

To...28th February...1918.

VOLUME. IV

[signature]

Lieut. Colonel.

Commanding 2nd Bn. Duke of Wellington's Regt.

.4./.2./.....1918.

Army Form C. 2118.

Original

WAR DIARY
or
INTELLIGENCE SUMMARY.
(Erase heading not required.)

Instructions regarding War Diaries and Intelligence Summaries are contained in F. S. Regs., Part II. and the Staff Manual respectively. Title pages will be prepared in manuscript.

Place	Date	Hour	Summary of Events and Information	Remarks and references to Appendices
			1918	
BOIS SUPPORT TRENCHES	FEBRUARY 1		The Battn relieved the 2nd ESSEX REGT in the LEFT SUB SECTOR the relief being successfully carried out.	N.A.
LEFT SUB SECTOR	2		A raid was successfully carried out by 2 Officers (2/Lt CALDWELL & party) and 2/Lt McDOUGALL) and 60 O.R. + 4 Stretcher bearers. Time commenced 3.00am 5 Prisoners of the 139 I.R. were brought in. See Appendices B + C.	B. C.
	3		The Battn holding the Line. Strong enemy own artillery fire 10.00	4
	4		GAS SHELLS in enemy SUPPORT and RESERVE lines. The Battn holding the line. 2/Lts CARD and CAPON joined Battn	
	5		The Battn relieved by CAMERON HIGHLANDERS. Relief successful. After relief proceeded to SCHRAMM BARRACKS, ARRAS.	D
SCHRAMM BARRACKS	6		The Battn moved by march Route to BERNEVILLE via DOULLENS RD.	E
ARRAS			Rest Billets.	
BERNEVILLE	7		The Battn cleaning up. A draft of 191 O.R. joined from the Div. DEPOT.	
"	8		A draft of 158 O.R. and the following officers joined from the 8th Battn B.W. Regt. CAPT. L. SHAW M.C., LIEUT H. LIVESAY, 2/Lts. G.S. COVAX, N. SUSMAN, F. GRIGGS, F. CHARLESWORTH, R.W. LEE, L. MORRIS.	

Army Form C. 2118.

WAR DIARY
or
INTELLIGENCE SUMMARY.
(Erase heading not required.)

Instructions regarding War Diaries and Intelligence Summaries are contained in F. S. Regs., Part II. and the Staff Manual respectively. Title pages will be prepared in manuscript.

Place	Date	Hour	Summary of Events and Information	Remarks and references to Appendices
	FEBRUARY		1918	
BERNEVILLE	9		The Battn reorganising dispositions Inspection of Trays.	
	10		The Battn left the 13TH INFANTRY BDE and joined the 10TH INFANTRY	F
			Bde. Composition of Latter Bde. now as follows 2ND BATT OF WELLINGTONS R.	
			1ST ROYAL WARWICKSHIRE REGT and 2ND SEAFORTH HIGHLANDERS.	
			The Battn proceeded by french Route to ECOLE COMMUNALE ARRAS	G
			CAPT DUNCALFE & left Regiment on transfer home to 10TH Bde.	
ECOLE COMMUNALE	11		The Battn in Rest Billets. Interior economy carried out.	
			LT HAYS U.S.R rejoining from hosp.	
ARRAS	12		As for previous day. Bathing & reports.	
"	13		Nothing to report. Training.	
"	14		Training. Draft of 14 O.R Joined. 2/T CROZWELL awarded the	
			military cross for good work on the R.O.D carried out on the 2nd inst	
	15			

James Redd [signature]

[signature] Lt Col

Army Form C. 2118.

WAR DIARY
or
INTELLIGENCE SUMMARY.
(Erase heading not required.)

Instructions regarding War Diaries and Intelligence Summaries are contained in F. S. Regs., Part II. and the Staff Manual respectively. Title pages will be prepared in manuscript.

Place	Date	Hour	Summary of Events and Information	Remarks and references to Appendices
ECOLE COMMUNE PONT	16		Battalion training. Anything to report.	
	17		R.E. Short parade taking to shop.	
	18		Bde Gde duty & walk into town. 2nd Lt SUSMAN transferred to Bn from the R.F.C.	
	19		Anything seen today.	
	20		do	
	21		do	
	22		do	2.Lt. KILBOURNE & STATIONS R.O.S attached to Battn from base camp
	23		Lewis gun carried out. 4 B.Tos	
	24		Bn 1 Coy Parade. Bn was bombing.	
	25		Battalion training.	
	26		do	
	27		do	
	28		do. A buy corn Both Bayonet & Bullet Competition	

SECRET. Copy No. 11

2nd Bn. Duke of Wellington's Regt. OPERATION ORDER No. Z.58.
@@

In the Field, 31st January, 1918.

1. INTENTION.

The Battalion will relieve the 2nd Essex Regt. in the LEFT SUB-SECTOR tomorrow, 1st February, 1918.

2. ORDER OF RELIEF.

    No. 3 Coy. Dukes will relieve B. Coy. Essex Regt. LEFT FRONT.
    No. 2 Coy. ———do——— A. Coy. ——— RIGHT FRONT.
    No. 1 Coy. ———do——— D. Coy. ——— LEFT SUPPORT.
    No. 4 Coy. ———do——— C. Coy. ——— RIGHT SUPPORT.
    H.Q. ———do——— H.Q. ———

O.C. No 4 Coy. will detail 1 Platoon to go to HILL SUPPORT and 1 Platoon to go to SADDLE SUPPORT.

3. ROUTE.

    No. 3 Company via VINE AVENUE.
    No. 2 Company via PICK AVENUE.
    No. 1 Company via VINE AVENUE.
    No. 4 Company via PICK AVENUE.

4. GUIDES.

One Guide of the 2nd Essex Regt. will report at the Coy. H.Q. of Nos. 2 & 3 Coys. at 5 p.m.
Nos. 1 & 4 Companies will not be provided with Guides.
Officers in Command of C. D. & E. Stong Points will each detail 1 Guide to report to B. Coy. H.Q., 2nd Essex Regt., HILL SUPPORT at 5 p.m. and Officer Commanding B. Strong Point will send 1 Guide to report to A. Coy. H.Q., Essex Regt. SADDLE SUPPORT at 5 p.m.

5. ADVANCE PARTIES.

Companies will send Advance Parties consisting of :-
1 Officer, 1 N.C.O., and 1 Signaller.
Headquarters. Sgt. J. Ward, and 1 Signaller.
They should report to the Coy. H.Q., and Bn. H.Q., respectively at 2 p.m.

6. LEWIS GUNS, ETC.

Lewis Gun Personnel and Observers will relieve with the Battalion.

7. DOCUMENTS.

Documents, Trench Stores, etc, should be taken over.

8. GUM BOOTS.

Gum Boots will be carried. Great care should be taken with these Gum Boots, and when not in use they should be collected and sent to Bn. H.Q.

9. CERTIFICATES.

Officers Commanding Companies will render a certificate to the Adjt. that all Dug-outs and Latrines have been handed over clean and in a sanitary condition.

10. MAPS OF DISPOSITION.

Sketch Maps of dispositions will be forwarded to Bn. H.Q. by 12 noon, 2nd. inst.

11. RELIEF COMPLETE.

Relief Complete will be reported by any sentence containing the word "LUCK".

(Sgd) W.S. Newroth, Captain.
Adjutant 2nd Battn. The Duke of Wellington's Regt.

DISTRIBUTION.

No. 1 C.O.   9 T.O.
    2 Bn. H.Q.   10 R.S.M.
    3 Essex Regt.   11 - 12 War Diary.
    4 - 7 All Coys. 13 File.
    8 Q.M.

SECRET.   Copy No. 10
2nd Bn. Duke of Wellington's Regt. OPERATION ORDER No. Z.59.
@@
                                         In the Field, 1st February, 1918.
Ref. MONCHY TRENCH MAP 1/10,000.

1. STRENGTH.
    Two Officers and 60 Other Ranks and 4 Stretcher Bearers will raid BAT, BADGER, BUCKLE and STRAP, on February 2nd.

2. OBJECT OF RAID.
    Object of Raid is to take Prisoners, secure Identification, kill Germans, capture M.G, and destroy Dug-outs.

3. ORGANIZATION OF PARTY.
    4 Blocking Groups, Nos. 1 to 4 :: 19 men.
    6 Fighting Groups, A to F.   :::39 men.
    2 Orderlies.   2 men.
                                        60

4. OBJECTIVES.
    Parties will go to places as follows :-
    No. 1. junction of BAT and STRAP.
    No. 2.   "   " BAT and BUCKLE.
    No. 3.   "   " STRAP and BADGER.
    No. 4.   "   " BADGER and BUCKLE and PUN.

    A & B   to STRAP TRENCH.
      C   to BAT   Trench.
    F.E.& D. to BUCKLE Trench.

5. FORMATION.
    Parties will go in three waves from 4 exits.

6. COMMAND.
    2Lieut. R.A.McDowall will be in charge of the leading wave.

7. WITHDRAWAL.
    2Lieut. N.G.Coldwell (O i/c Party) will go on with the last wave.
    At Zero plus 12, 2Lieut. N.G.Coldwell will order the bugle to be sounded. A bugle will also be sounded from No. 4 Sap and VERY LIGHTS will be fired from the FRONT LINE.

8. WITHDRAWAL BARRAGE.
    Groups A. B. C. & No. 1 will cover withdrawal with R.G.Barrage.

9. ARMS AND ORGANIZATION OF PARTY.
    Arms and Organization of party as previously detailed.

10. PRECAUTIONS RE IDENTIFICATIONS.
    Special Identity Discs will be issued on February 1st and all marks removed from their clothing which might give information to the enemy.

11. ASSEMBLY AFTER RAID.
    After the Raid the men will assemble in PICK CAVE. They will wait in FRONT LINE until barrage on PICK has died down.

12. MEDICAL.
    Stretcher Bearers Post junction of PICK and FRONT LINE.
    DRESSING STATION for walking cases in SADDLE SUPPORT.
    REGIMENTAL AID POST in PICK CAVE.

13. SYNCHRONISATION OF WATCHES.
    Watches will be synchronised at PICK CAVE at 6.30 a.m. FEBRUARY 2nd.

                                        (Sgd) W.S.Newroth, Captain.
                                                          Captain
                              Adjutant 2nd Battn. The Duke of Wellington's

D I S T R I B U T I O N.

```
No. 1 C.O.              No. 8 T.O.
    2 Bn. H.Q.              9 R.S.M.
    3 - 6 All Coys.        10 - 11 War Diary.
    7 Q.M.                 12 File.
```

SECRET.   Copy No. 10

2nd Bn. Duke of Wellington's Regt, OPERATION ORDER No. Z.60.
@@

In the Field, 1st Feby. 1918

1. **INTENTION.**
    If the word "FUSS" is sent by wire the following action will be taken.

2. No. 2 Coy. will evacuate the FRONT LINE except for 2 Sentries in each POST. 1 Section Commander for each alternate post and 1 N.C.O. or 1 Officer on duty.

    No. 3 Coy. will reduce each post to 4 men and 1 Section Leader per alternate post. 1 Officer and 1 N.C.O. on duty.

4. Evacuation to be commenced at 7.45 a.m. and to be completed by 8.15 a.m.

3. The evacuated men will go into deep Dug-outs in HILL & SADDLE SUPPORT.

5. Officers Commanding Companies will examine accommodation and arrange with O.C. No. 4 Company for evacuation of Dug-outs if necessary.

(Sgd) W.S.Newroth, Captain.
Adjt. 2nd Duke of Wellington's Regt.

After order — No.4 Sap will be evacuated and M.G. Coy. establish a post there.

DISTRIBUTION.

No. 1 C.O.   No. 8 T.O.
    2 Bn. H.Q.   9 R.S.M.
    3 - 6 All Coys.   10 - 11 War Diary.
    7 Q.M.   12 File.

SECRET.   Copy No. 10

2nd Bn. Duke of Wellington's Regt. OPERATION ORDER No. Z.61.
@@@

                                       In the Field, 2nd February, 1918.

1. INTENTION.

Nos. 1 & 4 Companies will relieve Nos. 3 & 2 Companies in the FRONT LINE tomorrow, 3rd inst., as follows :-
        No. 1 Coy. will relieve No. 3 Coy. LEFT FRONT.
        No. 4 Coy. will relieve No. 2 Coy. RIGHT FRONT.
Nos. 3 & 2 Companies will each find a Platoon for CLOSE SUPPORT in HILL & SADDLE SUPPORTS respectively.

2. TIME OF RELIEF.

No. 4 Company will commence their relief at 2 p.m.
No. 1 Company time to be notified later which will depend upon fog, etc.
All other arrangements will be made direct between Officers Commanding Companies.

3. RELIEF COMPLETE.

Completion of Relief will be reported by any sentence containing the word "BOX".

                                            (Sgd) W.S.Newroth, Captain.
                                      Adjt. 2nd Duke of Wellington's Regt.

D I S T R I B U T I O N.

No. 1 S.O.	No. 8 T.O.
2 Bn. H.Q.	9 R.S.M.
3 - 6 All Coys.	10 - 11 War Diary.
7 Q.M.	12 File.

SECRET.   Copy No. 11
         2nd Bn. Duke of Wellington's Regt. OPERATION ORDER No. Z.62.
         @@@
                                                 In the Field, 4th February, 1918.

1. INTENTION.
         The Battalion will be relieved on the LINE tomorrow, 5th inst., by
the 7th Cameron Highlanders.

2. ORDER OF RELIEF.
         RIGHT FRONT Coy. 7th Cameron Highlanders via PICK relieves No. 4 Coy. in the
                                                                         FRONT LINE.
              (   ) 7th Cam. Hldrs. via PICK relieves 1 Platoon No. 2 Coy. in
                                                                         SADDLE SUPPORT.
         LEFT FRONT Coy.   "   "   "   "   VINE   "   No. 1 Coy. in FRONT LINE.
              (   )   "   "   "   "   "   "   1 Platoon No. 3 Coy. in
                                                                         HILL SUPPORT.
         Bn. Headquarters   "   "   "   "   PICK   "   Bn. Headquarters.

         2 Platoons LEFT SUPPORT Coy. via VINE relieves 1 Platoon No. 3 Coy. in
                                                                         SHRAPNEL TRENCH.
         1   "   RIGHT   "   "   PICK   "   1 "   No. 2 Coy. in
                                                                         PICK CAVE.
         1   "   8th Seaforth Highlanders via PICK   )
              (   )   ) PICK CAVE.

3. GUIDES.
         4 Guides each with a paper marked Serial No. 5 to be at MONCHY DUMP
at 5.30 p.m. 3 of the above will be provided by No. 4 Coy. One from No. 2
Coy., Platoon in SADDLE SUPPORT.
         4 Guides each with a paper marked Serial No. 6 to be at MONCHY DUMP
at 5.30 p.m. 3 of the above will be provided by no. 1 Coy. One from No. 2
Coy. Platoon in HILL SUPPORT.
         One Guide with a paper marked Serial No. 7 from No. 2 Coy. in PICK
CAVE at FOSSE CAVE at 6.15 p.m.
         2 Guides each with a paper marked Serial No. 8 from No. 3 Coy. in
SHRAPNEL TRENCH at FOSSE CAVE at 6.30 p.m.
         One Guide with a paper marked Serial No. 4 from No. 2 Coy. in PICK CAVE
at FOSSE CAVE at 6.0 p.m.
         Each guide to be given instructions to lead his party to the trench
which he left.

4. ROUTE AFTER RELIEF.   proceed
         On being relieved Coys. will ~~be relieved~~ as follows to FOSSE FARM and
em-bus.   Nos. 4 & 2 Companies via PICK.
         Nos. 1 & 3 Companies via VINE, FORK, & PICK, or via VINE & HUSSAR LANE.

5. GUM BOOTS.
         All dry Gum Boots to be handed over to the relieving unit, receipts
being obtained. Receipts should be handed to the Adjutant on 6th inst. All
damp boots not handed over must be taken out.

6. CERTIFICATES.
         Certificates that all Dug-outs, Cubby-holes, Cookhouses and Latrines
in the vicinity of trenches have been handed over thoroughly clean and in a
sanitary condition will be forwarded to the Adjutant by 10 a.m. 6th inst.

7. DOCUMENTS AND WORK IN HAND.
         Officers Commanding Companies will hand over all Photographs, Trench
Maps, and Schemes, receipts being obtained.
         All work in hand will be handed over.

                                                                         P.T.O.

8. REAR PARTY.

Officers Commanding Companies will each detail 1 Officer per Coy. and 1 N.C.O. per Platoon to remain behind with the relieving unit until Noon 6th inst. The party will meet Lorries at the FEUCHY-CHAPEL Cross Roads at 2 p.m. the same date and will be conveyed to BERNEVILLE.

2Lieut. J.Cooke will remain behind for H.Q.

9. LORRIES.

Lorries will be at FEUCHY-CHAPEL Cross Roads and will come to FOSSE FARM when sent for by Platoon Commander. Two Lorries are allotted to each Platoon and One Lorry for Bn. H.Q., and One Lorry for Officers Servants.

10. OFFICERS SERVANTS.

All Officers servants and One Officers Mess cook per Coy. will parade at the Bn. H.Q. DUMP at 6 p.m. under Sergt. W.Wild who will march them to LES FOSSES FARM and there em-bus them. No servants to leave prior to above time.

11. EM-BUSSING PARTY.

2Lieut. J. Heskett and one runner to be detailed by Bn. H.Q. will report to Capt. E.C.Coke at FEUCHY-CHAPEL Cross Roads at 5.30 p.m.

Sergt. J.Ward will parade the Guides at MONCHY DUMP at 5.30 p.m., seeing that each guide is provided with a paper showing Serial No., etc.

12. TRANSPORT.

Officers Mess Cart will be at 300 Yards WEST of FOSSE at 6.30 p.m.

13. FEET WASHING.

Officers Commanding Companies will arrange that all men wash their feet on arrival in barracks. Hot water will be provided.

14. RELIEF COMPLETE.

Relief complete will be reported by the word "ROW".

(Sgd) W.S.Newroth, Captain.
Adjt. 2nd Duke of Wellington's Regt.

DISTRIBUTION.

No. 1 C.O.
    2 Bn. H.Q.
    3 7th Cameron Highlanders.
    4 - 7 All Coys.
    8 Q.M.

No. 9 T.O.
    10 R.S.M.
    11 - 12 War Diary.
    13 File.

SECRET.   Copy No. 10

    2nd Bn. Duke of Wellington's Regt. OPERATION ORDER No. Z.63
@@

                                                  In the Field, 5th February, 1918.

1. **INTENTION.**
    The Battalion will move by March Route to BERNEVILLE tomorrow, 6th inst., to be billeted there.

2. **TIME OF PARADE AND DRESS.**
    The Battalion will parade in Marching Order at 1.45 p.m.

3. **ROUTE.**
    DOULLENS Road, BAC DU NORD, R.8.c.

4. **ORDER OF MARCH.**
    H.Qrs., Drums, Nos. 1. 2. 3. & 4 Companies and Regtl. Transport.
    200 Yards will be maintained between Battalions and 1st Line Transport and between other Battalions.

5. **ADVANCE PARTY.**
    An Advance Party consisting of :-
2Lieuts. Capon & Card, 4 C.Q.M.Sergts., Arm.Staff.Sergt. and one man per Company, will report to the Staff Captain, 12th Inf. Bde., at the Town Majors Office, BERNEVILLE, at 9.30 a.m. on 6th inst.

6. **BLANKETS, ETC.**
    All Blankets and Company Stores will be stacked at the Q.M. Stores at 10 a.m.
    Officers Kits, 12 Noon.
    Officers Mess Kits, 1 p.m. Mess Cart will be outside Officers Mess SCHRAMM BARRACKS at that hour.

7. **SICK PARADE.**
    Sick Parade will be at 10 a.m.

8. **DINNERS.**
    Dinners will be served at 12.30 p.m.

                                           (Sgd) W.S.Newroth, Captain.
                                        Adjt. 2nd Duke of Wellington's Regt,

DISTRIBUTION.

No. 1 C.O.	No. 8 Q.M.
2 T.O.	9 R.S.M.
3 Bn. H.Q.	10 - 11 War Diary.
4 - 7 All Coys.	12 file.

SECRET.   Copy No. 10

2nd Bn. Duke of Wellington's Regt. OPERATION ORDER No. Z.64.
==

                                        In the Field, 9th February, 1918.

1. **INTENTION.**

    The Battalion will proceed to ARRAS tomorrow, 10th inst, by March Route via WARLUS, on transfer to the 10th Infantry Brigade.
    Leading Company to pass Lanc. Fus. Guard Room at 11 a.m.

2. **ORDER OF MARCH.**

    Headquarters, No. 3 Coy. Drums, Nos. 4. 1. & 2. Companies.
    The Battalion Qr. Guard and an Officer detailed by Officer Commanding No. 2 Company will march in rear of the Battalion and pick up stragglers.

3. **ADVANCE PARTY.**

    An Advance Party consisting of :-
    2Lieuts. G.W.Hanna, E.G.Capon, and H.G.Card, 4 C.Q.M.Sergts., Sgt. W.Wild, and servants as detailed by Officers, will parade at Guard Room at 8.30 a.m.

4. **BLANKETS, ETC.**

    Drummers Rifles and Packs and Companies Blankets and Stores will be at the Q.M.Stores by 9 a.m.
    Officers Kits at 10 a.m.
    Mess Cart at 10 a.m.

5. **DINNERS.**

    Dinners will be served on arrival at ARRAS.

6. **REAR PARTY.**

    A Rear Party consisting of :-
    2Lieut. J.Cooke and 2 Sanitary Men per Company and H.Q. will remain behind and report to Town Major, BERNEVILLE.
    On completion of duty they will proceed to ARRAS.

                                                    Captain.
                                        Adjt. 2nd Duke of Wellington's Regt.

                        D I S T R I B U T I O N.

        No. 1 C.O.   No. 8 Q.M. & T.O.
            2 Bn. H.Q.   9 R.S.M.
            3 Town Major.   10 - 11 War Diary.
            4 - 7 All Coys.   12 File.

12th Infantry Brigade No. J. 32/18.

1 King's Own.
2 Lan. Fus.
2 D of W.R.
2 Essex R.
12 M.G.Coy.
12 T.M.Batty.

With reference to 4th Division No. G.A. 13/5.

The Brigadier has much pleasure in forwarding the above letter of the G.O.C., to Units.

He has already expressed to C.O's his appreciation of the good work done in the trenches and the fine patrolling that has been carried out and asked them to convey his thanks to all ranks.

9th February, 1918.

Captain,
Brigade Major, 12th Infantry Brigade.

PRELIMINARY EXAMINATION OF 5 PRISONERS OF 139th I.R
24th DIVISION (SAXON) CAPTURED IN A RAID ON STRAP TRENCH
BETWEEN BAT AND BADGER TRENCHES, 2nd FEBRUARY 1918

Four men belong to the 3rd Coy, 139th I.R and 1 man to the 8th Coy. The latter was visiting a friend in the 3rd Coy and was unable to escape when our bombardment commenced.

Our attack this morning was a complete surprise, although in view of our wire cutting operations, prisoner suspected that an attack was in contemplation.

The front line garrison did not "Stand to" this morning. Front line troops only "Stand to" when specially ordered to do so.

RELIEFS. The 1st Bn relieved the 3rd Bn on the night 31st Jan/1st Feby. The tour of duty is 6 days.

Prisoners have no knowledge of a pending Divisional relief.

STRENGTH. The trench strength of the 3rd Coy is said to be about 75. Coys have been maintained at approximately this strength during the whole time the Division has been in this sector. Reinforcements have been young men of 18 tr or years who are said to be of poor quality and prone to run away as soon as they come under fire.

The Coy has only 1 Officer, the Platoons being commanded by Feldwebel.

Each Coy has 3 light M.Gs.

DISPOSITIONS. The right flank of the 3rd Coy is about the junction of BAT Trench and the front line. No 1 Coy is on the right and Nos 4 and 2 Coys on the left of No 3 Coy. A Coy front is said to be about 350 yds.

The 3rd Coy had 30 to 40 men in the front line and the remainder in the support line by day. At night the front line is reinforced from the support line.

Of the 3 light M.Gs of the Coy, 2 are in the front line and the 3rd in the support line.

One M.G is located at O.8.d.50.65. Another is near the left flank of the Coy. The third is beside the Coy H.Q about O.8.d.7.9.

Coy H.Q is in a deep mined dug-out in BUCKLE Trench about O.8.d.7.9.

The Support Bn is located in dug-outs in front of and S.W of BOIRY. One prisoner had been in dug-outs near the Chalk Pit at O.4.central, another in the dug-outs at O.11.a.65.55.

The resting Bn is at BELLONNE.

TRENCHES. The front line is in fair condition but not deep. Movement by day is possible only by crouching.

The front trench has recently been duckboarded and partially revetted.

Short mine shafts about 6 steps deep exist in the front line, but there is little or no chamber at the bottom. One such shaft had to accommodate about 8 men.

The Sap at O.8.d.4.2 is said to be no longer used.

BAT Trench is said to have fallen in and to be in bad condition. BADGER Trench is in good condition. BUCKLE Trench is good and contains dug-outs.

WIRE. New wire was put out in front of STRAF Trench last night.

Between the front line and BUCKLE Trench a certain amount of old wire still stands, but no new wire has been put up.

Work on trenches and wire is said to be done by Pioneers who live in or around BOIRY.

Rations have to be collected from field railhead every night. The locality varies, sometimes being at O.11.c.55.66 and sometim at BOIRY.

The light railway no longer runs along STIRRUP LANE.

The Bn H.Q which were at one time located in the Chalk Pit O.4.central, are said to have been removed to a deep dug-out probably about O.4.d.70.55.

10th Inf.Bde.
4th Div.

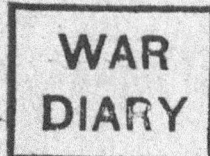

2nd BATTN. THE DUKE OF WELLINGTON'S (WEST RIDING REGIMENT).

M A R C H

1 9 1 8

10/4

S E C R E T.
ooooooooooooooooOOOOOooooooooooooooo

W A R D I A R Y.

of

2nd Bn. Duke of Wellington's Regt.

From... 1st March ...1918.

To... 31st March ...1918.

VOLUME.

W. G. Officer   Lieut. Colonel.
Commanding 2nd Bn. Duke of Wellington's Regt.

3rd April 1918.

Army Form C. 2118.

10/4 2 W Riding 23
Vol 42

WAR DIARY
or
INTELLIGENCE SUMMARY.

(Erase heading not required.)

Instructions regarding War Diaries and Intelligence Summaries are contained in F. S. Regs., Part II. and the Staff Manual respectively. Title pages will be prepared in manuscript.

Place	Date	Hour	Summary of Events and Information	Remarks and references to Appendices
ECOLE COMMUNALE ARRAS	MARCH 1918 —			45F 7 week
	1		Battalion training. 2/Lt. G.W. Hancox proceeded to England for one month under the "Lived Officers Scheme"	
	2		Field day. Baggage scheme. Nothing to report.	
	3		Day of Rest. Church parade.	
	4		Battalion training. Nothing to report.	
	5		Battalion practise moving forward into position according to "DEFENCE SCHEME" area vicinity of ST LAURENT BLANGY.	
	6		Battalion training. Nothing to report.	
	7		— do —	
	8		— do —	
	9		Battalion training. Major W.G. Bifford joined from 9th D of W R.	
	10		Rest. Church parade. Nothing to report.	
	11		Battalion training. Going on "BUTTE de TARN"	
	12		— do — Major W.G. Bifford to commanded the Battalion	
			Lt. Col. P.L.E. Walker left Battn. for leave to England to proceed to the WORCESTERSHIRE REGT.	

Army Form C. 2118.

WAR DIARY
or
INTELLIGENCE SUMMARY.
(Erase heading not required.)

Place	Date	Hour	Summary of Events and Information	Remarks and references to Appendices
ECOLE COMMUNAL ARRAS	MARCH 1916			
	13		Battalion training. 2nd Lt S.K. MADDRELL struck off strength. (AF/10/312.)	
	14		— do — Major P.&F. WALKER to ROYAL WARWICKS	
"	15		— do — 2nd Lt HARNELL joined the Battn from 9th D. of W. Regt	
"	16		— do —	
"	17		Field Firing practices on WAILLY F.F. RANGE.	
"	18		Battalion training.	
"	19		Battalion relieved 2nd SCOTS GUARDS in ROVER SECTOR, N. of SCARPE RIVER. Relief successful.	
TRENCHES ROVER SECTOR	20		10% of the Battn left out, as per S.S. 135.	
			Holding the line. Fairly quiet. Nothing to report.	
	21		Holding the line. Enemy offensive extended further South. No action on our front.	
	22		Division on our Right (South of River SCARPE) withdrew over a mile and a defensive flank was formed by us on the North bank of the river. No change in situation. A party of the enemy, on tor groups each about 8 strong entered our front line during the day. After a lengthy encounter they were finally forced out. Casualties (ours) 2. O.R. killed. 5 wounded.	
	23			2nd Lt S.P.G. BILHAM to hospital. Septic knee.

WAR DIARY
or
INTELLIGENCE SUMMARY.
(Erase heading not required.)

Army Form C. 2118.

Place	Date	Hour	Summary of Events and Information	Remarks and references to Appendices
	MARCH -1918-			
TRENCHES	24	—	Holding the line. Situation the same.	
ROUEX SECTOR	25		Relieved in turn by 2nd SEAFORTH HIGHLANDERS and moved to GORDON CAMP. B & C Coy moved to INVERGORDON TRENCH H.29.a (TRVES-SHEET 57c NW 2/4) in support to 1st WARWICKS.	
GORDON CAMP	26		Moved forward at dawn to ARMY LINE & occupied same until 4 pm. then returned to camp.	
"	27		Same as for 26th inst. 2 OR killed in ROUEX CAVES (part of small detachment left behind when relieved by SEAFORTHS)	
"	28		Enemy shelled camp at 3 am with H.E. SHRAPNEL & GAS SHELLS. Bat'n left camp and moved up to Army Line. Enemy attacking very strongly on Battalion in front. About 2 pm troops in front commenced to fall back. Movement finished by 5 pm. on ARMY LINE a rearguard action being fought in BATTERY VALLEY. Enemy advance having occupied old battery positions in BATTERY VALLEY (H.29.a and c. and H.33.a.) At 6.30 pm Bat'n less 2 Coys with 2/3 Coy on support 21st WEST YORKS on left and 4/5 K.O.S.B on right moved forward & took west side of BATTERY VALLEY. Little opposition was encountered. M.G. fire fairly heavy	

Army Form C. 2118.

WAR DIARY or INTELLIGENCE SUMMARY.
(Erase heading not required.)

Place	Date	Hour	Summary of Events and Information	Remarks and references to Appendices
ARMY LINE	MARCH - 1918 - 28 (cont)		Casualties were 2nd Lt R.G. McDOWALL wounded also 4.9 O.R. wounded. 8 O.R. missing and 9 O.R. killed. Capt. W.S. NEWROTH and 2nd Lt BRUHM to hospital with LETHAL GAS POISONING. Details left behind formed into a company & taken into action N. of River SCARPE.	
EAST OF BATTERY VALLEY	29		Battalion relieved at night by 1st ROYAL WARWICKS. R. 2. OR attached. Moved back to ARMY LINE	
ARMY LINE	30		No. 3 Coy moved up at dusk to outpost WARWICKS. 2nd Lt E. Q. GRAY and 2nd Lt F. CHARLESWORTH to hospital sick. 6 NCOs proceeded to England for exchange. Capt F. SLAUGHTON transferred to Division.	
	31		Army strength at strength. 31/3/18. No 3 Coy moved back to ARMY LINE at dusk. SEAFORTHS relieved WARWICKS in front.	

2nd Duke of Wellington's Regt.

1. 1/R. War. Regt. relieve our 3 Coys in the new line tonight.

2. After relief positions will be — No. 4 Coy. Right Front Line, No. 3 Left Front Line, No. 1 Right Support, No. 2 Left Support.

3. Right Boundary — 15th Divn.
    Left " — Sunken Road about 200x S. of Railway.
    Inter-Company Boundary — an East & West line through original Bn. H.Q.
    All references are to the Army Line which we have been occupying recently. Coys. are responsible for keeping touch on both flanks.

4. 9f Seaforths will be on our left.

5. Nos. 1 & 2 Coys. will each send 2 guides and No. 3 Coy. will send 2 guides to be at junction of Front Line Trench Army Line, and sunken road 200x South of Railway Line. 1/R. War. R. are taking over with one company from our Nos. 1 & 2 Coys. and with one Company from our No. 3 Coy.

6. As soon as R. War. Regt. move out of the front line trench in front of him the O.C. No. 4 Coy. will occupy the Front Line; he must therefore keep touch with the R. War. Regt. in the front line.

7. Nos. 2, 3, & 4 Coys. must be careful to bring out of the line all petrol tins; these must be sent back to the Transport tomorrow.

8. Rations will probably be ready for Companies tonight at new Bn. H.Q. by the time the relief is over.

9. Completion of relief to be reported by runner.

W.L. Officer Major

7.45 pm.
29.3.18

10th Brigade.

4th Division.

2nd BATTALION

DUKE OF WELLINGTON'S (West Riding) REGT.

APRIL 1918.

S E C R E T.

WAR DIARY.

of

2nd Bn. Duke of Wellington's Regt.

From 1st April 1918.

To 30th April 1918.

VOLUME. IV

[signature]
Lieut. Colonel.
Commanding 2nd Bn. Duke of Wellington's Regt.

3rd May 1918.

Army Form C. 2118.

WAR DIARY
or
INTELLIGENCE SUMMARY.
(Erase heading not required.)

Instructions regarding War Diaries and Intelligence Summaries are contained in F. S. Regs., Part II. and the Staff Manual respectively. Title pages will be prepared in manuscript.

Place	Date	Hour	Summary of Events and Information	Remarks and references to Appendices
ARMY LINE. (REVRS LONG & ARRAS-DOURT RLY)	APRIL-1918. 1		1st WARWICKS holding Outpost Line in front. The Battn holding the Army Line in support to them. Enemy shelling heavily.	
"	2		Battn still holding Army Line. Situation quiet.	
"	3		The Battn relieved by the 1st WARWICKS & 7/8th K.O.S.B. (15th DIV.), and moved back to INTERMEDIATE LINE on EASTERN outskirts of ST LAURENT-AU-BLANGY. Two companies in trenches, and Bn H.Q. & 2 companies in cellars in village	B.
INTERMEDIATE LINE	4		Brigade Reserve. Nothing to report.	A.
"	5		Battn moved up the line to LEFT BATTN SECTOR (from BROKEN MILL to RIVER SCARPE) and relieved 2nd SEAFORTH HIGHLANDERS. On our left SOMERSET L.I. and on the right 7/8. K.O.S.B.	
LEFT BATT. SECTOR	6		Battn holding the line; nothing to report	
"	7		" Advance party of CANADIANS arrived round (as 2 + 3 Offrs arrived & to in front) the line preparatory to taking over.	B1.
"	8		Battn relieved on the line by the 13th CANADIANS and proceeded by march route to ST LAURENT-AU-BLANGY, from there the Battn moved in motor lorries to AGNEZ-LE-DUISANS.	C.
AGNEZ LE DUISANS	9		Battalion resting. Cleaning war equipment &c.	
"	10		at Reorganising sections &c.	

46 F
30 Sheet

under heading 17."

"2nd Seaforths on right 1st Royal Warwickshires on left" should read
1st Royal Warwickshires on right 2nd Seaforth on left

(cf the other battalion diaries)

JMM
15/8/30

Army Form C. 2118.

WAR DIARY or INTELLIGENCE SUMMARY.

(Erase heading not required.)

Instructions regarding War Diaries and Intelligence Summaries are contained in F. S. Regs., Part II. and the Staff Manual respectively. Title pages will be prepared in manuscript.

Place	Date	Hour	Summary of Events and Information	Remarks and references to Appendices
	APRIL - 1918 -			
AGNEZ-LE-DUISANS	11.		Battalion training. LT. BILHAM. joined the Battn.	
"	12.		Battn proceeded in motor lorries to BURBURE (near LILLERS) and thence by march route to L'ECLEME.	
L'ECLEME	13.		Battalion proceeded (march route) to LANNOY. Battn H.Q. CHATEAU de NEPPE.	
LANNOY	14.		The 10TH INF BDE relieved 96TH INF BDE on WEST bank of LA BASSEE CANAL. The Battn moved to LE VERTANNOY in support. Battn H.Q. at W.14.F.3.4. (SHEET 36.a.S.E.)	D.
LE VERTANNOY	15.		The Battalion moved forward to the CANAL bank (proceeding via BERNENCHON.) preliminary to making a joint attack with the WARWICKS on PACOUT WOOD. At 6. p.m the Battn commenced to cross the bridge, PONT LEVIS Q.32.c.4.8. (SHEET 36.a.S.E.) to get into position to attack the wood from the WEST, the WARWICKS attacking it from the SOUTH and S.E. The operation was not a success. Officer casualties were. KILLED 2/LT HUGHES. T.N., HESKET J. 2/LTS. J.K. STOCK T.D. DIED OF WOUNDS. CAPT. T.S. BROWNING, 2/LTS. N.G. CALDWELL M.C., H.G. CARD, W.H.ROY, R.E. HENDERSON WOUNDED, and A. KING. OTHER RANKS. WOUNDED 149. MISSING 4. 32 KILLED.	
TRENCHES IN vicinity of PACOUT WOOD	16		Battalion dug in in the open ground west of PACOUT WOOD. Relieved by KINGS OWN R.L. REGT. (12TH BDE) and then moved to trenches on canal bank round HINGES. LT. S. WALLER missing. (congratulatory message received from G.O.C.	L
TRENCHES in CANAL BANK near HINGES	17		Holding the line. 2° SEAFORTHS on the right, 1ST ROYAL WARWICKS on the left. 2/LT. J.W. HUGHES awarded the M.C. (KILLED on 15TH). PTE NAYLOR awarded M.M. (Killed on 15TH)	

Army Form C. 2118.

WAR DIARY
or
INTELLIGENCE SUMMARY.
(Erase heading not required.)

Place	Date	Hour	Summary of Events and Information	Remarks and references to Appendices
TRENCHES on CANAL BANK near HINGES	18		Holding the line. Enemy bombarded whole Brigade front, heavily, from 1.30am to 5.30 am. No attack on Battalion frontage but SEAFORTHS on left attacked by large numbers who were beaten off. Lt. Col W.G. OFFICER wounded but remained at duty.	
"	19		Holding the line. Lt. Col W.G. OFFICER again wounded. 2'Lt MORRIS wounded but remained at duty. Battn relieved by 1st RIFLE BDE & 1st HANTS and then proceeded to BENSE-LA-VALLEY.	F.
BENSE LA VALLEY	20		Major F.J. Berkeley takes over command of the Battn. Lt HAYS U.S.R sick to hospital. 2'Lt CAPON sick to hospital. Battn moved by march route to GONNEHEM. Lt. BROWN R.A.M.C. attached to Batt.	
GONNEHEM	21		10th INF BDE in reserve. Battn reorganising. Working parties being provided.	
"	22		Still in Reserve. Nothing to report.	
"	23		Enemy shelled the village during night 22/23rd. Casualties 2 O.R killed & 4 wounded. Two companies (Nos. 9 + 2) sent into the line & occupied part of BOIS du PACOUT under orders of 11th Bde. 4TH Divn mentioned in despatches 22/4/18.	G.
"	24		Remainder of Battn sent into line. Nos 4 + 2 Cys back to Battn. Dispositions now 2 + 4 Coy in PACOUT WOOD and 1 + 3 Cys East of RIEZ du VINAGE. 2. SEAFORTH HIGHLANDERS on left and SOMERSET L.I. on right.	C.
RIGHT BDE SUB-SECTOR LEFT BDE SECTOR	25		Battn holding the line. Situation quiet.	

Army Form C. 2118.

WAR DIARY
or
INTELLIGENCE SUMMARY.
(Erase heading not required.)

Place	Date	Hour	Summary of Events and Information	Remarks and references to Appendices
	– APRIL – 1917 –			
LEFT B.O.R. SECTOR	26.		Holding the line has 4 + 2 Co'ys in PACOUT WOOD moved over to support of	
RIGHT BATT SUB-SECTOR.			4 I. Coy sent to 3 Coy on Immediate Support, the Batt now holding a one company	
			frontage on Q.26 & d. (Sheet 36a S.E.)	
"	27.		Holding the line. LT. COL F. PAWLETT, CANADIAN ARMY, S.R. even command of the Batt.	
			14 new officers joined the Batt. 8 coming up line and 6 assigned at 2nd Div. summer wing	
			names as follow. Lieut W.A. CROXSON, 2Lieuts J.T. McCULLOCH, J.A. BLACKBURN, S. JOHNSON	
			J.H.GAN, H.H.ANSON, G.F. CRAVEN, H. FILLINGHAM, B. HESELTHWAITE, W.G. McFARLANE	
			A.W. LITTLE, H. BUTLER, A.K. MORGAN, W. TUNSTALL, V. BIDDLE.	
	28		Holding the line. Situation quiet. Battn HQ moved to ILL of LE BASSEE CANAL	
	29		"	No. 2 Coy relieved h.L in front line and sho in Coy relieved H.	
			No. 3 Coy in Immediate Support. LIEUT. W.A. CROXSON sent to hospital. 2nd Lt. M. BADHAM	
			joined Batt from hospital. Major Beatty M.C. left the line and proc.	
			Regimental Details.	
	30.		Holding the line. Batt HQ moved back to DUCKS CREAK F.Y. South of LE BASSEE	
			CANAL	

Copy No 8   (A)

2nd Duke of Wellington's Regt

Operation Order No 76

Ref Map
61st N.W.   5.4.18

1. <u>Intention</u>   The Batt. will relieve the 2nd Sea. High^{rs}
                in the outpost line to-night

2. <u>Dispositions</u> Right front No 1 Coy. from "C" Coy Sea High^{rs}
                Left front No 4 Coy   " "D" "   "   "
                Right Support No 2 "   " "A" "   "   "
                Left Support No 3 "   " "B" "   "   "
                Posts will be taken over as held at present
                Bn. H.Q. in Railway cutting at H.20.c.7.9.
                Out Post at Railway Triangle

3. <u>Guides</u>   As arranged by O.C. companies

4. <u>Route</u>   BLANGY – FEUCHY Road or by the Railway
                if road is shelled. Movement will be by
                platoons at 200 yds distance.
                Companies will move in following order –
                No 1, No 4, No 2, No 3. No 1 Company
                will move off at 4.30 p.m or as soon
                thereafter as rations have been issued

5. **Rations &** The Cooks will move to GORDON CAMP
   Cooking to-night. A hot meal and tea
   will be sent up nightly to the two
   front companies. A hot meal only to
   the two support companies.
   No 2 Coy will carry for No 1 Coy
   No 3 "   "   "   " No 4 "
   There will be no movement for this
   purpose till after dark. Companies
   ~~support~~ must be careful not to
   give away their position by movement
   or smoke

6. **Blankets &c** All blankets and other stores to
   be stacked in a hut at cross roads
   East of Bn. H.Q. and returned to
   Transport lines to-night.
   To be stacked by 6 p.m.

7. **Completion of** To be reported by runner to
   Relief Bn. H.Q.

8. ACKNOWLEDGE
   Copy No 10 to Bn. H.Q.
   Copy Nos 1 to 4 Companies   R.C. Edwards
   "   No 5 " R.S.M   Lieut & a/Adjt
   "   No 6 " 2nd Sea. High.   2nd Duke of Wellington's Regt
   "   No 7 " War Diary
   "   No 8 " File   Issued by Runner
   "   No 9 " Q.M. & T.O   at 11. a.m.

2nd DUKE OF WELLINGTON'S REGT.   Copy No. 6.
Ref. map: OPERATION ORDER No.
5¹ᴮ N.W.   (B)   3/4/18.

1. The Battalion will be relieved in the line on night of 3/4 inst by the 1 ROYAL WARWICKS ARMY and 7/8 K.O.S.B. The first named on the left & the latter on the right.

2. Details of relief to be arranged by Company Commanders concerned.

3. After relief dispositions will be as follows :—
   No. 2 Coy in INTERMEDIATE ARMY line from C.30.b.90.45 to the Railway inclusive at C.24.d.3.6
   No. 3. Coy from the Railway exclusive along the INTERMEDIATE Army line to BRAIVGY LOCK
   Nos. 1 & 4 Coys in cellars about C.24.a.2.4.
   Battn H.Q. at C.24.a.3.2.

4. All TRENCH STORES are to be handed over to incoming units and receipts obtained and handed in to Battn H.Q. by 10 a.m. 4/4/18

2.

5. Movements will be by platoons at 300 yds distance.

6. Rations will be dumped tonight on ARRAS-BLANGY RD near Batt'n H.Q. 2 limbers will be sent to present Batt'n H.Q. about 5 pm for the purpose of loading sabags, socks & tc.

7. Company Water Tins will be carried back by companies.

8. Cooks will move back to G.24.a. tonight

9. Completion of relief will be reported by runner to present Batt'n H.Q. in H.25.b. and occupation of new position will be reported by runner to new Batt'n H.Q. in G.24.a.

10. ACKNOWLEDGE.

Cooke W/ Maj
2nd Duke of Wellington

No 1 Copy to A Coy
2.   B.
3.   C.
4.   D.
5.   R.S.M.
6.   WAR DIARY
7.   FILE.

SECRET   Copy No 4.

OPERATION ORDERS No 48
2nd Duke of Wellington's Regt.

Ref. Map. 51ᴮ N.W.   8.4.18.

1. The battalion will be relieved to-night April 8th/9th by the 13th Canadian Batt. (R. H'ds).

2. Two guides from Bn. H.Q. one for each Coy H.Q. and one per platoon will meet the incoming unit at the Double Arch H.19.b.4.6. at 8 p.m. 2 Lt Cooke will be in charge of these guides.

3. All maps, photographs, defence orders, trench stores etc. will be handed over, the receipts obtained will be forwarded to Bn. H.Q. by noon to-morrow 9th inst. Advance parties to take over are expected to arrive during the afternoon.

4. The battalion will march to the embussing point G.18.c.20.40. by platoons at 200 yds distance. From this point lorries will convey the battalion to AGNEZ-LES-DUISANS where O.C. Details will have made arrangements for billets. Capt E.C. Coke will be in charge of the embussing. Lt S. Waller will report to this officer at 8.30 p.m. at the embussing point G.18.C.2.4. he will ascertain from Bn. H.Q. the strength of the Bn and will be responsible for meeting companies and embussing them in correct lorries

5. Hot meals must all have left GORDON CAMP by 4 p.m. The camp kettles must be returned as soon as possible to GORDON CAMP and loaded in limber which will be waiting there. Two other limbers will be there at 4 p.m. to remove Soyer stoves, camp kettles & water tins. All water tins not sent down for carriage by transport must be taken back by companies and not handed over

6. Completion of relief to be reported by runner to Bn H.Q.

7. ACKNOWLEDGE

P. E. Edwards Lt + a/Adjt
2nd Duke of Wellington's Regt

Distribution
Copy N° 1	N°1 Coy
" 2	" 2 "
" 3	" 3 "
" 4	" 4 "
" 5	R.S.M.
" 6	File
" 7	War Diary
" 8	Bn H.Q.

Issued by runner at 3.35 p.m.

A.T.R.

D

1/ 10th Brigade will tonight take over from 76th Brigade from PONT LEVIS at AVELETTE inclusive W.17 central. to road in W.3 a. 8.9 inclusive. 1st R Warwicks on RIGHT. 2nd Seaforth's on LEFT. 2nd Duke's in SUPPORT.

2/ The Battn will pass ROAD JUNCTION at V.4.c.0.0 at 5-30pm. Intervals of 50 yards between Platoons.
<u>Order of March</u>   No. 4 — 3 — 2 — 1 Coy's B.H.Q.

3/ <u>Route</u>. GONNEHEM — ROAD JUNCTION W.13.d — W.14. central.

4/ Lewis Guns will be carried by the men, but L.G. Limbers will be available at 3-30pm to carry Panniers.

5/ Rations will be at HINGES Church at 10pm.

6/ Further details follow.

7/ <u>AFTER ORDER</u>
Battn will be ready to move at 5pm.

13/4/18

P.E. Edwards Lieut.
A/adjt- Lung

G.O.C., 4th Division.

No. 937 (G.C.) 18th April, 1918.

The Corps Commander wishes to congratulate Major General MATHESON, C.B., and the 4th Division on the manner in which the German attack this morning was met and defeated.

The enemy attacked under cover of darkness and a very heavy artillery preparation but failed to make any progress in the face of the steadiness and fine fighting qualities displayed by all ranks.

The enemy's massed attacks were broken up by our rifle fire and his machine guns were engaged and silenced by our Lewis guns and riflemen.

The Corps Commander wishes to especially congratulate Lt-Col. LAING D.S.O., M.C., and the 2nd Battalion Seaforth Highlanders for their fine endurance under a very heavy bombardment by 5.9 Howitzers, and for the way in which they subsequently frustrated the enemy's attempt to cross the canal S. of PACAUT WOOD.

(Sgd) G.V. HORDERN,
Brigadier-General,
General Staff, I Corps.

War Ministry

4th Division No. G.S 208.

All units.

    Following received from General HORNE, Commanding First Army dated 18th begins AAA
    Please accept and convey to units which have fought to-day my admiration of the skill and determination displayed by Commanders, Staffs and all ranks AAA A very heavy attack pushed home by vastly superior numbers has been repulsed with heavy loss to the Germans AAA The troops have shown a splendid spirit and may well feel proud of their achievement AAA ends.

                                  Stanley Rogers Col
                                        Lieut Colonel,
                            General Staff, 4th Division.

4th Division No. G.A 156

To all units.

The following message has been received
by the G.O.C from G.O.C, XVIIth Corps -

" I am so very sorry the 4th Division has been
taken from us; it is a sad blow. I want to
thank you and your Staff, and the whole Division
for all you have done for us. You made a great
name for yourselves, and there is no Division
that I would sooner have with me for every
reason, individual or collective. The best
luck to you all "

H. Marshall

Lieut Colonel,

General Staff, 4th Division

Copy No. 7

2nd Duke of Wellington's Regt.
Operation Order No. 76
(A)   5. 4. 18

Refer Map
57 B N.W.

1. **Intention**. The Battn. will relieve the 2nd Sea. Highrs. in the Outpost line tonight.

2. **Dispositions**.
   Right Front — No. 1 Coy. — from "C" Coy. Sea. Hrs.
   Left   "   — " 4 "   " D "   "   "
   Right Support — " 2 "   " A "   "   "
   Left   "   — " 3 "   " B "   "   "

   Posts will be taken over as held at present.
   Bn. H.Q. in Railway Cutting at H20c7.9
   Aid Post at Railway Triangle.

3. **Guides** ~~As door~~
   As arranged by O.'s C. Companies.

4. **Route**
   BLANGY — FEUCHY Road or by the Railway if road is shelled. Movement will be by platoons at 200 yds. distance. Companies will move in the following order — No. 1, No. 4, No. 2, No. 3. No. 1 Coy. will move off at 7.30 p.m. or as soon thereafter as rations have been issued.

5. **Rations**
   & Cooking. The cooks will move to GORDON CAMP tonight. A hot meal and

Camp tonight. A hot meal and tea will be sent up nightly to the two front Companies, a hot meal only to the two support Companies. No. 2 Coy. will carry for No. 1 Coy. and No. 3 Coy. for No. 4 Coy. There will be no movement for this purpose till after dark. All Companies must be careful not to give away their positions by movement or smoke.

6. <u>Blankets</u>
&c.   All Blankets and other stores to be stacked in a hut at cross-roads East of Bn. H.Q. and returned to Transport Lines tonight; to be stacked by 6 p.m.

7. <u>Completion</u> <u>of Relief</u>   To be reported by Runner to Bn. H.Q.

8. ACKNOWLEDGE.

P.C. Edwards Lieut. T/Adjt
2nd Duke of Wellington's Regt

Copy No. 1 to No. 1 Coy.
"   " 2 " " 2 "
"   " 3 " " 3 "
"   " 4 " " 4 "
"   " 5 " R.S.M.   Issued at 11 AM
"   " 6 " 2/Sea.Hrs.   by Runner
"   " 7 " War Diary
"   " 8 " File
"   " 9 " Q.M. & T.O
"   " 10 " Bn. H.Q.

(B.1) Copy No 6

Operation Order No.
2nd Duke of Wellington's Regt.

1. **Intention** — Nos 2 and 3 Companies will relieve Nos 1 & 4 Companies in front line to night
No 2 Company will relieve No 1 Coy.
No 3   "   "   "   No 4 "

2. **Rations & Hot Food** — Nos 2 & 3 Companies will carry their own rations & hot food only at dark and will eat the hot food & issue rations before relieving.
O's C. No 1 & 4 Companies will each detail a ration party to carry their own rations at dusk. These rations will be brought to the support company HQ's and the parties will remain with them until companies are relieved. Hot food for the support companies will be carried up by them after relief.

3. **Ammunition** — The two extra bandoliers ~~per man~~ & two Mills No 5 grenades per man in Outpost line will be handed over. All stores documents etc to be handed over.

4. **Guides** — O's C companies will make their own arrangements as to guides.

5. **Relief complete** — To be report by runner.

6. ACKNOWLEDGE

Issued at a.m.
by runner
In the Field 9.4.18

P. E. Edwards, Lt & A/Adjt
2nd Duke of Wellington's Regt

Copies No 1 to 4 Companies
No 5 R.S.M.
No 6 War Diary
No 7 File

SECRET   C   Copy No 6.
                                        E.D.

OPERATION ORDERS No 78
2nd Duke of Wellington's Regt.

Ref. map. 51^B N.W.

                                8.4.18

1. The battalion will be relieved to-night April 8/9th by the 13th Canadian Batt. (R. H'rs).

2. Two guides from Bn. H.Q. One for each Coy. H.Q and one per platoon will meet the incoming unit at the Double Arch H.19.b.4.6. at 6 p.m. 2/Lt Cooke will be in charge of these guides.

3. All maps, photographs, defence orders, trench stores etc will be handed over; the receipts obtained will be forwarded to Bn H.Q by noon to-morrow 9th inst. Advance parties to take over are expected to arrive during the afternoon.

4. The battalion will march to the embussing point G.18.c.20.40 by platoons at 200 yds distance. From this point lorries will convey the battalion to AGNEZ-LES-DUISANS where C.C. Details will have made arrangements for billets. Capt. E.C. Coke will be in charge of the embussing. L+S. Waller will report to this officer at 8.30 p.m. at the embussing point G.18.c.20.40; he will ascertain from Bn. H.Q the strength of the Bn. and will be responsible for meeting companies and embussing them in correct lorries.

5. Hot meals must all have left GORDON CAMP by 4 p.m. The camp kettles must be returned as soon as possible to GORDON CAMP and loaded in limber which will be waiting there. Two other limbers will be there at 4 p.m. to remove Sawyer stoves, camp kettles & water tins. All water tins not sent down for carriage by transport must be taken back by companies and not handed over.

6. Completion of relief to be reported by runner to Bn. H.Q.

7. ACKNOWLEDGE

P.C. Edwards Lt & a/Adjt
2nd Duke of Wellington's Regt.

Distribution
Copy No 1 No 1 Coy.
  "   " 2   " 2 "
  "   " 3   " 3 "
  "   " 4   " 4 "
  "   " 5   R.S.M.
  "   " 6   FILE
  "   " 7   War Diary
  "   " 8   Bn. H.Q.
  "   " 9   M.O.

Issued by runner at 3.35 p.m.

SECRET   Copy No.
2/7 Bn Duke of Wellington's Regt
WARNING ORDER No 1

In the Field 23-4-18

1. The Dukes will relieve the 2nd Lanc. Fus. in the RIGHT FRONT line tonight.

2. Distribution of Companies:-
No 1 Coy RIGHT FRONT
No 2 " CENTRE
No 3 " LEFT FRONT
No 4 " on CANAL BANK from Q.33.c.00.45 to Pt LEVIS Q.32.c.6.9

3. Guides will be at W.13.a.2.7 at 8.30 p.m.

4. Order of March. No 3 Coy. No 2 Coy. No 1 Coy No 4 Coy & B.H.Q.
200 yards distance between Platoons.

5. Disposition Maps & lists of all Stores taken over to be sent to B.H.Q. by 12 noon tomorrow, 24th inst.

6. Blankets to be rolled in bundles of ten and stacked outside B.H.Q. by 4 p.m. Officers kits to be stacked at the same hour & same place.

7. All picks & shovels & bombs &c which have been issued to Coys are part of the man's equipment

7. and Coy Commanders are responsible for them. Very lights issued yesterday are to be kept at Coy H.Q. and only issued to the men when required.

8. Any further details will be issued later when available.

P.C. Edwards Lieut
Issued at 11-30 p.m.   Adjt. 2/4th Bn Wellington Regt
23-4-18

Distribution
No 1   BHQ   No 8   R.S.M
   2-5 All Coys   9-10 War Diary
   6   Q.M   11   File
   7   T.O

H.Q. P30061

"A" Form.
MESSAGES AND SIGNALS.
Army Form C.2121 (in pads of 100).

Prefix	Code	m.	Words	Charge	This message is on a/c of:	Recd. at .... m.
Office of Origin and Service Instructions.			Sent		E........... Service.	Date..............
			At .... m.			From ....
			To		(Signature of "Franking Officer.")	By ....
			By			

TO — 2/ D of W Rgt.

Sender's Number.	Day of Month.	In reply to Number.	AAA
L29	16	—	

Following has been received from 2nd Division
"Please convey to 1st R War Regt and
2/ D of W Rgt the G.O.C's appreciation of
gallant efforts they made today.
In spite of bad luck at start they
stuck to their task splendidly."

From 13th Inf Bde
Place
Time 8.20 am.

The above may be forwarded as now corrected.   (Z)   N Mansell Capt
Censor.   Signature of Addressor or person authorised to telegraph in his name.

SECRET. (F) Copy No 10

Operation Order No 79
2nd Bn Duke of Wellington's Regt

Map Sheet 28f.

In the Field 19 April 1918

1. The Battn will be relieved tonight by the 1st Rifle Brigade and 1st Hants Regt. The Boundary line between Bns. being the junction of Road & Canal Bank at W.14d.28. road inclusive to left Battalion.

2. Guides for the Rifle Brigade will be at Road Junction W.14.b.1.2. at 8.30 p.m. One Battn HQ guide, One Coy HQ guide & 4 Platoon guides will be required for this party.

Bn H.Q. will supply two guides, No 4 Coy. two & No 3 Coy. two.

Later 1st Coy. of the Rifle Brigade will occupy from Bn Boundary on left to 50 yds. S.E. of Destroyed Bridge in W.15.b.

Guides for the Hants Regt. will be at W.3.c.2.6. at 9-15 p.m. No 2 Coy will provide one Coy HQ guide & two Platoon guides. No 1 Coy., two Platoon guides.

The route for all parties will be that used by the Ration Parties.

All guides will report at Bn H.Q. at 7 p.m.

3:    All Picks & Shovels will be taken out of the line. Coys should have their tools at the Ration Dump W.3.c.2.6. by 10.15 p.m. B"H.Q. will furnish a small party to load these tools and those already at the Ration Dump.

4/   Four Lewis Gun Limbers will be at Cross Roads W.14.b.12 at midnight. If Platoons pass this point before Limbers arrive, two men will be left with Gun & Magazines.

5:    The B" will be accommodated at CENSE LA VALLEE (Vis d.) in empty billets. 2/Lt A Ehuilt-Browne and 1 N.C.O. per B"H.Q. & Coy will go on ahead as billeting party.

6:-   All S.O.S. flares, Rockets, Bombs & Ammunition will be handed over & receipts forwarded to H.Q. by 12 noon tomorrow, 20th inst.

7:-   Completion of relief will be reported by Runner to present B" H.Q.

8:-   Movement will be by Platoons at not less than 200 yards distance.

Issued by Runner   P.J. Edwards Lieut.
at   p.m.   A/Adjt Linfs

PRESS COMMUNIQUE, TROOPERS, London.

O.A.561/595   10.55 p.m.,   22nd April, 1918   AAA

SUPPLEMENTARY PRESS COMMUNIQUE   AAA

The number of divisions employed by the enemy against the British alone since the opening of his offensive on the 21st March already is 102 and many of these have been employed twice or three times AAA In resisting the heavy blows which such a concentration of troops has enabled the enemy to direct against the British Army all ranks, arms, and services have behaved with a gallantry, courage and resolution for which no praise can be too high AAA

Mention has been made in previous Communiques of certain British Divisions for conduct of outstanding gallantry AAA Many other Divisions also have greatly distinguished themselves AAA

The Guards Division, after five days of heavy fighting at BOIRY-BECQUERELLE, completely repulsed hostile attacks delivered in great strength on the 28th March, and again on the 30th March, inflicting heavy losses on the enemy AAA This Division, with the 31st and 3rd Divisions on its right and left, in severe fighting on these and other occasions, successfully resisted all the enemy's efforts to open out the northern flank of his attack AAA

Especially gallant service was performed also on the 28th March by the 4th Division north of the SCARPE, in assisting to break up the attacks launched by the enemy on that day for the capture of ARRAS and the VIMY Ridge AAA This Division also distinguished itself on the LYS battle front, on the night of the 14th/15th April, when in an admirably executed counter-attack it took the village of RIEZ du VINAGE with 150 prisoners and again on the 18th April, when it repulsed strong hostile attacks south-east of ROBECQ and took nearly 200 prisoners AAA

During the first two days of the enemy's offensive south of ARRAS, the 21st Division maintained its positions at EPEHY against all assaults, and only withdrew from the village under orders when the progress made by the enemy to the south rendered such a course necessary AAA Before this Division withdrew it inflicted great loss on the enemy, and the German official reports acknowledge the bitterness of the fighting AAA

The 25th Division was in close support when the German attack opened, and was at once sent into the battle in the neighbourhood of the BAPAUME - CAMBRAI Road AAA Though constantly attacked, it was not dislodged from any position by the enemy's assault AAA When withdrawn from the SOMME fighting the spirit of the Division was exceptionally high AAA It has since been heavily engaged in the LYS battle and has again performed distinguished service AAA

On the 13th April the 31st Division was holding a front of some 9,000 yards east of FORET de NIEPPE AAA The Division was already greatly reduced in strength as the result of previous fighting, and the enemy was still pressing his advance AAA The troops were informed that their line had to be held to the last to cover the detraining of reinforcements and all ranks responded with the most magnificent courage and devotion to the appeal made to them AAA Throughout a long day of incessant fighting they beat off a succession of determined attacks AAA In the evening, the enemy made a last great effort, and by sheer weight of numbers overran certain portions of our line, the defenders of which died fighting but would not give ground AAA Those of the enemy who had broken through at these points were, however, met and driven back beyond our line by the reinforcing troops which by this time had completed their detrainment AAA

After severe fighting in the neighbourhood of CROISILLES at the commencement of the battle, the 34th Division took over the ARMENTIERES sector and was in line there on the 9th April AAA The Division maintained its position intact throughout the first two days of the LYS battle and when the enemy's advance on either flank made it necessary to order the evacuation of ARMENTIERES, it withdrew from the town on the night of the 10th/11th April deliberately and in good order AAA Since that day it has been continuously engaged and has fought throughout with the greatest gallantry, yielding ground reluctantly and counter-attacking frequently AAA

In the fierce fighting at the end of March and early in April around BUCQUOY and ABLAINZEVILLE, the 42nd (East Lancashire) Division (T) and the 62nd (West Riding) Division (T) beat off many attacks and contributed greatly to the successful maintenance of our line in this important sector AAA

The 50th Division, though but recently withdrawn from a week of continuous fighting south of the SOMME, on the 9th April and subsequent days held up the enemy along the line of the LYS and by the stubbornness of its resistance at ESTAIRES and MERVILLE checked his advance until further reinforcements could be brought up AAA

The 3rd and 4th Australian Divisions, at MERICOURT l'ABBE and DERNANCOURT; the New Zealand Division at SERRE, and at a later date, the 5th Australian Division south of the SOMME, all performed most valuable and gallant service during the latter stages of the German attack on the SOMME AAA With their aid, the enemy's progress was definitely checked, and by the vigour of their defence all his attempts to continue his advance have been repulsed, with the heaviest losses to his troops.

CHIEF.   (Intd). J.H.D.

SECRET

Copy No.

2nd Bn. Duke of Wellington's Regt.
Operation Order No. 80

In the Field 29th April 1918

Map. Ref. 36^A S.E.

1. **INTENTION.** No. 2 Coy. will relieve No. 1 Coy. in Front Line ~~tomorrow~~ night ~~30th April/1st May~~

   No. 4 Coy. will relieve No. 3 Coy. in Close Support. tonight, 29/30th inst.

3. **INSTRUCTIONS.**

   (a) Time of Relief, 10. P.M.

   (b) <u>Guides.</u> The requisite number of guides will be detailed from Nos. 1 & 3 Coys. to report to O.C. Nos. 2 & 4 Coys. at 9-30 P.M.

   (c) <u>Work.</u> All Work in hand will be handed over. No. 1 Coy. will supply all men required by No. 4 Coy. on the requisition of O.C. that Coy. for work on Front Line.

   This work will be continued with immediately after relief.

   (d) <u>Relief Complete</u> will be reported by any sentence containing code word "PIG".

   (e) <u>S.A.A. BOMBS, ETC.</u> All S.A.A. Bombs, Maps, Documents, &c, will be handed over. S.A.A. and Bombs carried on the men will not be handed over.

3: All Picks & Shovels will be taken out of the line. Coys should have their tools at the Ration Dump W.3.c.2.6. by 10.15 p.m. Bn H.Q. will furnish a small party to load these tools and those already at the Ration Dump.

4/ Four Lewis Gun Limbers will be at Cross Roads W.14.B.1.2. at midnight. If Platoons pass this point before Limbers arrive, two men will be left with Gun & Magazines.

5: The Bn will be accommodated at CENSE LA VALLEE (V.14.d) in empty billets. 2nd A. Elliott-Brown and 1 NCO per Bn H.Q. & Coy will go on ahead as billeting party.

6: All S.O.S. flares, Rockets, Bombs & Ammunition will be handed over & receipts forwarded to H.Q. by 12 noon tomorrow, 20th inst.

7: Completion of relief will be reported by Runner to present Bn H.Q.

8: Movement will be by Platoons at not less than 200 Yards distance.

R. Edwards Lieut
A/Adjt Lincs

Issued by Runner
at   p m

S E C R E T

WAR DIARY.

of

2nd Bn. The Duke of Wellingtons Regt.

From : 1st May 1918.

To : 31st May 1918.

VOLUME.

S. Fawkes
Lieut. Colonel,
Commanding 2nd Bn. The Duke of Wellington,s Regiment.........

June 1 1918.

Army Form C. 2118.

WAR DIARY
or
INTELLIGENCE SUMMARY.

(Erase heading not required.)

Instructions regarding War Diaries and Intelligence Summaries are contained in F. S. Regs., Part II. and the Staff Manual respectively. Title pages will be prepared in manuscript.

Place.	Date	Hour	Summary of Events and Information	Remarks and references to Appendices
LEFT BDE SUB SECTOR. RIGHT BATTN SUB-SECTOR.	MAY 1918 1		Battn holding the line, quiet day. Battn H.Q.	MAP. 36.a.S.W.
"	2		Battn relieved at night by 1st HAMPSHIRE REGT and then moved back to L'EGLANTIER and further LOMAX entrances known to relief Brigade (10th) being in Reserve	A = 0.0.81
L'EGLANTIER	3		The Battn cleaning up equipment; bathing &c	SGT S. HOWLETT 23995 PTE T. GARDNER 2809 JAWARDED MILITARY MEDALS 18536 R. WOOD 13496 T. CARROL 24912 A. ROBINSON
"	4		C.O. inspected the Battalion by companies. A/R Division received congratulatory message from the 1st EAST LANCASHIRE REGT.	
"	5		Quiet day. Specialist training carried out. Ceremonial Parade for Medal Presentations cancelled owing to rain.	
"	6		Battalion relieved the 1st KINGS OWN REGT in Brigade Support. Battn H.Q. V.6.d Y.2.B. 0.0.82. B. + D. Coys in trenches W.I.C. A + C Coys trenches in W.I.b. and W.2.C.	
BELLERIVE BDE SUPPORT	7		Quiet during the day. Enemy shelled B + D Coys also Battn H.Q. from 9.30 p.m. to 11.30 p.m. 2nd LIEUT. WILDBOURNE, EAST YORKS att 2 DURS killed, 2nd MORGAN wounded 2nd McCullock shock - to hospital.	
"	8		Enemy attack anticipated. Battn moved up the line & took over Bois du Biscuit Brigade now holding the line with 3 battalions instead of 2 as before. 2nd BIDDLE wounded, 2nd SEAFORTHS on LEFT. 1st ROYAL WARWICKS on RIGHT 2nd McFARLANE wounded	C - OD 83
PROOT WEST	9		Very quiet day.	

Army Form C.2118.

WAR DIARY
or
INTELLIGENCE SUMMARY.

(Erase heading not required.)

Instructions regarding War Diaries and Intelligence
Summaries are contained in F.S. Regs., Part II.
and the Staff Manual respectively. Title pages
will be prepared in manuscript.

Place	Date	Hour	Summary of Events and Information	Remarks and references to Appendices
		1918		
PISTOL WOOD	MAY. 10.		Enemy gassed all back areas very heavily, but quiet on forward areas. Regimental Aid post hit with a gas shell. The M.O. (Lt Brown R.A.M.C.) and all personnel gassed.	
"	11		Holding the line. Quiet day.	
"	12		Holding the line. Enemy in the wood very quiet. Very little shelling	
"	13		- do -	Improving the defences.
"	14		- do -	
"	15		Enemy identification required. Small raid done by "C" Coy. at 8·30 am 1. NCO (Cpl. PHOSEY) and 6 men dashed over the drive at about G.33.d.4.4. and came upon an unoccupied enemy post. Pushing further ahead and slightly to the left they came across a post occupied by 3 of the enemy. One ran away, the other 2 surrounded. The raiding party then came back. During this operation which lasted 15 minutes the enemy were kept down by an intense concentration of Lewis gun fire on both flanks of the raided post. Prisoners belonged to the 5th R.I.R. and were a N.C.O. + a musketeer, both were of fairly good physique. The Battn relieved by 1st HAMPSHIRE REGT and proceeded to L'ECLEME.	D.10.0.84

Army Form C. 2118.

WAR DIARY
or
INTELLIGENCE SUMMARY. (3)

(Erase heading not required.)

Instructions regarding War Diaries and Intelligence Summaries are contained in F.S. Regs., Part II. and the Staff Manual respectively. Title pages will be prepared in manuscript.

Place	Date	Hour	Summary of Events and Information	Remarks and references to Appendices
L'ECLEME Bn in Reserve	MAY 1918 16		Battn cleaning up bathing &c. Capt D.G.R. BILHAM awarded the M.C. 9306 SGT TW BOURNE 36094 CPL. P.C. TUSTIN and 94488 SGT. T.R. OGDEN awarded the D.C.M.	
	17		Reorganisation of sections &c. changing details. B & D Coys sent forward to trenches on CANAL BANK P.36 b and Q.1.a.	
	18. 19.		DIVINE SERVICE in the morning. CEREMONIAL PARADE for presentation of MEDAL RIBBONS in the afternoon by CORPS COMMANDER. Battalion relieved the 1st KINGS OWN in F - OB 55. (LT GEN HOLLAND)	
	18 19		the NNNY LEFT BRIGADE SECTOR CENTRE BATT. SUB-SECTOR 2nd SEAFORTH HIGHLANDERS on the left and 1st ROYAL WARWICKSHIRE REGT on the right. Trenches in area G.25.b & d and G.26.a.b. & c. Bn H.Q. G.31.a. 05.50	
	18		Quiet day. Battn resting. System of Training & later Training for the men. Preserve up Bn & gen ins 1st day Battn rest & cleaning of the soldier & some — clothing. 2nd day 22 thorough of gas alert cleaning of Lewis gun B.A.R. LF lubing of men — briefing. Close order Rule. Batt. HQ — Issue of Ammunition & other necessities. Close order drill & ordering Lewis gun — Route march - 2nd day 3rd day Battn in Support & 1/2 day only for rest. Battalion holding the line. Lewis Aeroplane hung day. 4 WANE regained from hospital	
RIEZ de VINAGE	20			
	21.		Battalion holding the line. Very little hostile activity. Major BARKELEY M.C. left the battalion and rejoined his own unit, 1st HAMPSHIRE REGT.	
	22		Situation as on previous day. 2/Lt FILLINGHAM sick to hospital	

Army Form C. 2118.

WAR DIARY
or
INTELLIGENCE SUMMARY.

(Erase heading not required)

Place	Date	Hour	Summary of Events and Information	Remarks and references to Appendices
	MAY - 1918			
RIEZ-du-VINAGE AREA	23		Battalion holding the line. 2nd Lt COKE rejoined from hospital. 2nd Lt HUTCHINGS sick to hospital.	
"	24		Battalion holding the line. Very little hostile activity. Work being done on the Forward Positions - Consolidating - Erecting barbed wire entanglements - wiring - making fire-stops - digging - cleaning out Intelligence Dumps at Sanitary - Burying dead.	
"	25		Battalion holding the line. MAJOR CARR M.C. BORDER REGIMENT, joined the Battalion as 2nd in Command. 2nd Lt F.H. HILL rejoined the Battn. after tour of duty in England.	
"	26		Holding the line. Situation quiet. 2nd Lieut HUFFEN joined the Battn. Trench Strength 24 9.	F = 110.86
"	27		Battalion relieved by 1st RIFLE BRIGADE. After relief moved back to Brigade in Reserve Area. L'ECLEME.	
L'ECLEME	28		Battalion cleaning up, bathing &c. Village shelled. 1 O.R. killed & 1 wounded	
"	29		Battalion inspected by C.O. (4 companies). Draft of 59. O.R. for 6 Regular Battns. Reported to-day for the Battn. Battalion parade Bayonet Fighting - Bomb Throwing - Gas Drill - Grenades, Lewis Gun, Sniping.	
"	30		Battalion training. Building Rifle Range &c. Overhauling Gardens, jumping &c	
"	31		Battalion training. Work as on previous day.	

COPY

2nd Bn Duke of Wellington's Regt
Operation Order No 83

Information. 1. The 10th Inf Bde sector will be altered from a 2 Battalion to a 3 Battalion front to-night 8/9/ . Brigade Boundaries will remain the same. Centre sector will be taken over by 2nd Duke of Wellington's Regt.

Intention. 2. 2 Duke of Wellington Regt will hold centre sector as follows:—

(a) Front line Q.33.d.80.60 (No 3 post SE edge of PACAUT WOOD) — Q.33.d.40.90 cross roads inclusive with ride, from 1st R. Warwickshire Regt held by "C" Coy.

(b) Q.33.d.40.90 cross roads ride exclusive to Q.33.a.80.25 (N.W. edge of PACAUT wood) with 2 posts along NW edge of wood from Right Coy 2nd Sea Hrs by "A" Coy.

(c) Support line from SE edge of wood Q.33.d.50.20 — Q.33.d.10.53 (ride inclusive) from 1st R Warr R. and from Q.33.d.10.53 — NW edge of wood at Q.33.c.50.90 and one post on NW edge of wood from 2 Sea Hrs by "D" Coy.

(d) On canal bank from W.3.c.38.45 to Q.33.c.65.00 from 1 R War R. and from Q.33.c.65.00 to Q.33.c.10.40 from 2 Sea Hrs by "B" Coy.

~~All posts on NW wood will be under orders of O.C. D Company.~~

(2)

Instructions 3.

(a) Guides
  (i) 9 platoon guides of 1 R. War. R. will be at W.2.a.7.3 at 9 pm for C coy, right ½ of D coy, B coy less ½ platoon.
  (ii) 7 platoon guides of 2 Sea H'rs will be at W.2.a.7.3 at 9.30 pm for A Coy, left ½ D coy, ½ platoon of B Coy.
  (iii) Units are providing 2 coy HQ. guides for Coy HQ.

(b) Bombs
  3 boxes no 5 and 3 boxes no 23 with rods and cartridges, conduit will be dumped at W.3.a.7.6 and will be collected from this point after 1 am 9th inst.

~~Patrols~~
  on night 9/10th patrols will be sent out to discover any sign of enemy attack. Should patrols see enemy about to attack they will fire whilst very lights this till cause artillery to lay down our barrage when patrols must get back to our own line.

d) Completion of ~~which~~ will be notified to B.W.H.Q. ~~~~

AID POST   at W.2.a.7.6

3

(c) Completion of relief will be notified to Bty
rep. by same method as in order 82
of 6th inst by wire + return B14D number

A10PBT   with heads W.2.9.73

B14HQ   with heads V.5.6.72 until further
orders

acknowledge

C Para
15 A/Bde
All coys
Bn HQ
2 Sqn H Dr
1 RNcl R
Sig
nav

SECRET.

2nd Bn. Duke of Wellington's Regiment.
OPERATION ORDER No. 81.

Ref. Map. Sheet 36.A. S.E.   In the Field, 2nd May, 1918.

INFORMATION. 1.   The 2nd Bn. Duke of Wellington's Regt. will be relieved in RIGHT SUB-SECTOR of 10th Bde. Sector on the night of the 2nd May, 1918, by 1st Bn. The Hampshire Regt.

INTENTION. 2.   (a) The Bn. will proceed to Divisional Reserve Rest Billets at LECLEME by road P.36.b.1.5.15.-V.5.b.55.30.-CENSE LA VALLEE (by Cross Country Road not marked on map).
     Guides will meet each Coy. at P.36.c.4.4. Post also established under 2Lieut. G.HARNELL at V.5.b.55.55. until Bn. H.Q. have passed that point.

(b) The Front Line will be relieved by "A" Coy. 1st Hants.
     The Immediate Support Line will be relieved by "B" Coy. 1st Hants.
     The Right Support by "D" Coy. 1st Hants.
     The Left Support by "C" Coy. 1st Hants.

INSTRUCTIONS. 3

(a) Guides. One per Platoon, one for each Coy. H.Q., two per Bn. H.Q. will report to DUKES Bn. H.Q. at 6.15 p.m. for written instructions. Each guide will be in possession of a paper signed by Coy. Commander with the Sector of Trench to be occupied by the Platoon he is to guide.
     Guides will be taken to Cross Roads at P.36.c.4.4. under an Officer where they will meet the in-coming Battalion.

(b) Routes in.
     A & B Coy. 1st Hants. will be guided Cross Country Route, leaving CANAL BANK at P.36.b.2.7. to points arranged by O's C. B. & D. Coys. DUKES passing well to the WEST of SUPPORT Coy. H.Q. at Q.31.b.7.9.
     C. & D. Coys. 1st Hants will be guided by direct Route, BRIDGE (P.36.a.6.7.)-CANAL BANK-FORKED ROADS(Q.31.a.9.5.) to points arranged by O's. C. A & C Coys. DUKES.

(c) Routes out.
     Out-going Coys. will follow route of in-coming Coys.

(d) Movement to be by Platoons at 200 yards interval.

(e) All Maps, Sketches, Programmes of Work in Hand, and other written information with regard to the line will be handed over to Relieving Companies.

(f) Trench Stores will be handed over to relieving Coys., and Duplicate Lists made. One copy of receipt taken to be retained by each Coy. Commander.

(g) The units of the 11th Bde. have emergency dumps of S.A.A., Hand and Rifle Grenades at their present billets. These will be taken over on relief by the units of the 10th Bde.
     Statements of quantities taken over and additional quantities of Rifle and Hand Grenades required to bring these dumps up to the equivalent of Battn. Echelons and of S.A.A. to give each man an additional 50 rounds S.A.A. will be rendered to Bn. H.Q. with the lists of Trench Stores handed over.

INSTRUCTIONS. 3. (Contd)
    (h) Lewis Guns will be carried to CROSS ROADS at P.36.c.4.4.
    and handed over to N.C.O. who will superintend loading
    them in limbers.

    (j) Completion of Relief will be reported by wire to Bn. H.Q.
    by Code Words "MOOSE JAW".

                                               (Sgd) R.C.Edwards, Capt & A/Adjt.
Issued by Runner   2nd Bn. Duke of Wellington's Regt.
  at 1.45p.m.

DISTRIBUTION.

Copy No. 1 10th Inf. Bde.   Copy No. 8 T.O. & Q.M.
         2 - 5 All Coys.   9 1st Hants Regt.
         6 B.H.Q.   10 - 11 War Diary.
         7 M.O.   12 File.

SECRET.

2nd Bn. Duke of Wellington's Regt.

Copy No. 10

OPERATION ORDER No. 82.

Ref. Map. Sheet 36.A. S.E.
1/20.000

In the Field, May 6th, 1918.

INFORMATION. 1. The 2nd Duke of Wellington's Regt. will relieve 1st The King's Own Regt. in Bde. Reserve on the night 6/7th May 1918.

INTENTION. 2. (a) The Battalion will proceed by road via CENSE LA VALLEE – TRACK V.5.c.2.3. – ROAD to V.5.b.5.2.
Guides will meet each Company at V.5.b.5.2.
(b) A. & C. Companies will relieve Forward Trench.
B. & D. Companies will relieve Support Trench.
Battalion H.Q. will be V.6.d.70.20.

INSTRUCTIONS. 3. (a) Advance Party 1 Officer and 1 Runner per Company will report to Bn. H.Q. 1st King's Own Regt. at 4.30 p.m. 6th inst. These Officers will ascertain their Company dispositions and will meet their Companies on Arrival.
(b) Order of March B. D. A. C. Companies and Bn. HQ.
The leading Platoon of B. Company will cross the Bridge at V.10.a.0.9. at 9.15 p.m.
(c) Movement will be by Platoons at 100 Yards interval to point where Guides are met, thence by Platoons at 200 Yards interval.
(d) Guides 1 per Platoon, 1 per Company H.Q., 2 Bn.H.Q., will meet Battalion at V.5.b.5.2. at 10.15 p.m.
(e) Lewis Guns and 32 Magazines per gun will be carried by Limber to V.5.d.3.7. Lewis Gun Officer will arrange for an N.C.O. to accompany these Limbers and superintend distribution of guns to Companies.
(f) Maps, etc. All Maps, Sketches, etc. will be taken over. Sketch Maps shewing dispositions by Platoons will be forwarded to Bn.H.Q. by 6 a.m. 7th inst.
(g) Trench Stores will be taken over and a copy of receipt will be kept by Company Commanders.
(h) Rations for consumption on the 7th inst. will be carried on the man.
(i) Water. Water-bottles must be filled before leaving Billets. Water will be distributed in Petrol Tins to each Company nightly.
(j) Completion of Relief will be reported by wire to Bn.H.Q. by Clock Method.
Greatcoats will not be taken into the Line, but will be placed in men's packs and handed into Stores.
Present Billets will be handed over to representatives of 2nd Lanc. Fus. during afternoon, 6th inst.

TRANSPORT 4. Transport Officer will arrange :-
(a) To remove packs (with greatcoats) from Coy.H.Q. at 3 p.m.
(b) To remove Officers Valises, Mess Stores, etc., from Bn.H.Q. at 8 p.m.
(c) To convey Lewis Guns and Drums to V.5.d.3.7.

AID POST. 5. Aid Post will be established at Bn.H.Q.

Capt.
A/Adjt. 2nd Bn. Duke of Wellington's Regt.

Issued at

DISTRIBUTION.

Copy No. 1 Bn.H.Q.   Copy No. 9 T.O.
         2 - 5 All Coys.   10 - 11 War Diary
         6 10th Inf. Bde.   12 File.
         7 1st K.O's.
         8 Q.M.

SECRET.   D   No. 60

2nd Bn. Duke of Wellington's Regt.

OPERATION ORDER No. 84.

Ref. Map Sheet 36.A. S.E.   In the Field, 15th May, 1918.
    1/20,000

INFORMATION.   1.   The 10th Inf. Bde. will be relieved by 11th Inf. Bde in
                    the RIGHT SECTOR on the night 15/16th May, 1918.

INSTRUCTIONS. 2.   The 2nd DUKES will be relieved in the FRONT LINE CENTRE
                    by the 1st HANTS. REGT.
           (1) "B" Coy. Dukes will be relieved by "D" Coy. Hants.
               "C" "   ———————do——————— "A"
               "A" "   ———————do——————— "B"
               "D" "   ———————do——————— "C"
               Reliefs will take place in the above order.
           (2) On completion of relief the Bn. will occupy its old
               billets in L'ECLEME.
           (3) In the event of an attack or preliminary bombardment, all
               units of the 1st Hants., N. of the CANAL will occupy the
               nearest trenches and come under the command of the O.C.
               2nd Dukes.

INSTRUCTIONS. 3.(1) GUIDES, will be at ROAD JUNCTION. W.2.a.1.2. at 10 p.m.
                    Each Company will provide 4 guides for their relieving
                    Company.   HANTS. will arrive at rendezvous in the
                    following order :-
                         "D" Company HANTS.
                         "A"   "   "
                         "B"   "   "
                         "C"   "   "
           (2) All Trench Stores, Trench Maps, Programmes of Work in hand,
               etc., will be handed over to relieving units.
               A duplicate list of Trench Stores, etc., handed over
               signed by a representative of the relieving Company, will
               be forwarded to Bn. H.Q. by 9 a.m. 16th inst.
           (3) Relief Complete will be reported by same method as in order
               82 of 6th inst.
           (4) ROUTE. "A" & "D" Companies via the WEST BRIDGE
                      "C" Company   "   " EAST BRIDGE.
           (5) Companies will move to L'CLEME via Bn. AID POST -
               WINDMILL - Late Bn. H.Q. (V.6.M.75.30) - BELLERIVE Road -
               L'CLEME.
           (6) TRANSPORT. (Lewis Guns.)
               Lewis Guns will be carried to the WINDMILL at W.1.d.1.2.
               and there loaded on L.G.Limbers.

                                   (Sgd) E.G.J.Berkeley, Major, for
                              A/Adjt. 2nd Duke of Wellington's Regt.

                        D I S T R I B U T I O N.
                        ————————————————————————

    Copy No. 1 B.H.Q.   Nos. 2 - 5 All Coys.   No. 6 Hants Regt.   No. 7 QM & T.O.
           Nos. 8 - 9 War Diary   No. 1 0 File.

SECRET.   Copy No. 11

2nd Bn. Duke of Wellington's Regt. (E)
OPERATION ORDER No. 85

Ref. Map Sheet 36.A. S.E.
1/20,000
In the Field, May 19th, 1918.

INFORMATION.	1.	The 2nd Duke of Wellington's Regt. will relieve the 1st Bn. The King's Own Regt. in CENTRE SUB-SECTOR on night 19/20th May, 1918.
INSTRUCTIONS.	2.(a)	The Battalion less "D" and "B" Companies will proceed by ROUTE 4 to CROSS ROADS P.36.b.15.20. B. and D. Companies will proceed from CANAL BANK under their own arrangements. Guides will meet each Company at P.36.b.15.20.
	(b)	"B" Company and 1 Platoon of "D" Company will relieve FRONT LINE and will be under tactical command of O.C. "B" Coy. "D" Company less 1 Platoon and "A" Company will relieve the SUPPORT LINE. "D" Coy. on LEFT and "A" Coy. on RIGHT. "C" Company will relieve the RESERVE LINE. Battalion H.Q. will be at Q.31.a.6.5.
	(c)	Advance Party 1 Officer and 1 Runner per Company will report to Bn. H.Q. 1st King's Own Regt. at 6 p.m., 19th inst. These Officers will ascertain their Company Dispositions and will meet their Companies on arrival.
	(d)	Order of March "A", "C", Companies and Bn. H.Q.
	(e)	Time The leading platoons of "A" Company will move off from billets at 8.15 p.m.
	(f)	Movement will be by Platoons at 100 yards interval to point where Guides are met, thence by Platoons at 200 yards.
	(g)	Guides 1 per Platoon, 1 per Company H.Q., 2 Bn. H.Q. will meet battalion at P.36.b.15.20. at 10.15 p.m.
	(h)	Lewis Guns and 24 Magazines per gun will be carried by limber to P.36.c.50.45. Lewis Gun Officer will arrange for a N.C.O. to accompany these limbers and superintend distribution of guns to Companies.
	(i)	Maps, etc., All Maps, Sketches, etc., will be taken over. Sketch Maps showing dispositions by platoons will be forwarded to Bn. H.Q. by 6 a.m. 20th inst.
	(j)	Trench Stores will be taken over and a copy of receipt will be kept by Company Commanders.
	(k)	Rations for consumption on the 20th inst. will be carried on the man. Rations for future consumption will be brought by limber to Q.25.b.2.2. and will be met by guides at 11 p.m. nightly.
	(l)	Water. Water-bottles must be filled before leaving Billets. Water will be brought up in Petrol Tins nightly. Empty Tins must be sent down regularly.
	(m)	Indents for Ammunition and R.E.Material must reach Bn. H.Q. by 6 a.m. daily.
	(n)	Billets. will be handed over to 2nd Lanc. Fus. They will be left scrupulously clean and a certificate as to cleanliness will be obtained.
	(o)	Completion of Relief will be reported by wire to Bn. H.Q. by G.902 of 5th inst.
TRANSPORT	3.	Transport Officer will arrange :- (a) To remove Packs and Blankets from Coy. H.Q. at 3 p.m. (b) To remove Officers Valises, Mess Stores, etc., from Bn.H.Q. at 6 p.m. (c) To convey Lewis Guns and Drums to P.36.c.50.45.
AID POST	4.	Aid Post will be established at P.38.d.3.9.

P.C.Edwards Captain,
Adjutant 2nd Battn. The Duke of Wellington's Regt.

Issued by runner at 2 p.m.

DISTRIBUTION.

Copy No. 1 Bn. H.Q.　　　　　　Copy No. 8 Q.M.
　　　 2 - 5 All Coys.
　　　 6 10th Inf. Bde.　　　　　　　　 9 T.O.
　　　 7 1st K.O's Regt.　　　　　　　 10 - 11 War Diary
　　　　　　　　　　　　　　　　　　　 12 File.

2nd Bn Duke of Wellington's Regiment.

After Order to Operation Order No.85.   May 19th 1915.

Overcoats.   Overcoats will be brought up on the night of the 20th, on
ration limbers, and be deposited by carrying parties at Company Dumps.
They will be tied in bundles and care must be taken that each man
gets his own.

                                    Sgd . J.Cocke. 2 Lieut.
                            A/Adjt. 2nd Bn Duke of Wellington's Regt.

To all recipients of O.O. No.85.

SECRET.   Copy No. 10

2nd Bn. Duke of Wellington's Regt.
OPERATION ORDER No. 26.

Ref. Sheet 36.A. S.E.
   .1/20.000   In the Field, 26th May, 1918.
==

INTENTION. 1. (a) 2nd Bn. Duke of Wellington's Regt. will be relieved in the
                    line on the night 27/28th May, 1918, by 1st Rifle Brigade.
                (b) 2nd Bn. Duke of Wellington's Regt. will move on completion
                    of relief, to billets in L'ECLEME.

INSTRUCTIONS. 2. (a) B. & D. Coys. 2nd D.of W's. will be relieved in FRONT LINE
                    by C. Coy. 1st R.B. C. Coy. R.B. are taking over Coy. H.Q.
                    from A. Company.
                    A. Coy. 2nd D.of W's. will be relieved in SUPPORT by B. & I
                    Coys. 1st R.B. B. & I. Coys. R.B. are taking over B. & D
                    Coys. H.Q.
                    C. Coy. 2nd D.of W's. will be relieved in RESERVE by A. Coy.
                    1st R.B.
                    Completion of Relief will be wired to Bn. H.Q. as in Order
                    No. 25.
                (b) GUIDES. 1 guide per Platoon (1st R.B. have 3 Platoons per
                             1   "   Per Coy. H.Q.   Coy.)
                             2   "   per Bn. H.Q.
                    will be at Pt. LEVIS. P.36.a.85.75. at 11 p.m.
                (c) All Trench Stores, Trench Maps, Aeroplane Photos, Programme
                    of Work in hand, will be handed over to incoming units and
                    receipts taken.
                (d) Lewis Guns, Magazines, etc., will be carried to Pt. LEVIS,
                    P.36.a.85.75. where limbers will await them.
                    L.G.Officer will arrange for a N.C.O. to superintend loading
                    and off-loading at L'ECLEME.
                (e) Great-coats will be carried out rolled in bandolier fashion
                    unless weather is bad, when they will be worn on the men.
                (g) Each Company will send a runner to R.S.M. to report when
                    all Companies are in billets.
                    R.S.M. will report all present to Adjutant.
                (f) Companies will move to L'ECLEME with not less than 200 yards
                    between Platoons.
                (h) Quartermaster will arrange :-
                    (i) To take over billets in L'ECLEME from 1st Hampshire
                        Regt., also Reserve Dump of S.A.A., Bombs, Stores, etc.
                    (ii) with T.O. for packs and blankets, etc., being moved
                         from BUSNETTES.

TRANSPORT. 3.   Transport Officer will arrange :-
                    (i) with Q.M. for move of packs, blankets, Officers Kits,
                        etc. as detailed in h.ii. above.
                    (ii) to convey L.G.Magazines & Officers Mess Stores from
                         Pt. LEVIS. P.36.a.85.75. to Coy. Billets at L'ECLEME.
                    (iii) for a limber to be at xxxxxxxxxxxx Bn. H.Q.
                          Q.31.a.0.7. at 10 p.m. to carry Stores etc.

                                            (Sgd) E.C.Coke, Capt.
                                            A/Adjt. 2nd Duke of Wellington's Regt.

                            D I S T R I B U T I O N.

Nos. 1 - 4 All Coys. No. 5 Bn.H.Q. No. 6 1st R.B. No. 7 10th Inf. Bde.
  No. 8 T.O. & Q.M. Nos. 9 - 10 War Diary. No. 11 File.

S E C R E T

WAR DIARY.

of

2nd Bn. The Duke of Wellingtons Regt.

From: 1st June 1918.

To : 30th June 1918.

VOLUME.

Major   Lieut. Colonel,
Commanding 2nd Bn The Duke of Wellington's Regiment.

July 3rd 1918.

Army Form C. 2118.

WAR DIARY
or
INTELLIGENCE SUMMARY.
(Erase heading not required.)

Instructions regarding War Diaries and Intelligence Summaries are contained in F. S. Regs., Part II. and the Staff Manual respectively. Title pages will be prepared in manuscript.

Place	Date	Hour	Summary of Events and Information	Remarks and references to Appendices
	JUNE	1918		
Bde in Reserve BELENE	1		Training, musketry, L.G. etc. Fitting clothing. Working parties.	
"	2		Changing details, working parties. B⁰ moved forward to PACAUT WOOD sector ?/-	
Cature B⁰ in line PACAUT WOOD	3		B⁰ relieved 1/10 KING'S OWN. Relief complete 1.30 a.m. Two Coys front line, 1 Coy support, 1 Coy in CANAL BANK. B⁰ Hqr STINK FARM. Casualties shelling during relief. Casualties 1 K + 5 W.	A
"	4		Holding line. Situation quiet. German killed by snipe.	
"	5		" " Situation quiet by day. M.G. + grenade fire at night.	
"	6		German killed by sniper. Casualties 4 W.	
"	7		Situation quiet. Casualties 2 W.	
"	8		Situation quiet. 6" shell obtained direct hit on Bash [in] fort in WOOD. Some gas shelling at night. Quiet day. S.O.S sent up at 11.11. at 11.22 p.m. Enemy put down heavy barrage on CANAL BANK. B+D Coys relieved C+A Coys in front line. Casualties 3 men W.	B
"	9		Coy relief complete 2 a.m. Situation quiet. Casualties 3 men W.	

Army Form C. 2118.

WAR DIARY
or
INTELLIGENCE SUMMARY.
(Erase heading not required.)

Instructions regarding War Diaries and Intelligence Summaries are contained in F.S. Regs., Part II. and the Staff Manual respectively. Title pages will be prepared in manuscript.

Place	Date	Hour	Summary of Events and Information	Remarks and references to Appendices
	JUNE 1918.			
PACAUT WOOD.	10		Quiet day. 1/Lt ELNET BROWN + 2 men wounded at night.	
"	11		Situation quiet. Casualties 1 K + 3 W.	
"	12		Sn/o/Sgt enemy relief. Casualties 1 W.	
"	13		Considerable shelling at night. B^n relieved during day.	C
Bde in Rexerve ECLEME	14		by 1st B^n HAMPSHIRE REGT. Reld Complete 1.30 a.m. B^n marched to ECLEME taking over billets occupied. Bathing + disinfection of clothing	
	15		Divine Service was held under the Chaplain General. Also at night the Batt^n were formed up to witness a demonstration of Gas Projectors.	
	16		Training. Musketry. In the afternoon Batt. Sports were held. A draft of about 100 men joined the Batt^n. Two coy A + C relieved B + A^t^r + a Seaforth Highlanders in the Canal Switch, Right Bde Sector. Relief passed quietly.	D
	17		Training. Musketry + Bayonet Training.	
	18		Ditto —	

WAR DIARY
or
INTELLIGENCE SUMMARY.

Army Form C. 2118.

Place	Date	Hour	Summary of Events and Information	Remarks and references to Appendices
	JUNE 1918.			
IN THE LINE CENTRE BATTⁿ LEFT B^{DE} (RIEZ DU VINAGE SECTOR)	19.		Battⁿ relieved the 1st Bⁿ KINGS OWN REG^T in the line. A coy Front line. C coy Support. B left reserve and D. Coy. R^t Reserve. Relief complete 1.10 am. Slight shelling during relief. Three men wounded. 1st ROYAL WARWICKSHIRES on right, 2nd SEAFORTH HIGHLANDERS on LEFT.	E
"	20.		General situation quiet. Two men wounded.	
"	21.		Holding line situation still quiet. Several men admitted to hospital sick.	
"	22.		Enemy fairly active on the support line with 5.9's and 4.2's all during the day. 1 man wounded.	
"	23.		The Corps on our left did an attack. The enemy retaliated rather heavily on our reserve and support line. 1 man killed 3 wounded. 12 men admitted to hospital sick. The sickness which is very prevalent is characterised by an extremely high temperature and violent head ache. The effects seem to last about a week, but during this time it is very infectious.	
"	24.		Situation quiet. 1 man killed and one man wounded by enemy machine gun fire. Considerable amount of work being done in the line as regards improving the trenches.	
"	25.		Inter coy relief. D coy Front line. B coy Support. A Lt Reserve and C R^t Reserve. Relief completed by 1.30 am. No casualties. 17 men admitted to Hospital suffering from the new sickness.	F

Army Form C. 2118.

WAR DIARY
or
INTELLIGENCE SUMMARY.
(Erase heading not required.)

Instructions regarding War Diaries and Intelligence Summaries are contained in F. S. Regs, Part II. and the Staff Manual respectively. Title pages will be prepared in manuscript.

Place	Date	Hour	Summary of Events and Information	Remarks and references to Appendices
IN THE LINE CENTRE BATTN. LEFT BDE. (RIEZ DU VINAGE SECTOR)	JUNE. 1918. 26.		Situation quiet. Several enemy spotted by our snipers. 3 hits claimed. Enemy relief suspected as the enemy have to day a been very careful not to show himself. Now he seems quiet careless about it. 14 men to Hospital with new sickness.	
	27.		Situation quiet. 2/Lts TUNSTALL and HUFFEN to Hospital with new sickness, also 17 men with same.	
	28.		Heavy enemy retaliation in reply to an operation carried out on our Left. 1 man wounded.	
	29.		Very quiet day. 2/LT LAW and 9.O.R. to Hospital.	
	30.		The 1st BATTN ROYAL WARWICKSHIRE REGT on our right did a successful raid. 3 prisoners taken and a great number of the enemy killed. 9.O.R to Hospital.	

SECRET.   Copy.No. 11

2nd Bn Duke of Wellington's Regiment.
OPERATION ORDER No.27.

Ref Map Sheet 36a.S.E.   In the Field, 2nd June, 1918.
1/20,000

INTENTION. 1. The 2nd Bn Duke of Wellington's Regt. will relieve the 1st Bn, The King's Own in the CENTRE SUB-Sector, PACAUT SECTOR, on the night 2/3rd June. 1918.

INSTRUCTIONS.
    2.(a) RELIEFS.
        RIGHT FRONT LINE "C" Coy. D.of W.will relieve "D" 1st K.O.
        LEFT FRONT LINE   "A" Coy. ————do———— "B" ————
        SUPPORT LINE.   "D" Coy ————do———— "A" ————
        RESERVE LINE.   "B" Coy.————do———— "C" ————

    (b) GUIDES. One per platoon, one per Company H.Q., two per Bn H.Q., will be at W.8.a.1.8. at 9.45.p.m.

    (c) ORDER OF MARCH. as in para (a).
        First Platoon of "C" Coy. will pass Bridge V.10.a.10.85.at 8.45.p.m. 100 yards distance between platoons will be maintained.
        A marching out state will be sent to R.S.M. when Coys move off.

    (d) DRESS. Fighting Order. Overcoats rolled Bandolier fashion.

    (e) ROUTE. One guide per Coy. will report at Bn.H.Q. at 4.p.m. to reconnoitre route and guide the Coy up at night.

    (f) Trench Stores. All Trench Stores, Maps, Programmes of Work, Defence Orders, etc., will be taken over and a list kept.

    (g) COMPLETION OF RELIEF. will be notified to Bn H.Q. as in Order No.25.

    (h) DEFENCE. In the event of an attack or a preliminary bombardment developing during the relief, all troops South of the Canal will occupy their Battle Positions in accordance with Battalion Defence Scheme.

    (i) DISPOSITIONS. Maps showing Dispositions will be forwarded to Bn.H.Q. by 8.a.m. 3rd inst.

    (j) ADVANCE PARTY. 2Lieut. J Cocke. 2Lieut J.T.Ickringill and 1.N.C.O. per Coy. and BN.H.Q. will report to 1st King's Own during afternoon 2nd inst.

    (k) LEWIS GUNS. and 24 Magazines will be carried by limber to W.8.a.1.8. The L.G.O. will detail a N.C.O. to accompany limbers and superintend distribution to Companies.
        Lewis Guns and Magazines will be collected from Coys at 8.p.m.

    (l) RATIONS. for consumption 3rd inst, will be carried on the man. All water bottles will be filled before leaving billets.

    (m) BILLETS. The Q.M. will arrange to hand over billets to 2nd Lancs. Fusrs. at 3.p.m. 2nd inst.
        All billets must be left scrupulously clean and certificates to that effect will be obtained from 2nd Lancs. Fusrs.

    (n) STORES. Salvage etc, will be collected at 2.p.m.
        Mens' Packs must be stacked at Coy.H.Q. by 3.p.m.
        Officers Kits must be stacked at Coy.H.Q.by 8.p.m.
        Mess Stores————————do———————————9.p.m.

    (o) PIONEERS. 6 Pioneers will march with "B" Coy and be accommodated by that Coy for 24 hours.

TRANSPORT.   Transport Officer will arrange:-
    (a) for collecting stores, etc, as shown in para (n).
    (b) for removal of Cookers and Maltese Cart.
    (c) to collect Lewis Guns and Magazines at 8.p.m. from Coy H.Q. and convey same to W.8.a.1.8.

BATTALION.H.Q.   willbe at W.8.d.1.6.
AID POST.   will be at W.2. a. 8.2.

                                    R. C. Cocke.
                                          Captain,
                            Adjutant 2nd Battn. The Duke of Wellington's

DISTRIBUTION.

```
Copy No. 1. BN.H.Q.           Copy No. 8. Q.M.
         2.-5 all Coys.                9. T.O.
         6. 1st King's Own R.          10-11. War Diary.
         7. 10th Infy Bde.             12. File.
```

SECRET.   B   2nd Bn. Duke of Wellington's Regt.   Copy No. 9
                            (OPERATION) ORDER No. 88
Ref MS Sheet 36.a. S.E.
       1/20,000   In the Field, 8th June, 1918.

INTENTION.   1. An Inter-Company Relief will take place on the night
                 8/9th June, 1918.

INSTRUCTIONS. 2. Relief.
        (a) B. Coy. will relieve C. Coy. in RIGHT FRONT LINE, C. Coy.
            will become RESERVE COMPANY. This relief will be
            complete when rear of C.Coy. passes D.Coy. H.Q.
            O.C. C. Coy. will inform O.C. B. Coy.
        (b) On completion of (a) D.Coy. will relieve A.Coy. in LEFT
            FRONT LINE, A.Coy. will become Company in SUPPORT.
        (c) Rations All empties must be at B.Coy. by 8 p.m.
            B.Coy. will carry empties to Ration Dump and pick up
            Rations for B. A. & D.Coys.
            A. & D.Coys. Rations will be carried to SUPPORT Line
            where A.Coy. rations will be left under a Guard of D.Coy.
            when D.Coy. move forward for relief carrying their own
            rations with them.
            C.Coy. on completion of relief (a) will send 1 N.C.O. and
            10 men to fetch their rations from Dump.
        (d) WORK Each Company will arrange to take over Programmes
            of Work in daylight. C.Coy. will send C.S.M. to take
            over ration arrangements of succeeding nights from C.S.M.
            B.Coy.
        (e) STORES Signed receipts for Stores, etc. taken over and
            handed over will be kept by all Companies.
        (f) Completion of Relief will be wired to Bn. H.Q. as in
            Operation Order No. 87.
        (g) ATTACK. In the event of an attack developing, all troops
            EAST of CANAL who have completed relief, will man their
            own trenches, but the moving Companies will, if not
            already in position, man CANAL BANK immediately.

                                (Sgd) E.C. Colge, Captain.
                        A/Adjt. 2nd Duke of Wellington's Regt.

                        DISTRIBUTION.

        Copy No. 1 B.H.Q.   Copy No. 7 T.O.
                 2 - 5 All Coys.   8 - 9 War Diary.
                 6 Q.M.   10 File.

SECRET. C   2nd Bn. Duke of Wellington's Regt.   Copy No. 10
                                  (OPERATION) ORDER No. 89
Ref. Map Sheet 36.a. S.E.
     1/20,000   In the Field, 13th June, 1918.

INTENTION.   1.(a) The Battalion will be relieved in the Centre Sub-sector
                     PACAUT SECTOR, on the night 13/14th June, 1918, by 3
                     Companies 1st Hampshire Regt.
                 (b) On Completion of Relief the Battalion will move into
                     Billets at L'ECLEME.

INSTRUCTIONS. 2.(a) Relief.
                     FRONT LINE. B. & D.Coys. 2nd D.of W's Regt. are being
                                 relieved by B. Coy. 1st Hampshire Regt.
                     SUPPORT LINE. A. Coy. 2nd D.of W's Regt. is being
                                 relieved by D. Coy. 1st Hampshire Regt.
                     RESERVE LINE. C. Coy. 2nd D.of W's Regt. is being
                                 relieved by A.Coy. 1st Hampshire Regt.
                 (b) Guides.
                     The following Guides will be at W.8.a.1.8. at 10 p.m.
                     1 per Platoon (each Coy. 1st Hampshire Regt has 4 Pltns)
                     1 per Company Headquarters.
                     2 per Battalion Headquarters.
                 (c) Completion of Relief will be notified by wire to
                     Bn. H.Q. as ordered in Operation Order No.88.
                 (d) March. Companies will move to Billets as vacated on
                     June 2nd, and will move with 100 yards between Platoons.
                 (e) Attack. In the event of Hostile Attack or heavy
                     preliminary bombardment,
                     i. Unrelieved troops will stand to in their own trenches
                     ii.Relieved troops will man the battle positions
                     and notify Bn. H.Q. at once.
                 (f) Trench Stores, etc. All Trench Stores, Maps, Programmes
                     of Work, etc. must be handed over and a signed receipt
                     obtained and kept.
                 (g) Lewis Guns Capt. J.Cooke will detail 1 N.C.O. to
                     superintend the on and off loading of Lewis Guns,
                     Magazines, etc. at W.8.a.1.8.
                 (h) Water Tins, Stores, etc. Empty Water Tins, Stores, etc.
                     will be carried to W.8.a.1.8. and loaded on limbers.
                 (j) Billets. Q.M. will arrange for billeting parties to
                     report at Town Major's Office, L'ECLEME at 2 p.m. to
                     take over billets from 1st Hampshire Regt, and to
                     distribute men's packs at respective billets. He will
                     take over the Reserve S.A.A. and Bombs at L'ECLEME.
                     He will request such transport as may be required from
                     Transport Officer.

TRANSPORT.   3.   Transport Officer will arrange for :-
                 (a) Limbers to be at W.8.a.1.8. to fetch Lewis Guns, empty
                     water tins & containers, & spare stores, etc. and convey
                     these to Company Headquarters.
                 (b) 1 G.S. Waggon and 1 Limber to be at Bn. H.Q. at 10.30 p.m
                 (c) To supply Q.M. with Transport as he may require under
                     para. (j).

                                          (Sgd) E.C.Coke, Captain.
                                       A/Adjt, 2nd Duke of Wellington's Regt.

DISTRIBUTION.

```
Copy Nos 1 - 4  All Coys. & H.Q.      Copy No. 7   File
          5    1st Hants Regt.                 8   T.O.
          6    10th Inf. Bde.                  9   Q.M.
                                          10 - 11  War Diary.
```

D

SECRET   2nd Bn. Duke of Wellington's Regt.   Copy No. 8

(OPERATION) ORDER No. 90

Ref. Map Sheet 36.a. S.E.
1/20,000   In the Field, 16th June, 1918.

INTENTION. 1.   "A" & "C" Companies, 2nd D.of W's Regt. will relieve "B" & "A" Companies, 2nd Seaforth Highrs. in the CANAL SWITCH on the night 17/18th inst.

INSTRUCTIONS. 2.(a) "A" Coy. 2nd D.of W's Regt will relieve B.Coy. 2nd S.Hrs
             "C" ---------------------do---------"A"----------

(b) <u>Order of March.</u> "C" - "A" Companies. Head of Column will pass BRIDGE at V.10.a.1.8. at 9.15 p.m.

(c) 100 yards distance will be maintained between Companies

(d) <u>Guides.</u> 5 Guides per Company will meet Companies at Road Junction P.36.b.1.2. at 10.30 p.m.

(e) Capt. M.C.Hoole will be in charge of the 2 Companies and will ensure that all Trench Stores, Maps, Programmes of Work, etc.1 are taken over.

(f) <u>Rations.</u> for consumption on the 18th will be carried on the men.

(g) <u>Stores.</u> Packs and Officers Kits will be stacked at H.Q. by 3 p.m.
Officers Mess Boxes at Q.M. Stores when finished with.

(h) <u>Completion of Relief</u> will be reported by wire, using the Code Word "SWITCH".

                                       P.C.Edwards Captain.

                         A/Adjt. 2nd Duke of Wellington's Regt.

D I S T R I B U T I O N.

Copy No. 1 B.H.Q.   Copy No. 6 Q.M.
       2 - 3 A & C Coys.   7 - 8 War Diary.
       4 2nd Sea. Hrs.   9 File.
       5 T.O.

SECRET.   E   2nd Bn. Duke of Wellington's Regt.   Copy No. 11
                         (OPERATION) ORDER No. 91.
Ref. Map Sheet 36.a. S.E.
     1/20,000   In the Field, 19th June, 1918

INTENTION 1. (a) The 2nd Bn. Duke of Wellington's Regt. will relieve the 1st
                   Bn. The King's Own Regt. in Centre Battalion CENTRE BRIGADE
                   SECTOR.

INSTRUCTIONS. 2. (a) <u>Relief</u>
                   A.Coy. 2nd D. of W's will relieve A.Coy. K.O's in FRONT LINE
                   C.Coy. ——————do—————— C.Coy ———————SUPPORT LINE.
                   B.Coy. ——————do—————— B.Coy ———————RESERVE.
                   D.Coy. ——————do—————— D.Coy ———————RESERVE.
               (b) <u>Order of Relief</u>. A. C. B. D. Companies.
                   Guides will be at DOUCE CREME Farm at 10.30 p.m. for A & C
                   Companies, and at 11 p.m. for B.& D. Coympanies & H.Q.
               (c) O.C. A.Coy. will arrange to hand over CANAL SWITCH to 2 Coy
                   K.O's. and will arrange march to DOUCE CREME for A. & C.Coy
               (d) <u>Order of March</u> H.Q., B. & D. Companies.
                   Head of Column will pass B. Coy's Billet at 10 p.m.
                   100 yards distance will be maintained between platoons.
               (e) <u>Advance Party</u> Capt. J.Cooke & 1 Officer & 1 N.C.O. per Coy
                   and B.H.Q. will report to 1st King's Own at 3 p.m. to take
                   over.
               (f) <u>Trench Stores</u> All Trench Stores, Maps, Programmes of Work,
                   Defence Schemes Orders, etc. will be taken over and receipts
                   in duplicate forwarded to Bn. H.Q. by 9 a.m. 20th inst.
               (g) <u>Completion of Relief</u>. will be notified to Bn.H.Q. as in
                   Operation Order No. 90.
               (h) <u>Dispositions</u> Maps showing dispositions will be forwarded
                   to Bn. H.Q. by 6 a.m. 20th inst.
               (j) <u>Lewis Guns</u> & 24 Magazines will be carried by limber to
                   P.36.a.8.7. The L.G.O. will detail 1 N.C.O. to accompany
                   limber & superintend distribution to Companies.
               (k) <u>Rations</u> for 20th inst. will be carried on the man. All
                   water bottles will be filled before leaving billets.
                   15 tins of water per Coy. & H.Q. will be carried up on
                   a separate limber from the Transport lines. Water for
                   Coys. will be dumped at Bn. Dump at Q.25.b.2.2. For
                   Bn. H.Q. at DOUCE CREME Farm.
               (l) <u>Billets</u>. The Q.M. will arrange to hand over billets to
                   2nd Lanc. Fus. at 3 p.m. on 19th inst.
                   All billets must be left scrupulously clean and
                   certificates obtained from 2nd Lanc. Fus.
               (m) <u>Stores</u> Packs, Stores, Salvage, Canteen barrels, etc. must
                   be stacked at Coy. H.Q. by 3 p.m.
                   Officers Kits & Baths must be stacked at Coy. H.Q. by 8 p.m
                   Mess Stores when finished with.

TRANSPORT.   3. (Transport Officer will arrange.
                    (a) for collecting stores as above.
                    (b) for removal of Cookers, Water Carts & Maltese Cart at 7 p.m
                    (c) to collect Lewis Guns & Magazines at 9.15 p.m.

BATTALION H.Q.   will be at Q.31.a.0.5.
REGTL. AID POST   will be at P.36.d.3.9.

                                                         Captain,
                                           A/Adjt. 2nd Duke of Wellington's Regt.

DISTRIBUTION

```
Copy No. 1  B.H.Q.                Copy No. 8   I.O.
         2 - 5 All Coys.                   9   M.O.
         6  1st King's Own R.              10 - 11 War Diary
         7  15th Inf. Bde.                 12  File.
```

SECRET F   2nd Bn Duke of Wellington's Regiment.   Copy. NO. 10

Ref, Map
Sheet. 36a.S.E.   OPERATION ORDER. No.92.
1/20,000.
                                        In The Field. 25th June.1918

INTENTION. 1. An inter-company relief will take place on the night
              25/26 June.1918.

INSTRUCTIONS. 2. RELIEF.
    (a). "D" Coy. will relieve "A" Coy. in the Front Line.
         "A" Coy. will move back to Left Reserve Line evacuated by
         "D" Coy.
         "B" Coy. will relieve "C" Coy in the Support Line.
         "C" Coy will move back to Right Reserve Line evacuated by
         "B" Coy.
         O.C."C" Coy. will arrange to provide the extra L.Gs,and
         teams in the Front Line at present found by "B" Coy.
         Relief will commence about 12.30 A.M. 26/6/18. "D" Coy.
         to move first and "B" Coy immediately afterwards.
         Details to be arranged by O.C.Companies.
    (b). RATIONS.
         Rations will be at Ration Dump at 11p.m..Companies to
         make own arrangements as to disposal.
    (c). WORK.
         Each Company will arrange to take over Programmes of Work
         in daylight. All Working Parties will be taken over with
         the exception of the party at Bn. H.Q.. The party at Bn.H.Q.
         will be returned but not relieved at present.
         Parties will be provided on night 25/26 as on previous
         night.
    (d). Stores.
         Signed receipts for stores will be taken over and kept
         by all companies.
    (e). Completion of Relief will be reported wired to Bn.H.Q.,
         Code Word "Margaret" being used.
    (f). Attack.
         In the event of an attack before relief is complete, all
         troops in the Front Line will come under the command of
         O.C."A"Company.
    (g). ACKNOWLEDGE.

                                  (Sd) J.COOKE, Captain,
                        A/Adjt 2nd Bn Duke of Wellington's Regiment.

DISTRIBUTION. Copy. No.1. Bn.H.Q.   Copy. No.7. Q.M.
              "   2-5. All Coys.   "   8. T.O.
              "   6. 10th Bde.   "   9-10.War Diary.
              "   11.File.

S E C R E T

WAR DIARY.

of

2nd Bn. The Duke of Wellingtons Regt.

From: 1st July. 1918.

To : 31st July. 1918.

VOLUME.

S. Lawton
Lieut. Colonel,
Commanding 2nd Bn The Duke of Wellington's Regiment.

2/8/18. 1918.

Army Form C. 2118.

WAR DIARY
or
INTELLIGENCE SUMMARY.
(Erase heading not required.)

Place	Date	Hour	Summary of Events and Information	Remarks and references to Appendices
CENTRE SUB-SECTOR. RIEZ DU VINAGE.	JULY 1918 1.		The Battn. was relieved in the line by the 1st RIFLE BRIGADE. Heavy shelling during the relief.	A.
REST BILLETS in L'ECLÈME	2.		Relief complete by 2 am. Bn. marched to L'ECLÈME and took over neat billets there. Bathing, Kit inspection, changing of clothing etc during the day.	
"	3.		Training. Musketry and Bayonet Training. 2/Lt J.H. LAW joined from Hospital.	
"	4.		Battalion training. Working parties found for crop cutting in front of the reserve line RIEZ DU VINAGE sector.	
"	5.		Battalion training. Bn. boxing competition in the afternoon. L'ECLÈME shelled by H.V. gun during the night. No casualties.	
"	6.		Battalion training. Changing details.	
"	7.		The Bn. relieved the 1st King's Own Regt. in the CENTRE SUB-SECTOR PACAUT WOOD SECTOR. A.Coy. Lt.Front, B.Coy. Support, C.Coy. Rt.Front D.Coy. RESERVE.	B.

Army Form C. 2118.

WAR DIARY
or
INTELLIGENCE SUMMARY.
(Erase heading not required.)

Place	Date	Hour	Summary of Events and Information	Remarks and references to Appendices
	JULY. 1918.			
CENTRE SUB-SECTOR, PACAUT WOOD SECTOR.	8.		Relief completed by 2 a.m. Heavy shelling during the relief. 1 man Killed, 2 men wounded. Everything very quiet during the day. 4 men sick to hospital.	
"	9.		Quiet day. At 11 p.m. an R.E. Special Coy. liberated 5 tons of liquid gas in projectors from the Canal Bank. There was no retaliation. 1 O.R. sick to hospital, also 1 O.R. sick to hospital from details.	
"	10.		Situation very quiet.	
"	11.		Situation very quiet during the day. Enemy heavy artillery very active round Batt. HQ. during the night. 1 O.R. wounded, also 1 O.R. sick to hospital. Snipers claim to have killed several of the enemy.	
"	12.		Inter Coy. Relief. B. Coy. LT FRONT. D. Coy. RT FRONT. A. Coy. Support (in the wood). C. Coy. RESERVE (on the CANAL BANK). 5 officers and 200 O.R. taken out of the line for special training at BUSNETTES. Quiet day.	C.

Army Form C. 2118.

WAR DIARY
or
INTELLIGENCE SUMMARY.
(Erase heading not required.)

Instructions regarding War Diaries and Intelligence Summaries are contained in F. S. Regs., Part II. and the Staff Manual respectively. Title pages will be prepared in manuscript.

Place	Date	Hour	Summary of Events and Information	Remarks and references to Appendices
	JULY 1918			D + E.
CENTRE SECTOR. PACAUT WOOD SECTOR.	13		Relief of Batt. complete by 1 a.m. Situation very quiet. Lt LUCAS marked unfit by a medical board and sent off the strength of the Battalion.	
"	14		Very quiet day. Snipers claim to have killed one of the enemy. 2 O.R. sick to hospital. Lt SKELTON M.C. joined the Battalion.	
"	15		Situation quiet during the day. The enemy shelled Batt. H.Q. very heavily during the night. 2 O.R. sick to hospital.	
"	16		Situation very quiet.	
"	17		Situation quiet. Batt. H.Q. shelled rather heavily during the night.	
"	18		In accordance of the Bn O.O. taken out of the line for a period of special training on the 17th July carried out an extremely successful raid on PACAUT WOOD. 29 Prisoners were taken, and 1 Machine gun captured and 3 destroyed. Our casualties were 5 killed, 25 wounded, and 2 missing (known to be killed) Zero was 2.30 p.m., and the enemy	

WAR DIARY or INTELLIGENCE SUMMARY

Army Form C. 2118.

Place	Date	Hour	Summary of Events and Information	Remarks and references to Appendices
	JULY 1918.			
CENTRE- SUB-SECTOR PACAUT WOOD SECTOR.	18.		retaliation barrage which consisted of shells of all calibres was put down at ZERO + 5 minutes.	
"	19.		Messages congratulating the Battn on their successful raid were received from the Army, Corps, Division and Brigade commanders, and also from the O.C. 1st KINGS OWN REGT. Very quiet day. Lt Parnell attached to the 10th BDE. TRENCH MORTARS.	
REST BILLETS in L'ECLÊME	20.		Situation very quiet. The Batt. was relieved in the Line by the 1st HAMPSHIRE REGT. A certain amount of shelling of tracks etc during the relief. Relief complete by 1 a.m. 1 man Killed during the relief. The Bn marched into rest billets at L'ECLÊME.	F.
"	21.		Cap badges (carrying of clothing) Kit inspection etc.	
"	22.		Battalion training. Musketry training, also the march past by companies.	
"	23.		A + D Coy on the Musketry Range at ALLOUAGNE. Officers on details changed over with the officers to be on details the next tour.	

Army Form C. 2118.

WAR DIARY
or
INTELLIGENCE SUMMARY.
(Erase heading not required)

Place	Date	Hour	Summary of Events and Information	Remarks and references to Appendices
	JULY. 1918.			
REST BILLETS in L'ECLEME	24.		Battalion training. Specialist training carried out. L'ECLEME shelled by H.V. gun.	
"	25.		Battalion training. Training at attacking in the open, also the Platoon in the attack.	
"	26.		B + C Coys on the musketry range at ALLOUAGNE. A + D Coys practising the attack in the open. LT + Q.M. HAY of the 4th DIV MACHINE GUN CORPS lectured the battalion on the advantages of burying W/S Singing Certificates.	
"	27.		Battalion training. Splendid response to War Savings Appeal. Battalion invests more than any other Infantry Battn in the Division. The Bn relieved the 1st KINGS OWN REGT in the CENTRE SUB SECTOR, RIEZ DU VINAGE SECTOR. A. Coy FRONT LINE, C. Coy SUPPORT LINE, B. Coy RIGHT RESERVE, D. Coy LT RESERVE. Relief complete by 1.30 a.m. 1st ROYAL WARWICKSHIRE REGT on our right. 2nd SEAFORTH HIGHLANDERS on our left. 1 OR killed 5 OR wounded.	G.
CENTRE SUB-SECTR RIEZ DU VINAGE SECTOR	28.			
"	29.		Situation Quiet during the night. Early morning the enemy carried out harassing fire. 1 OR killed. 1 OR wounded.	
"	30.		Holding the line situation quiet.	
"	31.		During the day the enemy shelled round Batt Hq. 3 OR killed 2 OR wounded.	

Signed
Lt Col
Cmg 27th 1st Dukes/Rgts W. Rgt

SECRET.   2nd Bn. Duke of Wellington's Regt.   Copy No. 11
                    OPERATION ORDER No. 93.
Ref. Map Sheet 36.a. S.E.
    1/20,000.   A   In the Field, 1st July, 1918.

INTENTION. 1. (a) The Battalion will be relieved in the CENTRE SUB-SECTOR
                   VINAGE SECTOR on the night 1st/2nd July, 1918, by the
                   1st RIFLE BRIGADE.
               (b) On completion of relief the Battalion will move into Billets
                   at L'ECLEME.

INSTRUCTIONS. 2. (a) FRONT LINE. D.Coy. D of W's Regt. are being relieved by
                                                    "I" Coy. 1st R.B.
                     SUPPORT LINE. B.Coy. D of W's. Regt are being relieved by
                                                    "C" Coy. 1st R.B.
                     LEFT RESERVE LINE. A.Coy. D.of W's Regt. are being relieved
                                                    by "A" Coy. 1st R.B.
                     RIGHT RESERVE LINE. C.Coy. D.of W's Regt. are being relieved
                                                    by "B" Coy. 1st R.B.
                 (b) GUIDES.
                     Guides at the rate of one per platoon & one per Coy. H.Q.
                     will be at P.36.a.9.7. at 10.30 p.m.
                 (c) COMPLETION OF RELIEF will be notified by wire to Bn.H.Q.
                     as ordered in O.O. No. 89.
                 (d) MARCH. Companies will move to billets at L'ECLEME as
                     vacated on June 19th, and will move with 100 yards between
                     platoons. Coy. Commanders will report to Bn.H.Q. on
                     arrival at billets.
                 (e) ATTACK. In the event of Hostile attack or heavy preliminary
                     bombardment :-
                       i. Unrelieved troops will stand to in their own trenches.
                      ii. Relieved troops will man the RESERVE positions & notify
                          Bn.H.Q. at once.
                 (f) TRENCH STORES. All Trench Stores, Maps, Programmes
                     of Work, etc. must be handed over and a signed receipt
                     obtained and kept.
                 (g) LEWIS GUNS. A.Coy. will detail one full rank N.C.O. to
                     superintend the on and off loading of Lewis Guns, Magazines
                     etc.
                 (h) WATER TINS, STORES, ETC. Empty Water Tins, Stores, etc.
                     will be carried to Battn. Dump and loaded on limbers.
                 (j) BILLETS. Q.M. will arrange for billeting parties to report
                     at TOWN MAJOR'S Office L'ECLEME, at 2 p.m. to take over
                     Billets from 1st Hampshire Regt. and to distribute men's
                     packs at respective billets. He will take over Reserve Bomb
                     etc. and Bayonet Fighting Stores at L'ECLEME.
                     He will request such transport as may be required from the
                     Transport Officer.

TRANSPORT. 3.   Transport Officer will arrange for :-
                 (a) 11 p.m. 2 limbers at Battn Dump Q.25.b.15.30. for empties,
                     spare stores, etc.
                 (b) 11.30 p.m. 2 limbers at P.36.c.8.8. for Lewis Guns.
                 (c) 11 p.m. 1 G.S.Wagon at Bn.H.Q. Q.31.a.0.5.
                 (d) To supply Q.M. with transport required under para (j).

                                            (Sgd) J.Cooke, Captain.
                             A/Adjt. 2nd Bn. Duke of Wellington's Regt.

DISTRIBUTION.

Copy No. 1 Bn.H.Q.   Copy No. 8 1st Hants. Regt.
         2 - 5 All Coys.   9 Q.M.
         6 1st R.B.   10 T.O.
         7 10th Inf. Bde.   11 - 12 War Diary.
                                           13 File.

SECRET.   2nd Bn. Duke of Wellington's Regt.   Copy No. 5 11
OPERATION ORDER No. 94.
Ref. Map Sheet VIEILLE CHAPELLE
1/20,000   B   In the Field, 7th July, 1918.

___

INTENTION. 1. The 2nd Bn. Duke of Wellington's Regt. will relieve 1st The King's Own Regt. in the CENTRE SUB-SECTOR, PACAUT SECTOR on the night 7/8th July, 1918.

INSTRUCTIONS 2. **RELIEFS.**

(a) A. Coy. will have 2 Platoons LEFT FRONT LINE
                     2 Platoons LEFT SUPPORT LINE.
    B. Coy. will have 3 Platoons in SUPPORT on CANAL BANK
                     1 Platoon in LES HARRISOIRS.
    C. Coy. will have 2 Platoons RIGHT FRONT LINE
                     2 Platoons RIGHT SUPPORT LINE.
    D. Coy. will have 4 Platoons in RESERVE in LES HARRISOIRS.
    These dispositions concur with those of the 1st K.O's., Company for Company.

(b) **GUIDES.** will be at N.8.a.1.8. at 10.30 p.m.
    One per Platoon, one per Company H.Q.

(c) **ORDER OF MARCH** A. C. B. D. & H.Q.   Front Platoon of A. Coy. will pass BRIDGE at V.10.a.10.85. at 9.30 p.m.
    100 yards distance will be maintained between platoons.
    A marching out state will be sent to R.S.M. when Coys. move off.

(d) **DRESS.** FIGHTING ORDER, Greatcoats rolled Bandolier fashion.

(e) **TRENCH STORES** All Trench Stores, Trench Maps, Programmes of Work, Defence Orders, etc., will be taken over and a list kept.

(f) **COMPLETION OF RELIEF** will be notified to Bn. H.Q. as in Operation Order No. 93.

(g) **DEFENCE.** In the event of an attack or preliminary bombardment developing during relief, troops South of CANAL will occupy the Battle Positions in accordance with Defence Scheme, those North of CANAL will occupy the nearest trenches and place themselves under order of Bn. Commander, of 1st The King's Own Regt.

(h) **DISPOSITION** Maps showing dispositions will be forwarded to Bn. H.Q. by noon 8th inst.

(j) **ADVANCE PARTY.** Front Line Company Commanders and Signal Officer will bicycle to and report at Bn. H.Q. 1st K.O's at 6 p.m.
    Bicycles will be left at H.Q. for use of Bn. Runners during tour in the line.

(k) **LEWIS GUNS.** and 24 Magazines per gun will be carried to N.8.a.1.8. by limbers. Capt. Cooke will arrange for 1 N.C.O. to accompany this limber to distribute guns to Companies.

(l) **RATIONS** for consumption on 8th inst. will be carried on the man.
    15 Tins of Water per Coy. & H.Q. will be picked up as Coys.

INSTRUCTIONS 2.   pass Aid Post, W.2.a.8.1.
(Contd)
- (m) **BILLETS.** The Q.M. will arrange to hand over billets to 2nd Land. Fus. at 3 p.m., 7th inst. and will arrange with T.O. for necessary transport.
  All Billets must be left perfectly clean.
- (n) **STORES** will be collected by limbers as follows :-
  Workshops and Msns Packs .... 2 p.m. at Coy. H.Q.
  Stores, Baths, Canteen................... 7 p.m.
  Officers Kits............................ 8 p.m. at Coy. H.Q.
  Officers Mess Stores, etc................ 9 p.m. —do—
  Lewis Guns & Magazines........ 8.30 – 9 p.m. —do—
- (o) As a further preventative to fever, all Companies will spray their trenches, cubby-holes, and shelters as soon as relieved personnel have evacuated these and **before** men move into cubbies or dug-outs. A report that this has been done will be sent to Bn. H.Q. by first runner, 8th inst.
  Q.M. will find 1 Syringe per Coy & H.Q.
  M.O. will provide suitable chemicals.

TRANSPORT. 3.   Transport Officer will arrange :-
- (a) Collecting Stores, etc., mentioned in para 2 (n)
- (b) Collecting & carrying Lewis Guns according to para 2 (k)
- (c) Carrying Water Bins in accordance with para 2 (l)
- (d) Removal of Cookers, Water Carts & Maltese Cart from L'ECLEME.
- (e) will provide Transport for Q.M. in accordance with para 2 (m).

BATTALION H.Q. 4. will be at W.2.b.35.40.

AID POST. 5. will be at W.N. W.2.a.8.1.

                                    Captain.
                      A/Adjt. 2nd Bn. Duke of Wellington's Rgt

DISTRIBUTION

Copy No. 1 Bn. H.Q.   Copy No. 8 1st K.O's.
      2 – 5 All Coys.   9 10th Inf. Bde.
      6 Q.M.   10 – 11 War Diary.
      7 T.O.   12 File.

SECRET.

C

2nd Battalion Duke of Wellington's Regiment.   Copy No. 12

Ref Map Sheet. 1/20,000.   OPERATION ORDER. No 95.
VIEILLE CHAPELLE.   In the Field. 12th July 1918.

___

INTENTION. 1. (a) The front line 2nd System will be handed over to 1st
R. War. Regt. on the right and 2nd Sea. Highrs. on the
left, inter-Battalion Boundary W.3.a.05.40..
To be completed by 10.p.m. 12/7/18.

(b) An inter-Company relief will take place on the night
12/13 July 1918

INSTRUCTIONS. 2. (a) **RELIEFS.**

1. On completion of relief para 1.(a) D. Coy. will relieve
A. Coy. in left front line only. A. Coy will move into
all Support hunettes (occupied at present by one Platoon
A coy. and one platoon C.Coy.)

2. B. Coy will relieve C.Coy. in Right Front Line and will
move into Reserve on Canal Bank.

(b) **TRENCH STORES.**
Trench Maps, Programmes of Work, Defence Orders etc, will
be handed over to relieving Companies in all cases and
receipts will be kept.

(c) Completion of Reliefs will be notified to Bn.h.q. as in
O.O. No 94.

(d) **DISPOSITIONS.** Maps showing dispositions by platoons will
be sent to Bn.H.Q. by 6.p.m.13th inst.

(e) **RATIONS, WATER Etc.,**
(1) B and D Coys. will send thier own ration parties to
AID POST at 10.30.p.m. who will collect rations and water
and carry same to their own companies in their new positions
(2) A and C Coys will detail similar parties when their
reliefs are complete.

(f) **Special Training Platoons** will proceed to billets at
L'ECLEME as soon as as dusk, in parties of ten and
rendezvous at the Windmill W.1.a.1.2. Their rations are
being sent to billets and will therefore not come up
to the Line to-night.

AID POST 3.   will remain at W.2.a.8.1.

BN.H.Q. 4.   will remain at W.2.d.4.4.

            (sgd) B.C.COKE Captain
        A/Adjt 2nd Bn Duke of Wellington's Regiment.

        DISTRIBUTION.
Copy No.1. Bn.H.Q.   Copy No. 2 - 5 All Coys.
    "   6. 10th Bde.   "   7.   1st R.War Regt.
    "   8. 2nd Sea. Highrs.   "   9.   Q.M.
    " 10. T.O.   "   11 - 12. War Diary.
    " 13. File.

SECRET.   2nd Bn. Duke of Wellington's Regt.   Copy No.
                            (OPERATION) ORDER No. 96.
                  (To be read in conjunction with 10th Inf. Bde. O.O. No. 164.)
Ref. Map. Sheet Special Map.
           Ed. A. S.E. Case,
           1/10,000.   D.   In the Field, 17th July, 1918.

RECAPITULATION. 1. A detachment of the Battalion will carry out a raid on
                 19th July, 1918, under the Command of Capt. F.R.HILL, on
                 that sector of PACAUT WOOD lying North of WOOD LANE between
                 STRUTHER LANE and point L.34.c.0.45.

INTENTION.   2. To clear the above sector of the WOOD in two phases, and
                 capture the garrison, thus obtaining identifications and
                 causing casualties.
                 PHASE 1. Penetrating and clearing houses, orchards, and
                 enemy positions immediately outside the N.E. edge of PACAUT
                 WOOD between points L.34.c.10.70. and houses at L.33.b.65.65,
                 58.60.
                 PHASE 2. To penetrate and clear from N.E. to S.W. as much of
                 PACAUT WOOD as lies within the points L.34.c.10.70, L.33.b.
                 58.60., L.33.d.90.15., L.34.c.65.45.

INSTRUCTIONS.   3.(a) Force.
                 The force will consist of 5 Officers & 206 Other Ranks with
                 5 Lewis Guns, divided into 4 Platoons as follows :-
                 A. Platoon .. 2Lieut. G.E.CRAVEN with 50 O.R. & 1 L.G.
                 B. Platoon ..   "   M.BAUMER   with 50 O.R.
                 C. Platoon ..   "   J.P.MURRAY with 50 O.R. & 1 L.G.
                 D. Platoon ..   "   H.S.LITTLE with 50 O.R. & 1 G.H.L.G.
                 8 Sappers from 526th (Durham) Field Coy. R.E.
                 (b) Organisation.
                 Each Platoon is divided into 10 Groups of 5 Other Ranks with
                 an N.C.O. in charge of each Pair of Groups.
                 8 Sappers of 526 (Durham) Field Coy. will report at Bn. H.Q.
                 at 12 noon, 18th inst., and accompany party to assist in
                 demolition of Buildings, Cellars, Dugouts, etc., 1 Sapper
                 going over with each of B. C. & D. Platoons.
                 (c) March.
                 The Platoons will leave BURBETTES by double groups of 10,
                 the last group leaving at 11 a.m., 18th inst., and proceed
                 to assembly points by different routes, arriving not later
                 than 1.45 p.m.
                 Order and Routes to be notified later.

                 (d) Arms.
                     Each man will carry Box Respirator, Rifle & Bayonet,
                     Bandolier of 50 rounds S.A.A., and 4 Mills No. 5 Hand
                     Grenades (will be carried in the pocket.)
                     2 men in every 5 will carry wire cutters.
                     3 men in every 5 will carry Bill-hooks.
                     Horns will be distributed to C. & B. Platoons.
                     No titles, regimental patches, or other articles which
                     might cause identification are to be worn by any of the
                     party.
                     Special Raid Identity Discs are being issued.
                     White Bands will be worn on Left Arm.

                                                                    P. T. O.

INSTRUCTIONS. 3. (e) Assembly Points.
(Contd)
A, B, & C. Platoons will assemble in the FRONT LINE
TRENCH (FAMAUT SECTOR) between post 10 and post 5 with
A. on the Right, B. in the Centre, and C. on the Left.
D. Platoon under cover of, but also clear of, -- WOOD
in rear of posts Nos. 10 & 11.
Numbered Boards will be placed at positions groups are
to take up.

(f) Objectives.
(a) (PHASE 1) Platoon Objectives will be :-
A. ....Q.34.d.00.36.
B. ....Q.33.b.32. 2.
C. ....Q.33.b.99.60.
D. ....House at Q.33.b.63.70.
as shown on attached map "X".

(b) The Objectives of the Parties will be Enemy Defence
1 – 22, (as shown on attached map "X") and divided
as follows :-
A. Groups........Points Nos. 1, 2, 3, 4, 5, 6.
B. Groups........—do—— 7, 8, 9, 10, 11, 12.
C. Groups........—do—— 13, 14, 15, 16, 17, 18.
D. Groups........—do—— 19, 20, 21, 22.

(PHASE 2.)
A.B.C.& D. Platoons, WOOD LANE, Enemy Posts between
STIRITON LANE and Q.34.c.65.45., passing over these to
points of Assembly in our own lines.

(g) Action of Party. (PHASE 1.)
At ZERO, A. Platoon will go over the parapet followed by
B. C. & D. Platoons at 25 yards distance. The latter
leaving their Assembly Point by moving to the Right over
the open, forming up in rear of D. Platoon's Assembly
Point.
Each Platoon will move out from Assembly Trench in 10
Groups of 5 O.R., No. 1 Group on the Right and No. 10
Group on the Left, forming "a line of Groups in File",
with the Officer in the best position from which to
supervise.
Groups will work in pairs and follow as close up to the
barrage as possible in accordance with safety.
The various parties will capture their objectives and
when the last objective (the House at Q.33.b.7.6.) is
gained,
(PHASE 2)
the whole will advance S.W. through FAMAUT WOOD that
lies within points Q.34.c.10.70, Q.33.b.33.60.,
Q.33.a.98.15., – Q.34.a. 85.40.

(h) Action of Stokes Mortars.
To place a Barrage on Enemy's Front Line and Special
Points from ZERO to ZERO plus 12, with 20 guns in
accordance with orders attached.

(j) Action of Machine Guns.
To give covering fire on Right Flank, and to cover
Enemy Approaches by Indirect fire on Back Areas in
accordance with orders attached.

(m) Action of Artillery.
18 pdr. barrage commencing Q.34.c.10.58,– Q.34.c.60.68.
at ZERO and ending at ZERO plus 12 at Q.33.b.33.70,–
Q.33.b.60.69, at intervals of 100 yards lifting every
two minutes and will be followed by the attacking
parties.
Protective barrages are put down on the lines Q.33.b.28.
24,– Q.33.b.60.60,– Q.34.c.60.68,– Q.34.c.60.68.
6" Hows,– 60 pdrs,– 4.5" Hows., are also co-operating
on special targets and counter battery work in accordance
with programme.

INSTRUCTIONS. 3.
(Cntd)
(l) **Lewis Guns.**
    5 Lewis Guns and Ammunition will be distributed as follows:
    A. (No. 5 Party) 1 gun and 8 magazines.
    C. (No. 14 Party) ———————do———————
    D. (No. 21 Party) ———————do———————
    These guns assist the party in overcoming obstinate
    opposition before and after reaching their own objectives.

(m) **Action of our Front Line in PACAUT WOOD.**
    On arrival of the Raiding Party in their Assembly Position
    1st N.Zor.R. are withdrawing the garrison of the Front
    Line between points C.34.d.5.65. and C.34.c.30.85.
    Between ZERO and minus 20 minutes and ZERO minus 10
    minutes the garrisons of the Front Line Posts in the
    WOOD must be withdrawn into the Immediate Support
    Lunettes, with the exception of sufficient look-out
    men who must watch the approaches to the Front Line.
    A bombardment of Rifle Grenades will be carried onto
    same objectives as Stokes Mortars.

(n) **Action when Objectives of PHASE 1 are gained.**
    Every party as its objective is gained, will take a
    position in it or on the edge of the WOOD, in Houses,
    Shell-holes, and along fences, attending to and clearing
    vicinity. Select points of entrance to the WOOD, but
    not immediately advancing through the WOOD.
    One man will act as Sentry to keep a look-out for any
    pre-arranged signals from any other part of the line.
    (PHASE 2)
    At ZERO plus 20 when Final Objective of Phase 1 on the
    outside of the WOOD has been gained, the STOKES MORTAR
    barrage will cease, and a general advance through the
    WOOD towards our own lines will commence.
    The time for this advance will be given from the Right
    of D. Platoon by blowing horns, which will be taken up
    by the other Platoons in possession of horns.
    The advance will be as rapid as the bush will allow,
    care being taken against congregating in large numbers
    in Rides and Straight Paths.

(o) **Mopping Up.**
    All objectives outside and inside the WOOD when gained,
    must be carefully mopped up and no live enemy left.
    Prisoners taken outside the WOOD will be sent back under
    escort of not less than 6 prisoners to one man, to rear
    of Post 10.
    Escorts will, after handing over prisoners, immediately
    rejoin their platoons; in the WOOD all prisoners must be
    driven forward to WOOD LANE.

(p) **Points of Re-assembly.**
    On reaching our own Front Line the party will re-assemble
    on Ride in Rear of Front Line Posts as follows :-
    A Platoon immediately in Rear of No. 10 Post.
    B, ————————————do———————— No. 13 Post.
    C ————————————do———————— Nos 17 & 19 Posts.
    D ————————————do———————— Nos 25 Post.
    where O's C., B.& D. Companies 2nd Duke of Wellington's
    Regt. will detail Officer to collect, call the roll, and
    despatch them.
    If the situation allows, the platoons will return by
    small parties to BUSMETTES.

                                                    P.T.O.

4.

INSTRUCTIONS. 3.(q) Aid Post.
(Contd)
  The M.O. will provide 20 extra Stretchers and establish
  Relay Posts at the two bridges crossing the CAMBRIN on
  C. Company's D. of M's., Front.
  4 Stretcher Bearers will accompany the party and will be
  detailed by the M.O.
  All Stretcher Bearers of the 2nd Bn. Duke of Wellington's
  Regt. will report to M.O. at Bn.H.Q. at 12 noon on day
  of this operation.

(r) Synchronisation.
  Watches will be synchronised by all concerned at 10th Bde.
  H.Q. at NOISY WOOD - V.12.b.40.75. as follows :-
  On the 17th inst. at 6 p.m.
  On the 18th inst. at 8 a.m. and 12 noon.

(s) ZERO HOUR.
  will be at 2.30 p.m.

           (Sgd) F.Pawlett, Lieut.Colonel
       Commanding 2nd Duke of Wellington's Regt.

D I S T R I B U T I O N.

Copy No. 1 10th Inf. Bde.	Copy No. 7 O.C., B. Coy.
2 O.C. Raiding Party.	8 M.O.
3 O.C. 2nd D. of M's.	9 Q.M.
4 1st A.War.R.	10 File.
5 2nd Sea.Bdrs.	11 - 12 War Diary.
6 O.C., B. Coy.	

REPORT ON RAID BY 2nd Bn. DUKE OF WELLINGTON'S REGT.
ON 18th JULY, 1918,
BY COMMANDING OFFICER, 2nd Bn. DUKE OF WELLINGTON'S REGT.

Ref. Map Sheet 36A. S.E. Ed: 3. 1/20,000.
Special Map issued with O.O. No. 96.

E.

PRELIMINARY: To be read in conjunction with Scheme & 2nd D. of W's O.O. No.
RAIDING PARTY. 8 Officers, 201 Other Ranks formed into 4 Platoons,
8 Stretcher Bearers, and 3 R.E's, left Billets at BUSNETTES
(in groups of 10 and under) between 9.30 & 10 a.m. proceeding by
four different routes to the LA BASSEE CANAL in rear of PACAUT
WOOD, a distance of approx: 8 Kilometres, from there by twos
and threes across the CANAL by BRIDGE in rear of WOOD direct
to their Assembly Positions arriving at these between 1.20 &
1.45 p.m.
The Parapet in front of Assembly Trench had been previously
heightened to prevent Enemy Observation, and 20 Lanes cut
through the wire.
The party was formed up according to orders, three Platoons
in Assembly Trench and one Platoon in rear of WOOD, the latter
advancing across the open in rear of Assembly Trench as the
First Wave went over.
Simultaneously with the coming down of the barrage, punctually
at 2.30 p.m., the First Wave mounted the Parapet, in lines of
half groups in file, followed at 25 yards intervals by the
2nd Wave, the same distance separating the others, in the
following order :- A. B. C. & D. Platoons.
A. Platoon advanced advanced to within 50 to 60 yards of the
barrage, halting, and on the latter lifting each party rushed
on its objectives which included a known Enemy Machine Gun
Post marked "Point E". This was taken by Group No. 3 from
the rear, Groups No. 4 & 5 assisting, Groups No. 1 & 2
occupying Shell holes in the Right Flank and capturing
prisoners.
The other objectives allotted to Groups of B. C. & D. Platoons
were taken as per schedule, expected opposition not being
encountered from Orchard fence between Points E (Q.34.c.05.70)
and F (Q.34.c.00.90) (vide Special Map with Orders.)
These objectives were taken with little opposition and very few
few casualties, each Platoon in turn from front to rear
capturing their objectives and remaining on the ground gained
till the Final Objective (Phase 1) at House Q.33.b.68.60, was
reached. All Objectives were gained on schedule time, the
final one being reached at Zero plus 13, finishing Phase 1 of
the Raid.
The signal to advance S.W. through the WOOD, clearing the latter
with the objective our own lines on WOOD LANE (called Phase II
of the Raid) was given by blowing of horns, first by the
Commander of the Party and taken up along the Line, upon
which the advance through the WOOD was commenced.
The route was via Lanes showing plainly on Aeroplane Photographs, and in the bush itself, leaving behind a small number
to act in rear in the event of any enemy re-appearing.
The passage through the WOOD was in places extremely difficult
on account of the thick bush and it might have been possible
to miss a small number of the enemy on that account but it is
considered that the number would be very small.
Our own line in WOOD LANE was reached approx: at Zero plus 25
the whole operation occupying 30 minutes.

NOTES ON OPERATION.

1. The value and accuracy of Artillery, Heavy and Light T.M's, and M.G's cannot be over-rated, all ranks expressing their opinion as to its excellence. With reference to the latter it is the opinion of those who were on the Right Flank of the First Wave that they were firing rather near and it is thought that although there was no danger of any of our own party being hit, it might have been better had they been placed farther to the Right with a target more to their front.

2. Enemy Artillery Retaliation commenced about Zero plus 5 and mainly consisted of shells of all calibre firing from a wide front on our Immediate Support, Support Lines, and the CANAL BANK as well as the fronts of the Battalions right and left of the WOOD. This continued until about Zero plus 15 when a heavy barrage was put down on their own and our front line on their side of WOOD LANE. This was thought to have been brought down by an enemy firing a light breaking into two reds from a shell hole on enemy rear edge of WOOD about Zero plus 10. Enemy machine guns were active on the trenches on the right of the WOOD and into WOOD from the direction of the ORCHARD, Q.35.a.8.6.

3. Enemy Casualties. Stokes Barrage on their main line of resistance in the WOOD caused many enemy casualties; evidence of dugouts being blown in and killing occupants was apparent in many places. Some refused to surrender and were shot or blown up with Mills Grenades; in one case a machine gun and crew were thus disposed of. The estimated enemy casualties in that sector of the WOOD were between 30 & 40. In addition to the above, enemy were seen to run out from WOOD, N.E., in the direction of the other part of the WOOD, and N.W. past our final objective (Phase 1) House Q.35.b.6.60. These must have been caught in our protective barrage and some casualties would accordingly occur.

4. Wire. Very little wiring was noticed in the WOOD and what there was was either of poor quality or cut by our Artillery or T.M. fire.

5. The enemy were completely surprised and some of them dazed by the force of our Artillery, but nearer their own Front Line they had recovered sufficiently to put up resistance in small parties.

6. The enemy garrisons in the area raided has been estimated at between 100 & 125 and from these figures it is concluded that 30 to 50 must have rushed into our own barrage before being caught by the Raiding Party.

7. Number of Prisoners brought in were 29, being captured singly and in parties from 2 to 8.
One machine gun was captured and three destroyed.

8. Our casualties were 5 killed, 25 wounded, 2 missing believed killed. 25 per cent of these casualties occurred after crossing into our own lines. 50 per cent by enemy barrage N. of WOOD LANE, and 25 per cent by machine gun and artillery fire before reaching this point.

P.T.O.

9. Damage to Works, Etc. Some of the buildings in rear of WOOD show
signs of recent occupation. In large building, Q.35.b.65.80, three
cellars were found, two of which had been blown in by our artillery
but one large one containing about 20 beds was untouched. There were
also barrels of cement in this building.
The Engineers who accompanied this party demolished several dugouts
and cellars, that afforded protection, by the aid of Mobile Charges
which were carried by them. _including above one_
Wire, Dug-outs, and Bivouacs in WOOD were damaged by Stokes Mortars.

10. Training. The party had previously received approximately 4 days
training over a Course specially prepared in the Back Areas.
This Course was extremely well marked out by the Divisional General
Staff and represented as far as possible the actual ground of attack.
The Raid was carried out and objectives gained in exactly the same
manner as had been done on the training ground.
The importance of the strictest attention to the minutest detail
during training was demonstrated during the progress of the attack.
The interest and enthusiasm of the men was maintained to the last by
not too long and not too strenuous work.
Particular and strict attention paid to transmission of orders and
instructions through all ranks down to the men until all thoroughly
understand, was a feature of the training.

Lieut. Colonel.
Commanding 2nd Bn. Duke of Wellington's Regt.

20th July, 1918.

SECRET.   2nd Bn. Duke of Wellington's Regt.   Copy No. 10
             (OPERATION) ORDER No.97.
Ref.Map Sheet 36A.S.E.
    1/20,000   In the Field, 20th July, 1918

INTENTION. 1. (a) The 2nd Bn. Duke of Wellington's Regt. will be relieved in the CENTRE SUB-SECTOR of the PACAUT SECTOR, on the night of July 20/21st, 1918, by the 1st Hampshire Regt.
(b) The 2nd Bn. Duke of Wellington's Regt. will march to the billets at L'ECLEME vacated by the 1st Hampshire Regt.

INSTRUCTIONS. 2. (a) RELIEFS.
  (1) A.Coy. 1st Hampshire Regt. will relieve B.Coy. plus ½ A.Coy. 2nd D.of W's in LEFT FRONT LINE & SUPPORT.
  (2) C.Coy. 1st Hampshire Regt. will relieve D.Coy. plus ½ A.Coy. 2nd D.of W in SUPPORT & RIGHT FRONT LINE.
  (3) D.Coy. (2 Platoons) 1st Hampshire Regt. will relieve C.Coy. 2nd D.of W in SUPPORT on CANAL BANK.
  (4) B.Coy. plus 1 Platoon D.Coy. 1st Hampshire Regt. will relieve 2nd Sea. Highrs. & 1st R.War. Regt. in 2nd SYSTEM LES HARRISOIRS.

(b) GUIDES.
Guides for A.Coy. 1st Hampshire Regt. will be as follows:-
2 of B.Coy. Front Line, 1 of B.Coy. H.Q., 1 of A.Coy. Support.
For C.Coy. 1st Hampshire Regt., 2 of D.Coy. Front Line, 1 of D.Coy. H.Q., 1 of A. Coy. Support.
These Guides will be at CHELSEA BRIDGE at 10 p.m.
Guides for B.Coy. plus 1 Platoon D.Coy. 1st Hampshire Regt, will be found by Bn.H.Q., 1 per Platoon & 1 for Coy. H.Q.
For D.Coy. 1st Hampshire Regt. will be found by C.Coy., 1 for each Platoon and 1 for Coy. H.Q.
These guides will be at W.8.a.1.8 at 10 p.m.
Bridges to be used, Q.33.c.60.20. & Q.33.c.50.30.

(c) TRENCH STORES.
All Trench Stores, Trench Maps, Programmes of Work, Defence Orders, etc., will be handed over and a list kept.

(d) COMPLETION OF RELIEF. will be notified to Bn.H.Q. as in O.O. No. 95.

(e) DEFENCE.
In the event of the enemy attacking or a preliminary bombardment, all troops relieved will man the nearest trenches to the EAST; all unrelieved troops will "STAND TO". In all cases runners will be sent to Bn.H.Q. to report where Coys. are.

(f) LEWIS GUNS.
All Lewis Guns and Magazines will be carried to the MOUND and loaded onto the limber.
H.Q.Lewis Gun N.C.O. will superintend the on-loading & the off-loading of these, care being taken that each Coy. have the same amount off-loaded as they on-loaded.

(g) EMPTIES AND STORES.
All empty Petrol Tins and Stores, etc, will be carried to the MOUND and loaded on limber.

(h) MARCH.
A distance of 100 yards will be kept between each Platoon.

(i) IN BILLETS.
Each Coy. when in Billets will report to Bn.H.Q. by runner.

(j) BILLETS.
Special Party at BUSNETTES will move into Billets at L'ECLEME under Capt. F.H.HILL.

P.T.O.

INSTRUCTIONS 2. (j) BILLETS. (Contd)
(Contd)
        Quartermaster will:-
        (1) Take over all Billets at L'ECLEME vacated by 1st Hampshire Regt.
        (2) Arrange for men's packs, canteen stores, etc to be at L'ECLEME when the Battalion arrives.
        (3) To move Stores, etc, of Special Training Party from BUSNETTES to L'ECLEME.
        (4) To request T.O. to supply any Transport required.

    (k) TRANSPORT.
        The T.O. will arrange:-
        (1) for 1 Limber to be at AID POST W.2.a.8.2. at 10.30 p.m.
        (2) to collect all empty tins and stores, etc. at MOUND 11.30 p.m.
        (3) to collect Lewis Guns and Magazines at MOUND at 11.30 p.m.
        (4) to supply Q.M. with Transport regarding para. 2(j)
        (5) to move Cookers, Water carts, Maltese cart, etc. to L'ECLEME.

BATTALION H.Q. will be at V.3.c.99.62.

AID POST. will be at V.3.d.20.45.

                                          (Sgd) E.C. Coke, Captain.
                A/Adjt. 2nd Bn. Duke of Wellington's Regt.

DISTRIBUTION.

Copy No.	1 Bn.H.Q.	Copy No.	8 1st Hampshire Regt.
	2 - 5 All Coys.		9 10th Inf. Bde.
	6 Q.M.		10 - 11 War Diary.
	7 T.O.		12 File.

SECRET.　　　　　　2nd Bn. Duke of Wellington's Regt.　　Copy No. 12
　　　　　　　　　(OPERATION) ORDER No. 98
Ref. Map Sheet 36.A. S.E.
　　　20.000　　　　　　　G.　　　　In the Field, 27th July, 1918.

INTENTION. 1. The 2nd Bn. Duke of Wellington's Regt. will relieve 1st The King's Own Regt., in the CENTRE SUB-SECTOR, VINAGE SECTOR, on the night 27/28th July, 1918.

INSTRUCTIONS. 2. RELIEFS.
    (a) A. Coy. 2nd D.of W. will relieve C.Coy. 1st K.O. in FRONT LINE.
       C. Coy. ——————————————— A. Coy ———— SUPPORT LINE.
       B. Coy. ——————————————— B. Coy. ———— RIGHT RESERVE
       D. Coy. ——————————————— D. Coy. ———— LEFT RESERVE.

    (b) GUIDES.
       Guides will be at BLACKFRIARS BRIDGE (Pt. LEVIS) P.36.b.0.6 at 10.15 p.m.
       One per Platoon, One per Coy. H.Q., One per Bn. H.Q.

    (c) ORDER OF MARCH.
       A. C. B. D. Coys. and H.Q. Front Platoon of A. Company will pass corner at V.9.b.96.85. at 9.30 p.m.
       100 yards distance will be maintained between Platoons.
       A Marching Out State will be sent to R.S.M. as Coys move off.

    (d) ROUTE.
       By Road to V.9.b.96.85. - Junction of ROBECQ Road and Track 4, - Track 4 to BLACKFRIARS BRIDGE.

    (e) DRESS.
       Fighting Order, Greatcoats rolled Bandolier fashion.

    (f) TRENCH STORES.
       All Trench Stores, Trench Maps, Programmes of Work, Defence Orders, etc., will be taken over and a list kept.

    (g) COMPLETION OF RELIEF.
       Will be notified to Bn. H.Q. as in Operation Order No. 97.

    (h) DEFENCE.
       In the event of an attack or a preliminary bombardment developing during relief, troops South of Lines Q.32.c.55.85. - P.36.d.80.30. - P.30.c.90.80. will occupy the Battle positions in accordance with Defence Scheme, those North of CANAL will occupy the nearest Trenches and place themselves under orders of Bn. Commander, of 1st The King's Own Regt.

    (j) Dispositions.
       Maps showing dispositions will be forwarded to Bn. H.Q. by noon, 28th inst.

    (k) ADVANCE PARTY.
       Advance Party of 1 Officer and 1 N.C.O. per Coy, Intelligence Officer and 1 Signalling N.C.O., will report at H.Q. 1st K.O. by 6.30 p.m. 27th inst.

    (l) LEWIS GUNS and 24 Magazines per gun will be carried to P.36.b.0.6. B. Coy. will lend A.Coy. 2 guns, D.Coy. will lend C.Coy. 2 guns. Each Coy. will send 1 Lewis Gunner per gun under H.Q. L.G. N.C.O., to accompany Limber and have guns off-loaded and ready for arrival of Companies.

    (m) RATIONS.
       Rations for consumption on 28th will be carried on the man. 15 Tins of Water per Coy. & H.Q. will be picked up by Coys. at P.36.b.0.6.
       Each Coy.H.Q. & Bn.H.Q. will keep 4 Box Respirators in store to replace damaged ones.

                                                      P.T.O.

INSTRUCTIONS. 2. (b) BILLETS.
(Cont.)
The Q.M. will arrange to hand over Billets to 2nd Lanc.
Fus. at 3 p.m. 27th inst, and will arrange with T.O. for
necessary transport.
All Billets must be left perfectly clean.

(c) STORES.
Stores will be collected by limbers as follows :-
Workshops and Men's Packs................2 p.m. at Coy. H.Q.
Stores, Baths, Canteen...................4 p.m.
Officers Kits. ....8 p.m. at Coy. H.Q.
Officers Mess Stores, etc. ....9 p.m. ——— do ———
Lewis Guns & Magazines. ....8.30 - 9 p.m. ——— do ———

TRANSPORT. 3. Transport Officer will arrange :-
(a) Collecting Stores, etc. mentioned in para 2 (c).
(b) Collecting and carrying Lewis Guns according to para 2 (l)
(c) Carrying Water Tins in accordance with para 2 (m)
(d) Removal of Cookers, Water Carts & Maltese Cart from L'ECLE
ME.
(e) Will provide Transport for Q.M. in accordance with para 2
(n).

BATTALION H.Q. 4. will be at P.36.b.9.3.

AID POST 5. will be at P.36.d.30.85.

                                      Captain.
A/Adjt. 2nd Duke of Wellington's Regt.

DISTRIBUTION.

Copy No. 1 Bn. H.Q.   Copy No. 8 1st K.O's.
        2 - 5 All Coys.   9 10th Inf. Bde.
        6 Q.M.   10 - 11 War Diary.
        7 T.O.   12 File.

~~~~~~~~~S E C R E T~~~~~~~~~

W A R   D I A R Y.

of

2nd Bn. The Duke of Wellingtons Regt.

From : 1st Aug. 1918.
To   : 31st Aug. 1918.

V O L U M E.

S. Fawkes
Lieut. Colonel,
Commanding 2nd Bn. The Duke of Wellington,s Regiment.........

1918.

Army Form C. 2118.

WAR DIARY
or
INTELLIGENCE SUMMARY.
(Erase heading not required.)

Instructions regarding War Diaries and Intelligence Summaries are contained in F. S. Regs., Part II. and the Staff Manual respectively. Title pages will be prepared in manuscript.

Place	Date	Hour	Summary of Events and Information	Remarks and references to Appendices
CENTRE SUB-SECTOR. RIEZ DU VINAGE SECTOR.	AUGUST 1918.			MAP REF "VIEILLE CHAPELLE" 1:20000.
	1.		Very quiet day. Support line shelled a little during the evening. 3.O.R. killed, 3 O.R. wounded.	"
"	2.		Situation quiet. 1. O.R. wounded.	"
"	3.		Quiet day. Our patrols patroled the Barn and found it unoccupied. 1. O.R. wounded.	"
"	4.		At 9 a.m. the enemy attempted to raid the 2ND SEAFORTH HIGHLANDERS on our left. The enemy's barrage extended over our left front and support lines. The raid was a failure. Very quiet day otherwise. 2.O.R's wounded. LT HORSLEY joined the Battn.	"
"	5.		Strong suspicions that the enemy is evacuating this sector. Patrols sent out. One patrol of 4 men under 2/LT MORRIS located a Boche post. 1 prisoner was taken, and the remainder of the post killed. 2/LT ROY joined the Battn.	"
"	6.		Three patrols sent out. No enemy located. HUN FARM (Q20d95.55), the BARN (Q24a 2.8) and Lancashire FARM (Q24a 55.75) unoccupied. During the evening B. Coy. sent out patrols and took up a line along the ECOURANT DE HENNE B.C. One of our patrols and one of the 2ND SEAFORTH's patrol	"

Army Form C. 2118.

WAR DIARY
or
INTELLIGENCE SUMMARY.
(Erase heading not required.)

Instructions regarding War Diaries and Intelligence Summaries are contained in F. S. Regs., Part II. and the Staff Manual respectively. Title pages will be prepared in manuscript.

Place	Date	Hour	Summary of Events and Information	Remarks and references to Appendices
CENTRE SUB SECTOR RIEZ DUVINAGE SECTOR.	AUGUST 1918.		MAP. REF. "VIEILLE CHAPELLE 1.20000"	
	6.		occupied LA PIERRE-AU-BEURE (Q21 d.0.9). In touch with the 1st ROYAL WARWICKSHIRES on our right and the 2nd SEAFORTH HIGHLANDERS on our left. Enemy shelled HUN FARM and the area he had evacuated with 8" shells during the night. 1 man wounded.	A.
"	7.		At 2 p.m. A. Coy. went through B. Coy. and took up a line running from Q 21 & 7.7 to Q 22 c 30.85. The details moved to BURBURE. 3. OR wounded.	
"	8.		At 5 a.m. A. Coy attacked with the 1st WARWICKS on the right and 2nd SEAFORTHS on the left. The village of QUENTIN was captured and A. Coy dug in along the line of the RIVER TURBEAUTÉ from Q 17 C 4.4. to Q 23 a 4.4. C. Coy relieved A. Coy in the Front Line. Relief over by 11 p.m. A. Coy. did splendidly throughout the day under CAPTAIN M.C. HOOLE but suffered rather severely from enemy M.G. and T.M. fire. 7 OR Killed and 27 wounded.	A.
"	9.		During the early morning C. Coy. pushes forward their posts over the RIVER TURBEAUTÉ. The Batt.n was relieved in the line by all	B.

WAR DIARY
or
INTELLIGENCE SUMMARY.

(Erase heading not required.)

Army Form C. 2118.

Place	Date	Hour	Summary of Events and Information	Remarks and references to Appendices
CENTRE SUB-SECTOR. RIEZ DU VINAGE SECTOR.	AUGUST 1918. 9.		Three BATT^NS of the 11th. Bde. C+D Coys. stayed on the CANAL BANK. Relief complete by 1.30 am on the 10th. 2 OR killed. 2/LT SHEARME M.C. to hospital sick.	
CHATEAU-DU-QUESNOY.	10.		BATT^N marched to MOULIN ROUGE (U9 & 8.3) and at 2.30 pm crossed the roadrailway the KING faced. Men bathing and changing clothing. 3 OR killed 2 wounded.	M.F. REF Sheet 36A 1:40000
"	11.		Training in open warfare. A/CAPT. F.H. HILL, 2/LT. M. BANHAM, 2/LT. G.E. CRAVEN all awarded the MILITARY CROSS. No. 11051. SERGT. H. DENTON and No. 16212 PTE. W. MARSHALL awarded the DISTINGUISHED CONDUCT MEDAL. 4 OR joined the BATT^N.	
"	12.		BATT^N training. Demonstration by a special platoon fired an under Capy Relig. A+B Coys. rifle range O+D Coys on the Canal Bank.	
"	13.		BATT^N training. The OC 81st Wing R.A.F. gave a lecture to the officers and NCOs of the 10th Infantry Bde. Congratulatory message received from the G.O.C. on the work done during the last few days in the line. The B.G.C. also rendered his thanks for the splendid work done.	C.

Army Form C. 2118.

WAR DIARY
or
INTELLIGENCE SUMMARY.
(Erase heading not required.)

Place	Date	Hour	Summary of Events and Information	Remarks and references to Appendices
	August, 1918.			
CHATEAU-DU-QUESNOY.	14.		Battn training in open warfare. A party of officers & NCOs went to the 21st Squadron R.A.F. for the day. Here they were shown the workings of the R.A.F. and some had flights in an aeroplane. 2/Lt. ROY. to hospital sick.	D.
RIGHT SUPPORT POSITION PACAUT SECTOR.	15.		The Battn relieved the 1st Battn KING'S OWN REGT in the RIGHT SUPPORT POSITION of the PACAUT SECTOR. Relief over by 6.15 p.m. 2nd SEAFORTHS on our right, 1st ROYAL WARWICKSHIRES in front holding the outpost line.	
"	16.		Quiet day. Nothing to report.	
"	17.		Quiet day. 2/Lt. O.O. WATMOUGH joined the Battn. 1 O.R. wounded.	
"	18.		Quiet day.	
"	19.		Holding the line. Very quiet. Enemy trenches found vacated by the WARWICKS. The WARWICKS closely followed the enemy up. The 11th Bde to on the left also keeping in touch with the enemy. Inter Coy Relief. Relief over by 8.30 p.m.	E.
"	20.		The enemy still mixing closely followed by the 2nd SEAFORTHS who relieved the 1st WARWICKS. Their line now run along the PARADIS ROAD.	MAP. REF. Sheet 36a S.E. 1:20000.

Army Form C. 2118.

WAR DIARY
or
INTELLIGENCE SUMMARY.
(Erase heading not required.)

Instructions regarding War Diaries and Intelligence Summaries are contained in F.S. Regs., Part II. and the Staff Manual respectively. Title pages will be prepared in manuscript.

Place	Date	Hour	Summary of Events and Information	Remarks and references to Appendices
	AUGUST. 1918.			
RIGHT SUPPORT POSITION	21.		Very Quiet day. Much work being done building new breastworks.	
PRAÄUT	22.		Quiet day. More work on the breastworks.	
SECTOR.	23.		Division relieved in the line by the 19th Division. The Battn was relieved by the 2nd WILTSHIRE REGT and the 9th ROYAL WELSH FUSILIERS. Relief over by 3.45 am. Battn moved back to the CHATEAU-DU-QUESNOY. Details moved from BURBURE to LOZINGHEM.	F.
LOZINGHEM.	24.		The Battn marched to billets at LOZINGHEM.	
			Battn the corps commander congratulated the Divn on its good work. A draft of 49 O.R. joined the Battn.	MAP. REF HAZEBROUCK S.A. G.
MAISNIL ST POL.	25.		At 12.15 pm the Battn marched to PERNES and entrained. There at 6.15 we detrained at PT HOUVIN, and from there marched to MAISNIL ST POL (BATTN HQ and A+R Coys) and C+D Coys to NEUVILLE AU CORNET.	LENS 11. H.
MAISNIL ST POL.	26		Battn practising the attack by platoons, companies, and finally the whole Battn in the attack. At 6.50 pm the Battn marched to VILLERS-AU-BOIS arriving there at 3.15 am on the 27th.	I.
VILLERS -AU- BOIS.	27.		Battn cleaning up and changing underclothing, also resting after the long march of the previous day. Coy Commandant Bn Commander reconnoitred the sector round MONCHY.	J.

A7092. W4. W.125 9/M1793 750,000. 1/17. D.D. & L., Ltd. Forms/C2118/14.

Army Form C. 2118.

WAR DIARY
or
INTELLIGENCE SUMMARY.
(Erase heading not required.)

Place	Date	Hour	Summary of Events and Information	Remarks and references to Appendices
	AUGUST 1918.			MAP. REF. LENS I. Sheet 51.c. 1:40,000 K.
VILLERS-AU-BOIS.	28.		(for details) At 1 pm the Batt'n marched to MONT ST ELOI and from there entrained for unknown destination. At 2:30 pm we detrained at ST CATHERINE (near ARRAS). The Batt'n then marched to an assembly point at FEUCHY CHAPEL (N3 & B.2.). At 6:30 pm the Batt'n then marched in lines of platoons towards the front line keeping their right flank on the ARRAS – CAMBRAI RD. When they arrived at the front line they relieved the 43rd CANADIANS (4th CANADIAN DIVISION) who were holding the line there. The line we took over ran just in front of VIS EN ARTOIS along the west banks of the SENSÉE RIVER from O23c 6.9. to O23a 95.95. The 1st ROYAL WARWICKSHIRE REGT on our left and the WINNIPEG RIFLES on our right.	
	29.		Our patrols pushed forward in the early morning and captured HAUCOURT + occupied a line immediately in front of it. 3 O.R. killed 7 O.R. wounded.	

Army Form C. 2118.

WAR DIARY
or
INTELLIGENCE SUMMARY.

Place	Date	Hour	Summary of Events and Information	Remarks and references to Appendices
				MAP. REF.
HAUCOURT	AUGUST. 1918.			ETERPIGNY.
	30.	At 4 pm	At 4 pm the Battn. attacked. The men went forward magnificently and attained the final objective, but owing to the Tanks not putting up flares being in the air they fell back to the 1st objective (see operation order). 43 prisoners including 1 officer were taken. 2/Lts WARD and LITTLE were killed. 2/Lt TUNSTALL, HEBBLETHWAITE, MORRIS, BANHAM. M.C. and JOHNSON were wounded. 36 O.R. killed, 162 O.R. wounded, 7 missing, and 16 O.R. admitted to hospital. D. Coy of the 2nd SEAFORTHS were attached as our reserve coy.	L.
"	31.		*A small attack without barrage to capture the copse at O 2 4 & 9 6. was unsuccessful during the afternoon. But at dusk the men in splendid form carried everything before them and captured the copse (STIPE COPSE), ST SERVIN'S FARM and the final objective of the 30th (see operation order of the 30th). 45 prisoners including 2 officers were taken. A coy of the 1st ROYAL WARWICKSHIRES were attached to us during the evening. 2/Lt WATMOUGH and 2/Lt ANSON	"

Army Form C. 2118.

WAR DIARY
or
INTELLIGENCE SUMMARY.
(Erase heading not required.)

Place	Date	Hour	Summary of Events and Information	Remarks and references to Appendices
	AUGUST. 1918.		were Killed. 2/Lt JOHNSON died of wounds. 2/Lt BLACKBURN was gassed. Lt SKELTON M.C. was admitted to Hospital. 74 O.R. Killed, 36 O.R. wounded. 17 O.R. missing. 21 O.R. to Hospital. In the operation the Batt'n also took 9 enemy machine guns and one enemy field gun. ✱ The attack was successful but owing to depleted numbers, a heavy counter attack preceded by a violent bombardment drove our men out of Capron, and our patrols withdrew fighting.	

SECRET.　　　　2nd Bn. Duke of Wellington's Regt.　　　　Copy No. WD
　　　　　　　　　　　(OPERATION) ORDER No.
Reg. Map Sheet 36.A. S.E. Edition 8.
　　　　　　1/30.000　　　A　　　In the Field, 27th August, 1918.

In continuation of orders already issued, the Battalion will push on at dawn.

1. Boundaries of the Battalion are amended to :-
   N.:- Q.27.a.20.45 - Q.27.a.30.75 - Q.21.d.35.10.
   S.:- Q.20.d.65.70. - Q.21.c.10.65. - Q.21.b.05.30. - Q.21.b.75.70.

2. "A" Company will push forward at dawn, passing through B. & D. Coys., and will advance by dribbling sections forward, with 4 Platoons in Line and will endeavour to take up a line :- Q.21.b.0.3. - Q.21.d.2.8. - Q.21.d.25.40. - Q.21.d.40.15.
   When on this line and in trench with Right and Left Battalion, A. Coy. will report to Bn.H.Q. by wiring the Code Word "YELLOW", and will not advance beyond this line until ordered by Bn.H.Q., but Patrols may be pushed out preparatory to a further advance.
   During the advance to the above line "A" will have scouts out ahead of them and provide their own protection.

3. The Reserve Coy. left in Reserve Line will not move unless ordered by Bn.H.Q., and should make and carry forward as much concertina wire as possible.

4. Patrols must carry Aeroplane Flares and supporting troops should have sufficient S.A.A. - Bombs - Rifle Grenades - S.O.S. - Wire Cutters - Telephones and pigeons and each man a pick and shovel and a sandbag.

5. Line must be taken up as soon after daylight as possible.

6. All Coys. must inform Bn.H.Q. of any item of information gained, and all information as to positions of our own troops.

7. A Dump is being formed at Junction of RAILWAY ALLEY and old Front Line.

8. "A" Coy. will take over all previous orders issued reference the advance from O.C. "B" Coy.

　　　　　　　　　　　　　　　　　　　　　　(Sgd) E.C.Coke, Captain.
　　　　　　　　　　　　　A/Adjt. 2nd Duke of Wellington's Regt.
3.00 A.M.
7/8/18.

　　　　　　　　　　　　　D I S T R I B U T I O N.

Copy No. 1 Bn.H.Q.
     2 - 5 All Coys.

SECRET.   2nd Bn. Duke of Wellington's Regt.   Copy No. 12
           (OPERATION) ORDER No. 106.
Ref: Map Sheet 36.A. S.E. Ed:2
     1/20,000.   **B**   In the Field, 9th August, 1918.

INTENTION. 1. The Battalion will be relieved in the Centre Sub-sector, VINAGE SECTOR, on the night 9/10th August, 1918, by all three Battalions of the 11th Brigade, as below.
(2) On completion of relief Bn.H.Q., A. & B. Coys. will move to CHATEAU-DU-QUESNOY.
C. & D. Coys. to CANAL SWITCH. Capt. J. COOKE will be in command of the last two Companies.

INSTRUCTIONS. 2 (a) **OUTPOST LINES.**
C. & B. Coys. will be relieved by Coys. of 1st Rifle Bde. C. & B. Coys. will each be divided into two halves, Left front and Right front. These two half Coys. will be taken over by different half Coys. of the relieveing unit.
1st SYSTEM.
1st System will be divided as follows by line through Front Line - Post 59, - Support Line - S.53, - Reserve Line - B.62, inclusive to Right Battalion.
In each line A. & D. Coys. will be divided as above. The Right Half Portions of the Companies will be taken over by Companies of the 1st Hants. Regt. and Left Coys. by Coys of 1st Somerset L.I.

(b) **GUIDES.**

Regt.	Place & Time for Guides.	Bridges to be used.
1st Hants.	CHELSEA BRIDGE Q.32.c.65.95. 1 p.m.	CHELSEA BRIDGE.
1st Somersets.	BLACKFRIARS. P.36.b.0.5. 1 p.m.	BLACKFRIARS.
1st Rifle Bde. Right Front Support Coy.	BLACKFRIARS Q.20.d.5.3.	----do----

Guides will be at the rate of 1 per Platoon, 1 per Coy.H.Q. where relieveing Coy. Commander decides to have Coy.H.Q. in our Sector.

Regt.	Rendezvous.
1st Rifle Bde. Left Front & Left Support Coy.	Q.27.a.15.50. 8 p.m. Where Front Line System crosses NORTH Road.

(c) **COMPLETION OF RELIEF** will be notified as in O.O. No. 99. Two Companies moving to CANAL SWITCH will report their arrival to 10th & 11th Infy. Bdes. by wiring Code Word "SWITCH".

(d) **MARCH.**
On completion of relief A. & D. Coys will relieve the 1st Somersets in CANAL SWITCH. When C. Coy. have been relieved they in turn will relieve A. Coy. in CANAL SWITCH, and then on Final Completion of Relief A. & B. Coys. and Bn.H.Q. will move to Billets at CHATEAU-DU-QUESNOY.

(e) **TRENCH STORES.**
All Trench Stores, Maps, etc, will be handed over by Coys. Each Coy. will be responsible for handing over the stores at present on their charge to incoming units.
Signed receipts in duplicate will be forwarded to Bn.H.Q. by noon, 10th inst.

(f) **LEWIS GUNS.**
B. Coy. will detail one full rank N.C.O. to superintend the loading of Lewis Guns, etc.

P. T. O.

INSTRUCTIONS. 2. (g)
(Contd.) **WATER TINS, ETC.**
Empty Water Tins will be carried down and loaded in Limbers at P.36.c.8.8.
(h) **BILLETS.**
Q.M. will arrange for Billeting parties to report to Town Major's Office L'ECLEME at 2 p.m. 9th inst. He will take over Reserve Bombs, etc., & Bayonet Fighting Stores, and give a receipt for these.
He will request Transport, etc. for conveyance of Stores, etc. from Transport Lines to CHATEAU-DU-QUESNOY.

NOTE. Names of Relieving Coys. will be notified to Coys. as soon as representatives of 11th Bde. have been seen, also the proposed Coy. H.Q. to be taken over.

TRANSPORT. 3. Transport Officer will arrange :-
(a) 2 Limbers at P.36.c.8.8. for empties, spare stores, etc. at 10.30 p.m.
(b) 2 Limbers for L.G's. at 10.30 p.m. at P.36.c.8.8.
(c) 1 Limber at Battn. H.Q. at 10 p.m.
(d) Supply Q.M. as requested.

4. ACKNOWLEDGE.

(Sgd) D.G.R.BILHAM, Captain.
A/Adjt. 2nd Duke of Wellington's Regt.

D I S T R I B U T I O N.

Copy No. 1 - 4 All Coys.
         5   Bn.H.Q.
         6   10th Bde.
         7 - 9 Battns. of 11th Inf. Bde.
         10   Q.M.
         11   T.O.
         12 - 14 War Diary.
         15   File.

SECRET. 2nd Bn. Duke of Wellington's Regt.   Copy No. 9
(OPERATION) ORDER No. 101
Ref. Map Sheet 36. A. S.E. Ed:8.
1/20.000   In the Field, 11th August, 1918.

INTENTION. 1. An Inter-Company relief will take place on the night 12/13th August, 1918.

INSTRUCTIONS. 2. RELIEFS.
- A. Company will relieve C. Company
- B. Company will relieve D. Company.

(a) ORDER OF MARCH.   A - B Companies.
A. Coy. will leave billets at 6 p.m.
200 yards between Platoons will be maintained.

(b) DRESS.
Fighting Order, Overcoats rolled Bandolier fashion.

(c) GUIDES.
1 Guide per Platoon and 1 Guide per Coy. H.Q. will be at ROAD JUNCTION P.36.b.2.2½ at 6.45 p.m.

(d) COMMAND.
Lieut. W.E. HORSLEY will be in charge of the two Coys., and will ensure that all Trench Stores, Maps, Programmes of Work, etc., are taken over.

(e) RATIONS.
Rations for A. & B. Coys. will be delivered at the CANAL, and for C. & D. Coys. at LE QUESNOY.

(f) STORES.
Officers Kits of A. & B. Coys. will be ready for collection at 5.30 p.m.
Packs of A. & B. Coys. by 6.30 p.m.
Officers Kits of C. & D. Coys. by 6.30 p.m.

(g) DETAILS.
Details from BURBURE will rejoin their Coys. at 4 p.m. tomorrow.
Details of A. & B. Coys. will proceed to Line with their Companies.
Men from C. & D. Coys. for new details will be at Bn. H.Q. by 1.45 p.m.

(h) DRAFT.
The Drafts of C. & D. Coys. at present with A. & B. Coys. will join their Coys. tomorrow on their arrival at Billets.

(j) COMPLETION OF RELIEF. will be reported by wiring as in O.O. No. 100.

TRANSPORT. 3. Transport Officer will arrange :-
(a) Conveying Rations & Officers Kits of A. & B. Coys. to CANAL BANK.
(b) Conveying L.G's, & Kits of C. & D. Coys. to LE QUESNOY.

Captain.
A/Adjt. 2nd Duke of Wellington's Regt.

DISTRIBUTION.

Copy No. 1 Bn. H.Q.   Copy No. 7 Q.M.
         2 - 5 All Coys.   8 T.O.
         6 10th Inf. Bde.   9 - 11 War Diary.
                                        12 File.

SECRET.   2nd Bn. Duke of Wellington's Regt.   Copy No. 10
               (OPERATION) ORDER No. 102
Ref. Map Sheet 36, a. S.E.   D   August
     1/20,000   In the Field, 14th August. 1918.

INTENTION. 1. The Battalion will relieve 1st The King's Own Regt. in the
              Right Support Position of the PACAUT SECTOR, on the afternoon
              of 15th Instant.

INSTRUCTIONS. 2. RELIEF.
    (a) A. Coy will take over from B. Coy. 1st The King's Own Regt.
        B. Coy. ———————————————— C. Coy. ————————————————————
        C. Coy. ———————————————— A. Coy. ————————————————————
        D. Coy. ———————————————— D. Coy. ————————————————————

    (b) GUIDES.
        Guides will be as under :-
        For C. & D. Coys. at CHELSEA Bridge at 2.30 p.m.
        For A. & B. Coys. ———————————————— 3.30 p.m.

    (c) ORDER OF MARCH.
        Companies at LE SURMOY.
        C. Coy. will leave Billets at 2 p.m.
        D. Coy. ———————————————— 2.40 p.m.
        Bn. H.Q. ———————————————— 3 p.m.
        Interval of 10 minutes will be allowed between each Platoon.
        Companies on CANAL.
        A. Coy. leave CANAL SWITCH at 3.15 p.m.
        B. Coy. ———————————————— 3.35 p.m.
        Route.
        Route 4 - Track to CANAL Bank and thence along CANAL Bank
        - PACK Bridge (Q.33.c.3.3.)

    (d) DRESS.
        Fighting Order. Greatcoats rolled bandolier fashion.

    (e) TRENCH STORES.
        All Trench Stores, Trench Maps, Programmes of Work,
        Defence Orders, etc., will be taken over, and receipts
        in duplicate forwarded to Bn.H.Q. by 6 p.m. 15th inst.

    (f) COMPLETION OF RELIEF will be notified to Bn.H.Q. by
        Clock Face Method.

    (g) DEFENCE.
        In the event of a preliminary attack or a bombardment
        developing during relief, troops on the SOUTH of the
        CANAL will occupy their BATTLE Positions in accordance
        with Defence Orders Part III.
        Troops on the NORTH of the CANAL will occupy the nearest
        Trenches, and place themselves under orders of Battalion
        Commander 1st The King's Own Regt.

    (h) DISPOSITIONS.
        Maps showing dispositions will be forwarded to Bn.H.Q.
        by 8 a.m. 16th inst.

    (j) ADVANCE PARTY.
        One Officer & one N.C.O. per Coy. - Lieut. H. LIVSEY &
        two Signallers for Bn.H.Q., will proceed to take over
        Stores.
        C. & D. Coys. & Bn.H.Q. will leave present Billets at 8 A.M.
        A. & B. Coys. will leave at 9 a.m.

    (k) LEWIS GUNS.
        Lewis Guns of C. & D. Coys. with 24 Magazines per Gun,
        will be carried to (ROSE HOUSE) F.36.b.2.2.
        C. Coy. will detail a N.C.O. to accompany this Limber to
        distribute guns.

                                                              P. T. O.

INSTRUCTIONS 2. (1) **RATIONS.**
(Contd)   Rations for consumption on 16th inst. will be carried by
           C. & D. Coys. & Bn.H.Q. from Billets.
           Limbers will convey Rations for A. & B. Coys. to
           Q.3.a.75.90. Water for Coys. will be sent to this place
           also. Time to be notified later.
(m) **BILLETS.**
           The Q.M. will arrange to hand over Billets to 2nd Lanc.
           Fus. at 5 p.m. He will also hand over all Reserve S.A.A.
           Bombs, etc., that were taken over.
           All Billets must be left perfectly clean and a certificate
           to this effect obtained.
(n) **STORES.** will be collected by Limbers as follows :-
    (a) Men's Packs & Workshops at 9 a.m. at Coy.H.Q.
    (b) All remaining Stores at   1 p.m.
    (c) Lewis Guns at   1 p.m.
    Officers Kits & Cooking Utensils of A. & B. Coys. will be
    collected by Limbers that take up L.G's of C. & D. Coys.

TRANSPORT   3.   Transport Officer will arrange :-
    (a) Collection of Men's Packs, Stores, etc., mentioned in
        para. 2 (n).
    (b) Collection of Lewis Guns.
    (c) Carrying of Rations and Water.
    (d) Removal of Cookers, Maltese Cart, etc., from LE QUESNOY
        and CANAL BANK.
    (e) Will provide Transport required by Q.M.

BATTALION H.Q. 4. Will be at W.3.d.2.6.

AID POST   5. Will be at W.2.b.6.3.

                   ACKNOWLEDGE.

                                        Captain,
                                A/Adjt, 2nd Bn. Duke of Wellington's Regt.

D I S T R I B U T I O N.

Copy No. 1 Bn.H.Q.   Copy No. 8 Q.M.
         2 - 5 All Coys.   9 T.O.
         6 1st K.O's.   10 - 12 War Diary.
         7 10th Inf. Bde.   13 File.

2nd Bn Duke of Wellington's Regiment.   Copy No...10.

OPERATION ORDER. No., 103.
Ref. Map Sheet. 36.A.,S.E.
1/20.000. Edition. 8.   E   In the Field. 10th August 1918.

INTENTION.   1. An Inter-Company relief will take place on the evening of 19th inst

INSTRUCTIONS. 2. (a) RELIEF.
"A" Company will relieve "C" Company.
"B"   "   "   "   "D"   " .
All details of relief, Guides, etc, will be arranged by
Company Commanders concerned.
(b) ORDER OF RELIEF. "A" Company 6.p.m., "B" Company 6.30.p.m.
All movement by sections at 5 minutes interval. No movement
to take place on Tracks EAST of PACAUT WOOD.
(c) WORK.
All work and nature of usual working parties will be handed
over. O.C's. "C" and "D" Companies will hand over all details
as to work on Breastworks.
Working Parties will rejoin their companies in new position.
(d) All Stores, Maps, etc, will be handed over and receipts kept.
"A" Company will hand over baths to "C" Company.
(e) Completion of Relief will be notified in the usual manner.
(f) RATIONS.
Rations will be delivered and carried by the usual Companies
and will be dumped at new Company H.Q.

ACKNOWLEDGE.

(Signed) D.G.R.Bilham. Captain.
A/Adjt. 2nd Bn Duke of Wellington's Regiment.

DISTRIBUTION.

Copy No.1. Bn .H.Q.
       2.-5. All Coys.
       6.   Q.M.
       7.   T.O.
       8-10. War Diary.
       11. File.

SECRET.   2nd Bn. Duke of Wellington's Regt.   Copy No. 13.
           (OPERATION) ORDER No. 104.
Ref. Map.Sheet.36.A. S.E.
   1/20.000.   In the Field, 22nd August, 1918.

INTENTION. 1. (a) The 2nd D.of W's Regt. will be relieved in the Right Support
               Sub-sector of the PACAUT SECTOR on the afternoon of 23rd by the
               2nd Wiltshire Regt. & 9th Royal Welch Fusiliers.
           (b) On completion of relief Companies will march to billets as under:
               Bn.H.Q., A. and B. Companies - CHATEAU le QUESNOY.
                       C. and D. Companies   - CANTRAINE.

INSTRUCTIONS. 2. (a) RELIEFS.
                   A. Coy. will be relieved by D. Coy. 2nd Wilts. Regt. in FRONT
                       Line as far as Q.34.c.0.4. from the Right Boundary.
                       From the Left Boundary to Q.34.c.0.4. by the 9th R.W.
                   E. Coy Fusiliers.
                   D. Coy. will be relieved by B. Coy. 2nd Wilts. Regt.
                   Companies will be relieved in their "Stand to" positions.
                   B. & C. Coys. will not be relieved by anyone in the SUPPORT
                   Line and HARRISON'S Trench. They will vacate their positions
                   as soon as they see all A. Coy. have past their Lines.
              (b) GUIDES.
                   A. Coy. will supply 1 Guide for the 9th R.W.Fus: to be at
                   CROSS Roads LES HARRISOIRS (W.2.b.0.6.) at 2 p.m.
                   Guides from A. & D. Coys. for 2nd Wilts. Regt. will be
                   arranged by Officers Commanding these Companies with the
                   corresponding Company Commanders who will visit them today.
              (c) TRENCH STORES.
                   Trench Stores, etc., of A & D. Coys. will be handed over as
                   detailed in K.273.
                   B. & C. Coys. will form all their Stores into Dumps. The
                   location of these dumps will be forwarded to Bn.H.Q. by 1 p.m.
                   tomorrow, and list of stores on these dumps forwarded as already
                   detailed.
              (d) COMPLETION of RELIEF.
                   Completion of Relief - Time of Leaving in case of B. & C.Coys.
                   will be notified to Bn.H.Q. in the usual manner.
              (e) DEFENCE.
                   In the event of the enemy attacking or a preliminary bombard-
                   ment, all troops relieved will man the nearest trenches; all
                   unrelieved troops will "Stand to". In all cases runners will
                   be sent to Bn.H.Q. to report where Coys. are.
              (f) REAR PARTIES.
                   Each Company will leave behind a cleaning up party of one
                   N.C.O. & 2 men. 2Lieut. S.JOHNSON will be in charge of the
                   whole party and will go round all trenches and will satisfy
                   himself that they have been left clean.
                   He will see any parts that are not satisfactory are cleaned up,
                   and should he find any part too big for his party, he will
                   notify Bn.H.Q. when the Company in question will be required
                   to send up a party next day to clear its area.
                   2Lieut. S.JOHNSON will report to O.C. "A" Coy. before they
                   move off, and on his relief will meet parties for B.Coy. at
                   B.Coy.H.Q., D.Coy. at the BRIDGE, and "C" Coy. at Road by
                   "C" Coy. Trench.
                   Each Party from Front to Rear will await the arrival of 2Lieut
                   S.JOHNSON. On being satisfied that all trenches are clean
                   he will march the whole party back to billets and report his
                   arrival to Bn.H.Q.
              (g) LEWIS GUNS.
                   All Lewis Guns will be dumped at Bn.Ration Dump by 2.45 p.m.
                   Each Company will leave 1 Lewis Gunner to guard the Coy. Guns
                   until they have been loaded.
              (h) GREATCOATS.
                   All Greatcoats will be rolled in bundles and labelled by Coys.
                   and will be down at the Ration Dump by 2 p.m. ready to be
                   carried by Transport.   P.T.O.

INSTRUCTIONS. 2. (j) MARCH
A & B Coys. will move via BRIDGE (Q.33.c.3.3.) then along CANAL Bank to ROSE HOUSE and then via Route 4.
C. & D. Coys. will move via CROSS Roads (W.2.b.8.4.) - Road Junction W.8.d.a.4.4. - by track to NOISY NOOK.

(k) BILLETS.
Companies will report their arrival in billets by Runner.
Q.M. will arrange billets.

(l) PACKS.
Q.M. will arrange for Packs to be in billets on arrival.
All men will get their Caps and Cleaning Materials from their packs and pack their greatcoats in their packs.
Packs will then be returned to Transport Lines on the evening of the 23rd. inst.

TRANSPORT. 3. The Transport Officer will arrange:-
(a) Limbers to be at Ration Dump by 3.45 p.m. for all Coys. L.G's and Greatcoats.
(b) Supply Q.M. with Transport.
(c) Mess Cart and Limber to be at Bn.H.Q. at 2.15 p.m. for Stores.
(d) Move Cookers, Maltese Cart, etc.
(e) To take men's packs back to Transport Lines.

(Sgd) D.G.R.Bilham, Captain.
A/Adjt. 2nd Bn. D ke of Wellington's Regt.

D I S T R I B U T I O N.

Copy No. 1 Bn.H.Q.   Copy No. 8 9th R.W.Fus:
         2 - 5 All Coys.   9 Q.M.
         6 10th Inf: Bde.   10 T.O.
         7 2nd Wilts. Regt.   11 - 13 War Diary.
                                   14 File.

SECRET.   2nd Bn. Duke of Wellington's Regt.   G   Copy No. 11
          (OPERATION) ORDER No. 105
                                            In the Field, 23rd August, 1918.

INTENTION.   1   The Battalion will march to Billets at LOZINGHEM tomorrow,
                  (August 24th.)

INSTRUCTIONS. 2. (a) DRESS.
                      Battle Order with Steel Helmets.
                  (b) ORDER of MARCH.
                      Bn.H.Q., Drums, A. B. C. & D. Companies, and balance of
                      Transport at present Billets.
                  (c) STARTING POINT.
                      Starting Point will be Road Junction V.7.b.48.40.
                  (d) TIME. 10.30 a.m.
                  (e) ROUTE.
                      CHATEAU-QUESNOY - CANTRAINE to BAS RIEUX - BUSNETTES Road to
                      Track - HAUT RIEUX - ALLOUAGNE (C.12.a.) - LOZINGHEM.
                  (f) BILLETING PARTY.
                      C.Q.M.Sergts. and 1 N.C.O. from Bn.H.Q. will meet at C.Coy.
                      H.Q. on bicycles at 8 a.m. to take over billets and meet
                      Battalion at the outskirts of LOZINGHEM.
                  (g) BAGGAGE.
                      All Coys. L.G's, Stores, Tools, etc., will be stacked
                      outside Coy. H.Q. by 8.30 a.m. ready for collection.
                  (h) OFFICERS KITS.
                      Officers Kits, Valises, etc. by 9 a.m. at Coy. H.Q.
                  (j) MESS STORES.
                      All Mess Stores by 9.30 a.m. at Coy. H.Q.

REPORTS.   3.   Head of Column.

                                                        Captain.
                                       A/Adjt. 2nd Duke of Wellington's Regt.

              DISTRIBUTION.

        Copy No. 1 Bn.H.Q.   Copy No. 8 Q.M.
                 2 - 5 All Coys.   9 - 11 War Diary.
                 6 10th Inf: Bde.   12 File.
                 7 T.O.

ADDENDUM.

              INTERVAL.
              100 yards between Companies.
              100 yards between Rear of Column & Transport.

SECRET.　　　2nd Bn. Duke of Wellington's Regt.　　　　　Copy No. 11
　　　　　　　　(OPERATION) ORDER No. 106.
Ref. Map Sheet 36.b. & LENS 11.
　　1/40.000　　　1/100.000　　　　　　　　In the Field, 24th August, 1918.

INTENTION. 1. The Battalion will march to PERNES to entrain tomorrow.

INSTRUCTIONS. 2. (a) DRESS.
　　　　　　　　　　Full Marching Order and Steel Helmets to be worn.
　　　　　　　(b) ORDER of MARCH.
　　　　　　　　　　Bn.H.Q. Drums, C. D. A. & B. Companies with intervals as in Operation Order 105.
　　　　　　　(c) STARTING POINT.
　　　　　　　　　　C.17.d.80.35.
　　　　　　　(d) TIME.
　　　　　　　　　~~10.45~~ a.m.　12.15 p.m.
　　　　　　　(e) ROUTE.　　H.Q. of Central
　　　　　　　　　　AUCHEL - ~~FLORINGHEM~~ - PERNES.
　　　　　　　(f) SICK PARADE.
　　　　　　　　　　8. a.m.
　　　　　　　(g) BILLETING PARTY.
　　　　　　　　　　All C.Q.M.Sergts. and 1 N.C.O. for Bn.H.Q. will report to Lieut. H.LIVSEY at Orderly Room at 9.15 a.m. with Billeting Strengths.

REPORTS. 3. Head of Column.

　　　　　　　　　　　　　　　　　　　　　　Captain.
　　　　　　　　　　　　　　　　　A/Adjt. 2nd Duke of Wellington's Regt.

SECRET.　　　　　2nd Bn Duke of Wellington's Regiment.　　　　Copy No...10..

OPERATION ORDER NO. 107.

Ref Map. LENS.11.　　　　　　　　　　　　　In the Field 26th August 1918.

INTENTION. 1. The Battalion will march to Villers-au-Bois.

INSTRUCTIONS. 2. (a) Dress. Battle order. One pick or shovel per man, (exclusive of Specialists) to be carried.
(b) Order of March:- Bn,H.Q., "A" "B" "C" "D" Companies.
(C) Starting Point:- Road outside Bn. Orderly Room.
(d) Time:- 6.50.p.m.
(e) Route:- TERNAS- AVERDOINGT-TINCQUES-LAMONT ROUGE FARM=(South of Aubigny) -AGNIERES-CAMBLAIN L'ABBE-LE PENDU.
(f) Billeting Party.:- As detailed.

TRANSPORT. 3.　　Will follow in rear of Battalion.

REPORTS. 4.　　Head of Column.

　　　　　　　　　　　　Sgd D.G.R.Bilham. Captain.
A/Adjt 2nd Bn Duke of Wellington's Regiment.

DISTRIBUTION.

Copy No. 1. Bn H.Q.　　　　　　Copy No. 7. 10th Infy Bde
" " 2-5. all Coys　　　　　　　　" 8-10. War Diary
" 6. T.O.& Q M.　　　　　　　　" 11 File.

SECRET.   2nd Bn. Duke of Wellington's Regt.   **J.**   Copy No.
WARNING ORDER
In the Field, 27th August, 1918.

1. Probable time of move 1 p.m.

2. Rations for 29th inst. will be issued tomorrow morning, and will be carried on the man.

3. A good Dinner will be provided at 12 noon.

4. Water bottles must be filled. Carts will be available tomorrow morning for this purpose.

5. Arrangements will be made for A. B. & D. Companies Details to be separated from the rest of the Battalion during the morning. C. Company will make their own arrangements in the same way.
Packs of men for Details must be kept separate from others. Details will have dinners with their own Companies.

6. Bomb buckets are only to be issued to Rifle Bombers.

7. Four long-handled wire cutters are being issued to Companies; these will be Company Stores, and great care must be taken of them.

Captain.
A/Adjt. 2nd Duke of Wellington's Regt.

2Nd Bn Duke of Wellington's Regiment.   Copy No. 8

SECRET.

OPERATION ORDER. No., 108.

Ref. Map:- LENS.11.   K   In the Field. 28th August 1918.

INTENTION. 1. The Battalion (Less details) will embus to move to the assembly position.

INSTRUCTIONS. 2. (a) Dress :- Battle Order.
(b) Order of March:- H.Q., "C" "B" "D" "A" Companies.
(c) Starting Point.:- "C" Coys ,H.Q..
(D) Time:- 11.50 a.m.
(e) Details:- Detialsn will parade at "C" Coy H.Q., under Capt F.H.Hill.M.C. ,at 1.45.p.m. and will proceed to Arras, to pass present Bde H.Q., at 2.5.p.m.(follow 1st R.Warwicks Regt.)
Packs will be carried.
Billeting parties will meet them at Rond Point Arras.

TRANSPORT. 3. Transport will move independently at 10.a.m.

Sgd D.G.R.Bilham Captain
Adjt. 2nd Bn Duke of Wellington's Regiment.

DISTRIBUTION.

Copy. No., 1.   Bn.H.Q.,
2 to 5 Coys.
6.   Q.M.
7.   T.O.
8.to.10. War Diary.
11.   File.

SECRET.   2nd Bn. Duke of Wellington's Regt.   Copy No. 6
              WARNING ORDER No. 1
                                        20th AUGUST, 1918.

1. The Battalion will move forward to the First Objective in the following order :-
   FRONT LINE.   C. Company LEFT.   D. Company RIGHT.
   SUPPORT   B. Company in two lines of Platoons in small parties.
   RESERVE   A. Company.

2. At ZERO, B. Company will move forward and occupy present Front Line till First Objective is gained.
   On jumping off for Second Objective B. Company will move forward to First Objective, detaching two Platoons to reach Second Objective as soon as possible and support (thicken) C. & D. Companies, (4 Platoons/ each.) These will be under the command of O.C. Companies they join.

3. In the event of Counter Action becoming necessary on the part of the Front Line, the Senior Officer present will take command until further orders.

4. The action of B. Company less two Platoons when Final Objective is gained will be in order named :-
   1. Secure an unprotected flank.
   2. Reinforce in event of counter-attack.

5. "A" Company will be Tactical Reserve throughout, and will be one objective behind "B" Company until emergency arises for its use.

6. Battalion H.Q. will move as per order and further moves will be arranged as situation develops.

                                  (Sgd) D.G.R.BILHAM, Captain.
                           A/Adjt. 2nd Duke of Wellington's Regt.

              D I S T R I B U T I O N.
              ─────────────────────────

    Copy No. 1 Bn.H.Q.   Copy No. 6 - 8 War Diary.
           2 - 5 All Coys.   9   File.

2nd Bn Duke of Wellington's Regiment.   Copy No., 1.

SECRET.   OPERATION ORDER No. 109.

Ref Map.Eterpigny.   In the Field 30/8/18.

1. The Battalion will attack at 4p.m. to-day.

2. The Method will be the same as detailed in Yesterday's Warning, with the exception that "A" Coy will take over the role of "D"Coy, and "B"Coy will take over the role of "C"Coy. "C" and "D" Companies will reorganise during the bombardment, (as much to be done before as possible) and will be under the Command of Captain J.COOKE in Support, thus taking over the role of previously allotted to "B" Company.

3. The formation will then be:-
   "A" Company   RIGHT FRONT
   "B" "   LEFT FRONT.
   (XXXXXXXXXXXXXXXXXXXXXXXXXXX
   C & D, Coys (amalgamated) IN SUPPORT.

4. The disposition of C & D,Coys will remain the same in the meantime. During the afternoon "A" Coy will slowly dribble small bodies down to the assembly position.
"B" Coy will similarly reorganise so as to get the Company in their Jumping off position, (on the left sector of the Battalion Frontage).

5. The Formations will be the same Attacking,Coys as arranged for Coys yesterday.

6. BOUNDARIES.
   RIGHT. Road O.24.a.3.5. - O.24.d.25.65. - O.30.b.6.7. -and Main Road to P 25.a.30.45.
   INTER- Bn.O18.c.6.4. - O.24.b.30.95. - P.19.a.3.5. - P.19.b.50.00.

7. OBJECTIVES.
   1st Objective. TRENCH.O.24.d.25.65. - O.24.b 45.50. - O.18.d 8.1. P.13.c.2.5. - P.13.a.70.15.
   2nd Objective. Point on ARRAS- Cambrai Road. O.30.b.6.7.-St SERVINS FARM and WOOD P.19.c.0.6. - P.13.c.70.25. - P.13.d. 23.90.
   3rd Objective. P.25.a.30.45.- P.19.a.15.30.- P.19.b.50.70.- P.13.d.75.75.

8. BARRAGE.
   The attack will be carried out with a destructive and rolling barrage.

9. At ZERO hour a barrage will come down on the following line :- O.24.c.65.60.- O.18.d.65.43. - P.13.c.35.60. At ZERO plus 1 barrage lifts 100 yards and remains 5 minutes. At ZERO plus 6 barrage lifts 100 yards and continues to lift at the rate of 100 yards every 2 minutes until it is 200 yards clear of the second objective, where it will remain for 5 minutes. At ZERO plus 20,barrage will again move forward at same rate until Infantry reach final objective and will then lift on to Front System of the DROCOURT- QUEANT line including the M.G.Posts in front at P.26.a 35.25.-P.26.a.2.9. - P.20.c.15.12.

10. Companies will dig in on the Final Objective.

11. Bn. H.Q., will be "A"Coy. H.Q.

12. RESERVE COMPANY. "D" Company 2nd Seaforths under Capt Mackintosh- Walker,will take over the previous role of "A" Coy and will be in RESERVE.

                          (Sgd) D.G.R.Bilham.Captain
                A/Adjt. 2nd Bn Duke of Wellington's Regiment.

DISTRIBUTION.
Copy.No.1 Bn.H.Q.   Copy No.2-5 Companies.
      6. File.   7-9. War Diary.

SECRET

WAR DIARY.

of

2nd Bn. Duke of Wellington's Regt.

From... SEPT. 1st ...1918.

To... SEPT. 30th ...1918.
       inclusive.

VOLUME.

T. Pawlett
Lieut.Colonel.
Commanding 2nd Bn. Duke of Wellington's Regt.

Oct. 4 ...1918.

4th Division

2nd Battn Dukes of Wellington Reg

came from 10th Bde. Feb.

~~Sept. To December~~
~~1918~~

1918 SEP — 1919 JUN

Army Form C. 2118.

WAR DIARY
or
INTELLIGENCE SUMMARY.
(Erase heading not required.)

Place	Date	Hour	Summary of Events and Information	Remarks and references to Appendices
SEPTEMBER-1918				
HAUCOURT	1.		At 4.15 p.m. the Battn. in conjunction with the 1/6th ROYAL WARWICKSHIRE Rgt. attacked & captured PEAR TRENCH. The DIV. CMDR. came up to B.H.Q. specially to congratulate the Battn. on their magnificent work & the previous days— The Battn. was relieved by the 47 CANADIANS (10th CANADIAN Bde)	A.
	2.		Relief complete by 2 A.M. Battn. moved back to WHISTLE TRENCH— 11 A.M. Battn. moved forward into REMY TRENCH & became Battn. in DIV. RESERVE.	B. REF. MAP ETERPIGNY
	3.		CONGRATULATORY MESSAGES from CORPS COMMANDER. G.O.C. 4th DIV. B.G.C. 10th Bde. 2Lts HARVEY - SHAW - STARKEY - HOUGHTON & WOLFENDEN joined Battn. The Battn. was relieved by 1 GLOUCESTERS & 1st ROYAL WELSH FUSILIERS. Relief complete by 6 p.m. Moved back to trenches near GUENAPPE.	C. D. E.
	4.		The Battn. marched to TILLOY & there embussed at 1-15 p.m. for AVERDOINGT. Arrived at 5 p.m. 29 O.R. joined Battn.— Capt. J. COOKE took command of "D" Coy, vice Capt. C. SKELTON M.C. CONGRATULATORY MESSAGE from CORPS CM'D'R.	F. G.
AVERDOINCT	5.		The Battn. cleaning up & getting ready for COMMANDING OFFICER'S inspection. 25 OR joined Battn.	
	6.		Battn. in training. Musketry. Drill & attack practice. Lecture to all Officers at Bn. H.Q. Mess. 2 Lts. KAY - WALSH & Mc HUGH joined the Battn. 11 OR joined.	
	7.		Battn. in training. Lewis Gun instruction - Arms drill. Platoon attack. A Coy. Range. The Battn. passed through the Gas chamber.	

57 F
15 sheets

Army Form C. 2118.

WAR DIARY
or
INTELLIGENCE SUMMARY.
(Erase heading not required.)

Instructions regarding War Diaries and Intelligence Summaries are contained in F. S. Regs., Part II. and the Staff Manual respectively. Title pages will be prepared in manuscript.

Place	Date	Hour	Summary of Events and Information	Remarks and references to Appendices
	SEPTEMBER — 1918 —			
AVERDOINGT	8		The Battn in Training. Same as previous day. Demonstration in method of firing Rifle Grenade (No 36).	
	9		Battn in training. Lewis gun Class started under Sergt. WARD. 2Lt. BANHAM & 80 O.R. joined Battn —	
	10		Battn training. Arranged that Coy Cmdrs. should hold. half-an-hour conference daily with Platoon & Section Leaders — A Coy Rifle Grenadiers practised firing Rifle Grenadier —	
	11		Battn in Training — Battn bathed —	
	12		Battn in Training — Much Rain —	
	13		Battn in Training — CSM BROWN, Army Gymnasium Staff assisted Coys in B & P.T.	
	14		Battn in Training — 10-30 to 11-30 AM Battn Drill — 11-30 to 12 Noon Church Parade — 2 Lts BLACKBURN & H.W. SMITH M.M. rejoined from Hospital —	
	15.		Battn in training —	
	16.		Battn in training —	
	17.		Battn in training — Warning of a Battn move.	
	18.		The Battn relieved the 8th MIDDLESEX (56th Div) in the Right Sub-Sector (LECLUSE). Relief Complete by 11 pm. 7th MIDDLESEX on right.	MAP.S. 51.B.SENE. 1:20,000.
LECLUSE			ROYAL WARWICKS on Left. 2 Lt. T WALSH to Hospital.	H

2nd Bn. Duke of Wellington's Regiment.   Copy No 7
(OPERATION) ORDER No. 111.

Ref. Map ETERPIGNY.   A.   In the Field, 1st September, 1918.

INTENTION. 1. To clear ground of enemy N. of ARRAS-CAMBRAI Road between where SOUP Trench joins ARRAS-CAMBRAI Road at C.24.d.80.00 and P.25.a.3.5 N. to C.24.d.6.3. to P.25.a.70.65.

INSTRUCTIONS. 2. (a) FORCE — Two Platoons of 1st R.War.Regt. under Lieut. R.E. BARNWELL and   strengthened by Details from 2nd D:of W Regt.
(b) COMMANDER — Capt. J. COOKE, 2nd D.of W'S Regt.
(c) FORMATION.
One Platoon in the Front Line and one Platoon in immediate Support.
(d) Point of Assembly — SACK Trench.
(e) OBJECTIVE — Continuation of PEAR Lane (P.19.c.70.00) to P.25.a.3.5.

The Force will be supported by a Barrage on its Right Flank in Front of OBJECTIVE.
It will consolidate when OBJECTIVE is gained and will immediately get in touch with troops on its Left in PEAR Lane.

A CANADIAN Battalion is attacking on the S. side of the ARRAS-CAMBRAI Road the same time and same line of OBJECTIVE continued to the SOUTH.

Force will keep in touch and line with this Battalion and co-operate with it throughout.

TIME — ZERO HOUR will be notified later.

(Sgd) D.G.R.BILHAM, Captain.
A/Adjt. 2nd Duke of Wellington's Regt.

AFTER ORDER.

Your objective is now from P.19.d.2.4. — P.19.c.6.0. instead of as outlined in O.O. No. 111. and your Route will be from the same ASSEMBLY POINT N. of the GRID Line, EAST of the WOOD to P.19.d.2.4.— P.19.c.6.0.
The CANADIANS are operating on your Right, S. of the GRID Line from OLIVE Trench so that the barrage will come down S. of you instead of in front.
All troops N. of GRID Line and E. of the WOOD will be withdrawn NORTHWARDS 200 yards before ZERO HOUR.
Operate on Left of CANADIANS. Get liaison with them and keep in touch with their Right.

(Sgd) D.G.R.BILHAM, Captain.
A/Adjt. 2nd Duke of Wellington's Regt.

DISTRIBUTION.

Copy No. 1 Bn.H.Q.   Copy No. 6 - 8 War Diary.
        2 - 5 All Coys.   9   File.

WAR DIARY
or
INTELLIGENCE SUMMARY.
(Erase heading not required.)

Army Form C. 2118.

Place	Date	Hour	Summary of Events and Information	Remarks and references to Appendices
	SEPTEMBER – 1918 –			
LECLUSE	19.	8-40 & 10 A.M.	B. H. Q at P.10.b.9.1. heavily shelled by 5.9".	
	20.		Quiet day – 1 NCO missing believed killed – 2.O.R wounded on Patrol.	
	21.		Outpost line shelled during morning – remainder of day quiet.	
	22.		Left Coy heavily shelled around Maun line & Resistance – 1.O.R killed – 2.O.R wounded.	I
	23.		Quiet day. The Battn relieved by 2nd SEAFORTH HIGHLANDERS – Relief over by 11.30 pm. Battn moved into BRIGADE RESERVE.	
	24.		Bath in Bde Reserve – Quiet day – 1.O.R wounded –	
	25.		Quiet day –	
ST. SERVINS FM.	26.		Quiet day – Lt C. SKELTON M.C. to ENGLAND.	
	27.		Coys paraded 1 hour musketry + ½ hour gun drill – Quiet day –	
	28.		B. H. Q. heavily shelled between 6+7 p.m. with 5.9 + 4.2". No casualties.	
	29.		A + D Coys moved to Kinches in P.15 b + d.7 relieved the 7th MIDDLESEX – B + C did not move –	J
ORANGE HILL	30.		The Battn relieved by 1st ROYAL WARWICKS + moved to ORANGE HILL. Relief complete by 11 p.m.	K

Signed
Lieut Colonel
Comdg 2nd Battn The Duke of Wellington's Regt.

SECRET.   2nd Bn. Duke of Wellington's Regt.   Copy No. 9.
                            (OPERATION) ORDER No.
Ref: Map ETERPIGNY 51.b.   B.   In the Field, 1st September, 1918.

INTENTION. 1. The 2nd Duke of Wellington's Regt and Troops attached will be relieved by the 47th CANADIANS (10th CANADIAN Bde.)
The Brigade will move into Divisional Reserve in vicinity of WHISTLE Trench in O.15.b.

INSTRUCTIONS. 2 (a) The Boundaries between which the 47th CANADIANS will relieve will be :-
       North. GRID Line running W. & E. through O.24. & 19.
       South. GRID Line running W. & E. that divides square O.24. & 19
            and O.30. & 25. to point O.24.c.9.0.

(b) RELIEFS.
The relieving Battalion will relieve in attacking formation in the following order :-
RIGHT ASSAULT COMPANY........ B. Company.
RIGHT SUPPORT COMPANY........ A. Company.
LEFT ASSAULT COMPANY......... D. Company.
LEFT SUPPORT Company. .... C. Company.
The Companies will assemble in the above formation.
Right Assault Coy. SACK Trench & S. of SUNKEN Road.
Right Support in shell holes to rear.
Left Assault Coy. SACK Trench between two SUNKEN Roads in 24.d.
Support Company in shell holes.
From this position the Companies will be led forward in this formation into Front Line as it is.

(c) GUIDES.
4 Guides per Company will be provided by Bn.H.Q. to meet incoming units on CAMBRAI ROAD at ROMARY'S FACTORY, 15.d. from 9.45 p.m. onwards. These guides will lead Companies to report to 2Lieut. E.L.WOOLFORD at Advanced Report Centre.
Guides will be sent by Companies in the Line to report to 2Lieut. E.L.WOOLFORD at REPORT CENTRE at 10.30 p.m. as under:-
A. & D. Coys will supply guides for Right Assaulting Coys,
         (B. & A. Coys. Canadians). 4 Guides for each Coy.
         These guides will be detailed by Capt. M.C.HOOLE.
B. Coy. & D.Coy. 2nd Seaforth's will supply guides for Left
         Assaulting Coys. (4 for each Coy.) To be arranged
         by Lieut. L.SHAW,M.C. and Capt.J.R.MACINTOSH-
         WALKER mutually.
Guides must be men who know position of the new Front Line.
2Lieut. E.L.WOOLFORD will see that the relieving Battalion gets correct guides from Coys. and that relieving Battalion is led to SACK Trench correctly.

(d) TROOPS RELIEVED.
As soon as incoming Unit has relieved troops in Front Line, all other troops may leave.
O.C. "A" Company will inform tonight's attacking party on his Right when he is relieved.
When relieved, all troops must be collected by Units in parties under Officers or Senior N.C.O's. and brought down to Rendezvous posts.

(e) RENDEZVOUS. will be as follows :-
DUKE'S present Bn. H.Qrs.
SEAFORTHS, Seaforths present Bn.H.Q.
WARWICK'S, Warwick's present H.Q.
Guides will be at these points to direct Coys. and parties to their destinations.

(f) COMPLETION OF RELIEF. to be notified to DUKE'S H.Q. by all Coy. Commanders by Code Word "THANKS".

(g) STORES.
Companies will do their best to bring out L.G.Magazines and Water Tins, which are very hard to obtain.

(h) ACKNOWLEDGE.

                                           (Sgd) D.G.R.BILHAM Captain.

DISTRIBUTION.

Copy No. 1 B.H.Q.
        2 - 5 All Coys.
        6 Seaforths.

Copy No 7 47th Canadians.
        8 10th Inf: Bde.
        9-11 War Diary.
        12 File.

2nd Bn. Duke of Wellington's Regt.

CONGRATULATORY MESSAGES.

The following wire received from Corps Commander dated 2/9/18.

Please convey to all ranks of the 4th British Division and of attached Units my most sincere congratulations for the splendid success you achieved to-day. CURRIE. Ends.

4th Division No. G.A.85
10th Brigade No. B.M. 46.

10th Infantry Brigade.

The G.O.C. wishes me to express to you his appreciation of the excellent work performed by your Brigade during the past two days. Heavy fighting, after a particularly difficult and tiring relief has brought out the fine soldierly spirit and high quality of all ranks.

He asks me to remind you that there is still a great effort required and much to be done, and though he realises the strain, he is confident that all ranks will rise to the occasion which if successful will have far reaching results.

Will you please convey these remarks to all under your command.

(signed) LAURENCE CARR.
Lieut.Colonel.
1st September, 1918.   General Staff, 4th Division.

2nd Duke of Wellington's Regt.

Passed to you.
Please convey the Divisional Commander's remarks to all ranks under your Command.

(signed)   Captain.
Brigade Major,
2nd September, 1918.   10th Infantry Brigade.

4th Division G.A. 86.
10th Brigade No. B.M.45.

10th Infantry Brigade.

The G.O.C. wishes you to convey to Lieut.Colonel F. PAWLETT, and all ranks of the 2nd Duke of Wellington's Regt., his great appreciation of the magnificient way in which this Battalion has fought during the past days heavy fighting East of MONCHY.

The Battalion has shown fighting spirit worthy of the best traditions.

(signed) LAURENCE CARR.
Lieut.Colonel.
1st September, 1918.   General Staff, 4th Division.

O.C.
2nd Duke of Wellington's Regiment.

In forwarding the above letter of the G.O.C. I should like to express my deep appreciation and great admiration of the work done by all ranks of your Battalion, and I hope soon to have the opportunity of expressing my thanks to them personally.

(signed) J.GREENE,
Brigadier General
Commanding 10th Infantry Brigade.

SECRET. 2nd Bn. Duke of Wellington's Regt. Copy No. 6
(OPERATION) ORDER No.
Ref. Map ETERPIGNY.   D   In the Field, 2nd September, 1918.
_____

INTENTION. 1. The Battalion will move and occupy trenches running N. & S. in Square C.17.b. & d. at once.

INSTRUCTIONS. 2. (a) Companies will report as soon as they are ready to move off.
(b) GUIDES.
One Guide per Company will report to Lieut. H.LIVSEY at B.H.Q. at once.
Bn.H.Q. Coys. will be amalgamated. A & B called "A" Company, under Capt. H.C.HOOLE, M.C.
C & D called "C" Company under Capt. J.COOKE.
Guides will meet Companies at Junction of SUNKEN Road and CORY Trench.
(c) ORDER OF MARCH.
Bn. H.Qrs. A. and C. Companies.
(d) ACKNOWLEDGE.

(Sgd) D.G.R.BILHAM., Captain.
A/Adjt. 2nd Duke of Wellington's Regt.

DISTRIBUTION.
Copy No. 1 Bn.H.Q.   Copy No 6 - 8 War Diary.
       2 - 5 All Coys.   9   File.

SECRET.   2nd Bn. Duke of Wellington's Regt.   Copy No. 8
                         (OPERATION) ORDER No.
Ref. Map STEENIGNY.   E   In the Field, 3rd September, 1918.
_____

INTENTION.   1(a) Battalion is being relieved by 2nd WELCH Regt.
              (b) Orders as to destination will be sent as soon as received.

INSTRUCTIONS. 2(a) ORDER OF MARCH.
                   Companies will march off in order :- Bn.H.Q., C. & A. Companies.
                   100 yards interval will be maintained between Platoons.
                   Companies will be prepared to move at once.
              (b) STORES.
                   Lewis Guns and Stores as arranged.
                   All Bombs, Flares, etc., still in boxes and not issued will
                   be stacked in Company Dumps.
                   Receipts will not be required.
              (c) ADVANCE PARTY.
                   Advance Parties are going on to arrange Company Area.
                   Battalion is moving to area K.12.c. & d. and K.12.a.&b.
              (d) COMPLETION OF RELIEF. will be reported in the usual manner.

                                                (Sgd) D.C.R.BLURTON, Captain.
                                             A/Adjt. 2nd Duke of Wellington's Regt.

                         D I S T R I B U T I O N.
                         _____

              Copy No. 1 Bn.H.Q.   Copy No. 6 - 8 War Diary.
                   2 - 5 All Coys.   9 File.

SECRET.   2nd Bn. Duke of Wellington's Regt.   Copy No. 8.
                                (OPERATION) ORDER No.
Ref. Map 'LENS 11 CAMBRAI Road.   In the Field, 4th September, 1918.

INTENTION.   1. The Battalion will move by Bus to BAILLEUL-AUX-CORNAILLES.

INSTRUCTIONS.   2 (a) DRESS.
                      Battle Order, Steel Helmets, Covers to be worn.
                  (b) Order of March
                      Bn. H.Qrs., BROMS., A. & C. Companies.
                  (c) STARTING POINT.
                      Junction of TRACK and MONCHY-MARIERE Road at W.19.a.70.98.
                  (d) TIME.
                      12.15 p.m.
                  (e) BILLETING PARTY.
                      Two C.Q.M.Sergts. per Company and 1 N.C.O. for Bn.H.Q. will
                      proceed as Billeting Party and will meet the Battalion on
                      arrival in new area.
                  (f) DINNERS.
                      Dinners will be at 11.30 a.m. Camp Kettles will be carried
                      to the embussing point.

TRANSPORT.   3. Transport have moved under separate orders.

REPORTS.   5   Head of the Column.

                    ACKNOWLEDGE.

                                              (Sgd) D.G.R.BILHAM, Captain.
                                              A/Adjt. 2nd Duke of Wellington's Regt.

                            DISTRIBUTION.

        Copy No. 1 Bn.H.Q.   Copy No. 7 Q.M.
                 2 - 5 All Coys.   8 - 10 War Diary.
                 6 10th Inf: Bde.   11 File.

                            AFTER ORDER.

INSTRUCTIONS. 2 (a) ROUTE.
                     ARRAS Road thence (N.12.c.0.3.) thence N.W. along SUNKEN Road
                     to ARRAS-CAMBRAI Road at N.11.b.45%6., thence W. along Main
                     Road to embussing point on ST. POL - ARRAS Road between
                     TINQUES and TINQUETTES.
                 (b) INTERVAL.
                     100 yards distance will be maintained between Platoons.

                                              (Sgd) D.G.R.BILHAM, Captain.
                                              A/Adjt. 2nd Duke of Wellington's Regt.

G.

The G.O.C. has received the following letter from Sir H.S. HORNE, K.C.B., K.C.M.G., Commanding the First Army, which he wishes to convey to all ranks :-

"I am very anxious to tell you how well I think the 4th Division has done during the last fight.

From the moment you went in you commenced to work through and clear up a most difficult piece of country, and you finally, altho' very tired and worn and short in numbers, completed your task by capturing your portion of the DROCOURT-QUEANT LINE on September 2nd.

When one remembers how much fighting and how little rest has fallen to the chance of the 4th Division one feels that you may well be proud of yourselves.

If you care will you let all know how highly appreciated their XXXXXX great efforts and fine fighting have been by the Army".

SECRET.   2nd Bn. Duke of Wellington's Regt.   Copy No. 2
            (OPERATION) ORDER No. 116
Ref: Map Sheets 51.b.S E. & N.E.
        1/20.000   H   In the Field, 18th September, 1918.

INTENTION. 1. The 2nd Bn. Duke of Wellington's Regt. will relieve the 8th Middlesex Regt., 56th Division, in the RIGHT Sub-sector on the night of 18/19th inst.

INSTRUCTIONS. 2. (a) RELIEFS.
   D.Coy. D.of W. will relieve D.Coy 8th Middlesex Regt. as
                                          LEFT FRONT COMPANY.
   C.Coy. ————do———————— A.Coy. RIGHT FRONT COMPANY.
   A.Coy. ————do———————— B.Coy. in SUPPORT.
   B.Coy. ————do———————— C.Coy. in RESERVE.

(b) DRESS.
   Battle Order, Greatcoats to be carried, rolled bandolier fashion and fastened round Haversack.

(c) GUIDES.
   1 Guide per Platoon, 1 per Coy.H.Q., 2 for Bn.H.Q. & Aid Post will be at ST. SERVIN'S FARM at 7.30 p.m. Coys. are not to pass this point before this hour.

(d) TRENCH STORES.
   All Special Maps, Aeroplane Photographs, Trench Stores and Water Tins will be taken over. Receipts in duplicate will be forwarded to Bn.H.Q. by 8 a.m.19th inst.

(e) DISPOSITIONS.
   Coys. will forward by 8 a.m. 19th inst., Sketch Maps showing Dispositions of Posts and Platoons.

(f) COMPLETION OF RELIEF.
   Completion of Relief will be reported to Bn.H.Q. in the usual manner.

(g) RATIONS.
   Rations for the 19th inst. will be carried on the man.

(h) MOVE.
   (i)   The Battn. will move by Bus from TINQUES and will debus at ST. ROHART'S FACTORY.
   (ii) STARTING POINT. will be Road Junction C.2.c.15.00.
   (iii) TIME. 12.30 p.m.
   (iv) ORDER OF MARCH.
         Bn.H.Q., D. C. A. & B. Companies.

(j) DETAILS.
   Details will parade under Major R.N.CARR,M.C. outside the Orderly Room at 2 p.m.

(k) BILLETS.
   All Billets must be left scrupulously clean. Capt. M.C.HOOLE,M.C. will go round with the Billet Warden and will obtain a certificate that the billets have been left in a clean and sanitary condition.

TRANSPORT. 3. Transport will move independently to new lines at N.18.d.3.7. under instructions already issued.

BATTALION H.Q. 4. will be at P.10.b.9.1.

R.A.P. 5. will be at P.10.b.3.7.

   ACKNOWLEDGE.

                                   (Sgd) D.G.R.BILHAM. Captain.
                        A/Adjt. 2nd Duke of Wellington's Regt.

DISTRIBUTION.

Copy No. 1 Bn.H.Q.
        2 - 5 All Coys.
        6 10th Inf: Bde.
        7 8th Middlesex Regt.

Copy No. 8 Q.M.
        9 T.O.
        10 - 12 War Diary.
        13 File.

SECRET.　　　　　　　2nd Bn. Duke of Wellington's Regt.　　　Copy No. 11
　　　　　　　　　　　(OPERATION) ORDER No. 118//7
Ref: Map Sheets 51b N.E.　　　　　I　　In the Field, 23rd September, 1918.
　　　　　　　　51b S.E.

INTENTION. 1. (a) The 2nd D. of W's Regt. will be relieved by the 2nd Seaforth
　　　　　　　　　Highrs. in the Right Sub-sector of the L'ECLUSE SECTION on the
　　　　　　　　　night of the 24/25th September, 1918.
　　　　　　　(b) On completion of Relief the Battalion will move into Brigade
　　　　　　　　　Reserve.

INSTRUCTIONS. 2. (a) RELIEFS.
　　　　　　　　　C. Coy. Seaforths relieve B.Coy Dukes, RIGHT FRONT COY.
　　　　　　　　　B. Coy. —————————— C.Coy.Dukes, CENTRE FRONT COY.
　　　　　　　　　D. Coy. —————————— D.Coy.Dukes, LEFT FRONT COY.
　　　　　　　　　A. Coy. —————————— A.Coy.Dukes, in Battalion RESERVE.
　　　　　　　(b) GUIDES.
　　　　　　　　　Guides will be found by Coys. at the rate of 1 per Platoon
　　　　　　　　　and 1 for Coy. H.Q. as under :-
　　　　　　　　　For Right & Centre Coys. CROSS Roads at P.11.c.65.40 at 7.45
　　　　　　　　　For Left & Reserve Coys. ——do——　　P.10.b.3.8. at 7.45
　　　　　　　　　No Guides will be required for Bn. H.Q.
　　　　　　　　　O's. C. B. & C. Coys. will arrange for guides to be at their
　　　　　　　　　Coy. H.Q. for Posts No. 3, K1, K2, & Nos. 4. 5. 6. 7.
　　　　　　　　　respectively to guide the reliefs of these posts.
　　　　　　　　　C. Coy. will provide guide for Officer in charge of Village
　　　　　　　　　Posts.
　　　　　　　(c) TRENCH STORES.
　　　　　　　　　All Defence Schemes, Special Maps & Photographs will be hand
　　　　　　　　　handed over. List of Trench Stores handed over will be
　　　　　　　　　forwarded to Bn.H.Q. by 12 noon 25th inst.
　　　　　　　(d) COMPLETION OF RELIEF
　　　　　　　　　will be wired in usual Code.
　　　　　　　(e) MOVE.
　　　　　　　　　On Completion of Relief Coys. will move to the positions now
　　　　　　　　　occupied by 2nd Seaforth Highrs. and will take over accomoda
　　　　　　　　　tion of the Company of corresponding letter.
　　　　　　　(f) ADVANCE PARTIES.
　　　　　　　　　Advance Parties of 1 Officer, 1 N.C.O. & 1 Guide per Platoon
　　　　　　　　　and 1 per Coy. H.Q. and 1 Officer, 1 N.C.O. & 2 Guides from
　　　　　　　　　Battalion H.Q. will proceed to new area early in the after-
　　　　　　　　　noon to reconnoitre accomodation that they will be taking ov
　　　　　　　　　over and to take over Trench Stores.
　　　　　　　　　The Guides will be shown the route they are to take and
　　　　　　　　　after finding the way will rejoin their Coys. in order to
　　　　　　　　　guide them after relief.
　　　　　　　　　List of Stores taken over will be forwarded to Bn.H.Q. by
　　　　　　　　　12 noon, 25th inst.
　　　　　　　　　All parties will report to Bn.H.Q. of 2nd Seaforth Highrs.
　　　　　　　　　at P.13.d.6.4.
　　　　　　　(g) LEWIS GUNS, STORES, ETC.
　　　　　　　　　All Lewis Guns, Magazines, Water Tins of the Bn., (viz 15
　　　　　　　　　per Coy.) Stores, etc, will be dumped at old Battn.H.Q.
　　　　　　　　　Coys. will leave guards over their Coy. Lewis Guns.
　　　　　　　(h) COMPLETION OF MOVE.
　　　　　　　　　Completion of Move will be notified by wiring usual code on
　　　　　　　　　arrival in new area.
　　　　　　　(j) COOKERS.
　　　　　　　　　Cookers will be with Coys. in new positions.

　　　　　　　　　　　　　　　　　　　　　　　　　　　P. T. O.

TRANSPORT. 3. The Transport Officer will arrange Transport for :-
    (a) Stores mentioned in Para. (2) g. at 10 p.m.
    (b) To clear reserve L.G.Magazines.
    (c) One Limber for Bn.H.Q. at 8.30 p.m.

ACKNOWLEDGE.

                              (Sgd) D.G.R.BILHAM, Captain.
                A/Adjt. 2nd Bn. Duke of Wellington's Regt.

D I S T R I B U T I O N.

Copy No. 1	Bn.H.Q.	Copy No. 8	Q.M.
2 - 5	All Coys.	9	T.O.
6	10th Inf: Bde.	10 - 12	War Diary.
7	2nd Sea: Highrs.	13	File.

SECRET. 2nd Bn. Duke of Wellington's Regt.   Copy No. 10
(OPERATION) ORDER No. 118.
Ref: Maps Sheets 51.b. S.E.& N.E.   J
          1/40.000   In the Field, 20th September, 1915

INTENTION. 1. A. & D. Coys, D. of W's Regt. will relieve the 7th Middlesex
             Regt., less one Company in SUPPORT in the REDOUBT SECTOR.

INSTRUCTIONS. 2(a) RELIEF.
                 Companies will relieve as under in following order :-
                 D.Coy. Dukes will relieve D.Coy. 7th Middlesex.
                 A.Coy. Dukes will relieve A. B. & Bn.H.Q., 7th Middlesex.
             (b) Details of Relief have been arranged by Company Commanders
                 concerned.   leave
             (c) Relieving Coys will leave their present positions at :-
                 D. Company, 7 p.m.   A. Company, 7.30 p.m.
             (d) TRENCH STORES.
                 List of Trench Stores taken over together with Disposition
                 Maps will be forwarded to Bn.H.Q. by 9 a.m. tomorrow.
                 O.C. A.Coy. will arrange to take over papers and stores at
                 Bn.H.Q.
             (e) COMPLETION OF RELIEF.
                 Completion of Relief will be notified to Bn.H.Q. in the
                 usual manner.
             (f) RATIONS.
                 Rations will be carried up on the men.
                 Cookers of A. & D. Coys. will return to Transport Lines tonight
                 but cooking utensils will be sent forward for Companies.
             (g) Battalion H.Q. will remain in present Location.
             (h) WATER.
                 15 Tins of Water are being sent up with rations and will be
                 carried forward with Companies.

          3. ACKNOWLEDGE.

                                         (Sgd) D.C.R.BILHAM. Captain.
                                   A/Adjt. 2nd Duke of Wellington's Regt.

                         D I S T R I B U T I O N.

       Copy No. 1 Bn. H.Q.   Copy No. 6 7th Middlesex Regt.
            2 - 5 All Coys.   7 10th Inf: Bde.
                                              8 - 10 War Diary.
                                             11 File.

SECRET.　　　　　　　2nd Bn. Duke of Wellington's Regt　　　　Copy No. 10.
　　　　　　　　　　　　(OPERATION) ORDER No. 119.
Ref: Sheets Map 51.b.N.E. & S.E.　　K
　　1/20. 000.　　　　　　　　　　　　　In the Field, 30th September, 1918.

_____

INTENTION.　1. (a) The 2nd B. D.of W. Regt. will be relieved in the present
　　　　　　　　　　area by the 1st R. War: Regt. on the night of the 30th Sept/
　　　　　　　　　　1st Oct., 1918.
　　　　　　　(b) On completion of Relief the Bn. will move to the ORANGE HILL
　　　　　　　　　　Area, (V.5.2.3.4.).

INSTRUCTIONS. 2 (a) RELIEF.
　　　　　　　　　　A.Coy. Dukes will be relieved by C.Coy. 1st R.War: Regt.
　　　　　　　　　　D.Coy. ──────────── do ──────── D.Coy. ────────
　　　　　　　　　　B. & C.Coys. ──────── do ──────── B.Coy. ────────
　　　　　　　　　　O.C. B.Coy. will arrange to hand over both the accommodation
　　　　　　　　　　of both B. & C.Coys. to the incoming Company.
　　　　　　　　　　A.Coy., 1st R.War: Regt. will take over the accommodation
　　　　　　　　　　previously occupied by the 187th Infy. Bde. at F.10.b.3.3.
　　　　　　　(b) GUIDES.
　　　　　　　　　　(i)　Guides will be provided by D. & A.Coys. at rate of one
　　　　　　　　　　per Platoon and one per Coy.H.Q. So to at PROSPECT FARM at
　　　　　　　　　　6.30 p.m.
　　　　　　　　　　(ii)　B.Coy. will furnish two Guides to report at Bn.H.Q. at
　　　　　　　　　　5 p.m. for instructions.
　　　　　　　　　　(iii)　No other guides will be required.
　　　　　　　(c) ADVANCE PARTIES.
　　　　　　　　　　Advance Parties will report to Coys. during the afternoon to
　　　　　　　　　　take over Stores and Accommodation. These Advance Parties
　　　　　　　　　　of A. & B. Coys. of the 1st R.War: Regt. will be responsible
　　　　　　　　　　for showing their own Companies the accommodation.
　　　　　　　(d) TRENCH STORES.
　　　　　　　　　　All Trench Stores, Special Maps of the Sector, Defence Schemes
　　　　　　　　　　and all Petrol Tins will be handed over. Receipts in
　　　　　　　　　　duplicate will be sent to Battn.H.Q. by 9 a.m. 1/10/18.
　　　　　　　(e) MOVE.
　　　　　　　　　　B. & C.Coys., after handing over to representatives of 1st R.
　　　　　　　　　　War: Regt. relieving them, will not be required to wait, but
　　　　　　　　　　may move off by Platoons at 200 yards interval, starting with
　　　　　　　　　　B.Coy. at 7 p.m., C.Coy. 7.15 p.m.
　　　　　　　　　　Guides as already detailed will lead Coys to their new area.
　　　　　　　　　　D. & A.Coys. will move off as soon as relieved by incoming
　　　　　　　　　　unit.
　　　　　　　(f) COMPLETION OF RELIEF.
　　　　　　　　　　Completion of Relief will be notified to Bn.H.Q. in usual
　　　　　　　　　　manner.
　　　　　　　　　　B. & C.Coys. will similarly notify Bn.H.Q. when they leave.
　　　　　　　(g) ARRIVAL.
　　　　　　　　　　Coys. will report arrival in new area to new Bn.H.Q. at
　　　　　　　　　　N.5.c.3.3.
　　　　　　　(h) LEWIS GUNS.
　　　　　　　　　　All Lewis Guns will be stacked at present Bn.H.Q. by Coys. &
　　　　　　　　　　each Coy. will arrange to leave one Gunner with its Coy. Guns.
　　　　　　　(j) PACKS.
　　　　　　　　　　Q.M. will arrange to have Packs and Officers Valises dumped at
　　　　　　　　　　Coy.H.Q. in new area.

TRANSPORT. 3. Transport Officer will arrange.:-
　　　　　　　(a) To collect Cookers of B.& C.Coys. and Boilers of A.& D.Coys.
　　　　　　　　　　at 5 p.m.
　　　　　　　(b) To collect reserve L.G.Magazines, Canteen Stores & Bn.H.Q.
　　　　　　　　　　Stores at 4.30 p.m.
　　　　　　　(c) Collect all Lewis Guns at present Bn.H.Q. at 10.30 p.m.
　　　　　　　(d) Supply Q.M. with any Transport he may require.
　　　　　　　(e) Mess Cart to be at Bn.H.Q. at 6.30 p.m.

　　　　　　　　　　　　　　　　　　　　　　　　　　　Captain & Adjutant,
ACKNOWLEDGE.　　　　　　　　　　　　　　　　　2nd Bn. The Duke of Wellington's Regt.

DISTRIBUTION.

```
Copy No.  1  Bn.H.Q.                Copy No.  8   M.
          2 - 5  All Coys.                    9   T.O.
          6  10th Inf: Bde.                  10 - 12  War Diary.
          7  1st R.War.Regt.                 13  File.
```

WAR DIARY
or
INTELLIGENCE SUMMARY.
(Erase heading not required.)

Army Form C. 2118.

Place	Date	Hour	Summary of Events and Information	Remarks and references to Appendices
OCTOBER 1918.				
ORANGE HILL	1.		The Battn in Divl Reserve round ORANGE HILL. Battn in cleaning up & making Trench shelters. AWARDS - Bar to M.M. 1; M.M. 7.	LENS. 11.
	2.		The Battn bathed at ST. CATHERINE (ARRAS) - Trench shelters to Continental system of time came into force -	completed
	3.		The Battn in training. Inspection of Platoons. Close Order Drill. Attack practice in open warfare dealing with M.G. nest - Draft of 10. O.R. Lt SHEPHERD to C.C.S. CAPT COKE acting Q.M. Lecture by Educational	
	4.		The Battn in training as on previous day. At 1600. Officer to O.R.	X
	5.		The Battn marched to WAN QUENTIN. Paraded at 1200 - arrived at 1700. The Battn was met by the Brass Band of the 4 Battn who played them into the 2nd Battn Band took over - "Details" changed ARRAS.	
WANQUENTIN	6.		The Battn in training - Inspection of Platoons - Close Order Drill - P.T.~B.F. Bayonet attack in open - as a Platoon & as a Company -	M.S. 51. 2. 54.
	7.		The Battn in training.	51
	8.		The Battn in training - "Detail" came to WANQUENTIN.	B. Rawlent

Army Form C. 2118.

WAR DIARY
or
INTELLIGENCE SUMMARY.
(Erase heading not required.)

Instructions regarding War Diaries and Intelligence Summaries are contained in F. S. Regs., Part II. and the Staff Manual respectively. Title pages will be prepared in manuscript.

Place	Date	Hour	Summary of Events and Information	Remarks and references to Appendices
OCTOBER 1918.	9.		The Battn in training.	
WANQUENTIN	10.		The Battn in training. Night operations cancelled whilst in progress at 1800 - owing to warning order for Brigade to move in morning of 11th	
			The Battn moved by Bus 646 outside of CAMBRAI from there marched to St. OLLE. Embused at 1000 - Detrused at 1630.	A.
CAMBRAI.	11.			
St. OLLE	12.		The Battn rested in Billets at St. OLLE.	
	13.		The Battn marched to NAVES. Paraded 0800 - arrived 1100 -	B.
NAVES	14.		Rested in Billets. Village shelled during the night - No casualties -	
	15.		The Battn in Training. Company & Platoon in attack - Two B Coy. sent on locating Machine gun nests. Lt. B.B. MOXON & 2/Lt. F. GLEADOWN M.M. joined -	
	16.		Very wet day. Impossible to train in the open - A & B Coys. bathed in Bath Horse special up by the Battn -	
	17.		The Battn in training in the open - Coy & Coy v HQ. batted.	
SAULTZOIR	18.		The Battn relieved the 1/6th Battn Sea of Wellington on the SAULTZOIR sector - Relief Complete by 2230. B. H. Q. in VILLIERS EN CAUCHIES	C. N.S. 51 a. 1.40.10d

Army Form C. 2118.

WAR DIARY
or
INTELLIGENCE SUMMARY.
(Erase heading not required.)

Sheet. 51A NE & SE.

D.

Place	Date	Hour	Summary of Events and Information	Remarks and references to Appendices
OCTOBER 1918. SAULZOIR	18.		Covering period from 18th to 25th.	

On the night 18th October, this Battalion moved into LES VILLERS Area, taking over line from 1/6th Duke of Wellington's Regt. This line consisted of Outposts in SAULZOIR, guarding the approaches to the river all the Bridges over which were blown up. The remainder of the Battalion were on the Main front of Resistance on the hill in the rear.

The work of the Division was to press forward by stages on the line:

(I) MASPRES - SAULZOIR, (II) MONCHAUX - VERCHAIN - SOMMAING, (III) South of MAING - QUERENAING - ARTRES.

The first phase was given to 10th Brigade on Right, 11th Brigade on Left.

Second phase, 10th Brigade on Right, 12th Brigade on Left.

Third phase, 11th Brigade on Left, 12th Brigade on Right.

The two attacks affecting this Battalion covered a period from Oct 19 - 25th and were operations in the following manner.

On the night of the 19th and morning of the 20th, the battalion took SAULZOIR in advance of schedule time by crossing the river and

WAR DIARY or INTELLIGENCE SUMMARY

Army Form C. 2118.

Place	Date	Hour	Summary of Events and Information	Remarks and references to Appendices
	Period from 20th to 24th		peacefully penetrating the villages with slight fighting for the railway in P.27.	D.
SAULTZOIR.			Then at 3·10 hours at 04·00 hours, 20th October, the 2nd SEAFORTH HIGHLANDERS passed over, capturing the high ground in the neighbourhood of P.23, this Battalion assisting and taking up a position in SUPPORT; casualties were slight. The Brigade remained in these positions for four days. Further orders for his attack were issued on the 23rd October, for phase two which included a possible objective of QUERENAING.	E.
VERCHAIN.			At 04·00 hours, supported by a shrapnel barrage of one Brigade of Field Artillery, the 10th Brigade attacked, this Battalion on the Right and the 1st R.WARWICK.Regt. on the Left, Captured VERCHAIN the line of the river ECAILLON, the high ground in P.12.a.& c, and MURCopse in one operation. Disposition of Companies was :— LEFT - A Company, } Field - J.A.LENNON.M.C. RIGHT - D Company, } Capt. J.COOKE, M.C. supported by LEFT - C. Company, } Capt. F.H. HULL.M.C. RIGHT - B. Company, } Lieut. H. LIVSEY, M.C.	F.

Army Form C. 2118.

WAR DIARY
or
INTELLIGENCE SUMMARY.
(Erase heading not required.)

Place	Date	Hour	Summary of Events and Information	Remarks and references to Appendices
OCTOBER 1918.	19.		Other items which occurred during period 19th & 25th.	
	19. 20.		Casualties:- 2/Lt W. McHUGH. wounded -	
			Casualties:- Lt. G. JACKSON wounded - 6 - OR Killed - 30 - OR Wounded.	
	21st		Casualties:- 6 - OR wounded -	
	22nd		Awards. Published in Divisional Routine Orders - (For Gallantry at St. SERVINS FARM.)	
			D.S.O.
			Lt. Col. F. PAWLETT.
			Bar to M.C.
			Capt. M.C. HOOLE. M.C.
			M.C.
			Capt. J. COOKE
			Lt. H. LIVESAY.
			D.C.M.
			Sergt. W. REED
			Corpl. J.R. KLIBER
	24.		Casualties:- Capt. Hill M.C.
			Lt. LIVESAY. M.C.
			Lt. SHEARNE. M.C. } wounded -
			2/Lt KAY.
			2/Lt KILBURN.
			2/Lt WOLFENDEN - Killed -
			39 - O.R. Killed
			127 - O.R. Wounded.

Army Form C. 2118.

WAR DIARY
or
INTELLIGENCE SUMMARY.
(Erase heading not required.)

Place	Date	Hour	Summary of Events and Information	Remarks and references to Appendices
VERCHAIN MUR COPSE	24th		The enemy was in force, first line of railway, second, line of river, third, high ground R.12.b., fourth, Mur Copse high ground, fifth, Sunken Road on PIMPLE Q.1.0.5.5., and Sunken Road East of that point where they had dug a system of trenches and put up wire entanglements.	P.12.b. Q.1.c.55
			The country was extraordinarily difficult and the enemy were in force with numerous machine guns which were overcome in a marvellously efficient manner by the action of the Battalion and leadership of officers and N.C.O's.	
			At daybreak of the 24th found the Battalion hardly on its objectives of the PIMPLE, SUNKEN ROAD and trenches behind, the fight being in the air on account of the failure of the 61st Division to gain its objectives. In getting thus far we had to stand heavy casualties, and Division, whilst not meaning, intimated that it was vital to future operations to be in position of the PIMPLE and surrounding country including trenches behind. This led to a hastily organised attack in the afternoon at 16.45 hours under a shrapnel barrage.	
			This attack was entirely successful under the command of Right=Capt. J. COOKE, M.C., Left=J.A.LENNON,M.C. with the Battalion re-organized into 6=O Companies. They succeeded in capturing all the high ground and the	

Place	Date	Hour	Summary of Events and Information	Remarks and references to Appendices
VERCHAIN	24th		above mentioned) Trenches system, with many prisoners & machine guns, the casualties not being more than 5, although the losses in the later phase of capturing village, ridge, and HERMAN STELLUNG and the new one will amount. This ended the operations as far as the Battalion was concerned and can be looked upon as one of the most successful operations It has ever taken part in, for in addition to inflicting large casualties on the enemy, capturing over 350 prisoners, 31 machine guns and 2 minenwerfer, it was operated over the most difficult country and gained objectives of immense value to future operations, compelling the enemy to withdraw a distance of over 200 yards on the right of the 24th. This night the Brigade, less this Battalion, was relieved, the played on until the next phase of the operation had started.	
QUERENAING	25th		Patrols sent forward in the early morning discovered that the enemy had withdrawn and the Battalion established itself on its final objective in Q.2.a., the 11th Brigade passing over it and continuing the operation, this Battalion returning to its Billets in VERCHAIN in the afternoon.	Q.2.a.

Army Form C. 2118.

WAR DIARY
or
INTELLIGENCE SUMMARY.
(Erase heading not required.)

Place	Date	Hour	Summary of Events and Information	Remarks and references to Appendices
OCTOBER 1918	26.		The day was spent in complete rest - The whole Battⁿ bathed	
	27.		Reorganisation - Cleaning of Billets & equipment. Checking of battle equipment - All Coys detailed & salvage parties to collect Machine Guns etc captured by the Battⁿ during the operations -	
	28.		Light training carried out by Companies - Clothing refitted - Salvage work as on previous day -	
VERCHAIN	29.		The Battⁿ in training -	
	30.		The Battⁿ in training. Companies in the attack -
Extract from XVII Corps Summary No 62 -
"Captured documents show the great importance the enemy attached to holding the HERMANN STELLUNG which ran just East of the ECAILLON River - (vide Army Summary No 1384 of October 29th)"
Note. The HERMANN STELLUNG referred to above is the line captured by this Battⁿ on the 24th.	
	31.		The Battⁿ in Training.	

J. Paulson
Lieut. Colonel
2nd Battⁿ. the Duke of Wellington's Reg^t.

SECRET.   2nd Bn. Duke of Wellington's Regt.   Copy No. 9
                               WARNING ORDER No. 1.
Ref: Map LENS 11.   In the Field, 4th October, 1918.
_____

1.   The Battalion will move tomorrow to the HABARCQ – WANQUETIN Area.

2.   Companies will be prepared to parade at 1200 to march off.

3.   Dinners will be at 1100.

4.   Lewis Guns will be loaded on L.G.Limbers by 1030 ready for collection by
      the Transport Officer. Lewis Gun Limbers are already in possession of
      the Companies.

5.   All Packs will be stacked by Companies near D. Coy. H.Q. on the ARRAS –
      CAMBRAI Road by 0900.
      Officers Valises, Company Stores, etc, will be stacked at the same place
      by 0900.

6.   Instructions re Billeting will be sent out later but C.Q.M.Sergts. will
      be prepared to leave about 0900.
      Parties to take over the Camp will report in the morning, and all
      Trench Shelters will be left standing and receipts obtained for these by
      Companies and forwarded to Bn.H.Q. as soon as possible.

7.   The morning will be spent in thoroughly cleaning up the area and having
      a Foot Inspection. All men must change their socks.

8.   Dress for march will be Full Battle Order.

9.   Officers and men for new Details will parade at D. Company H.Q. under
      2Lieut. W.J.E.WHITELEY at 0900. and will move independently to Details
      Camp. Dress, Full Marching Order.
      Valises of Officers proceeding to Details will be sent by Bn.Transport
      from new area.
      This Transport will bring back the Valises of Officers who join the
      Battalion tomorrow from Details.

10.   Rations for men proceeding to Details will be issued at their new Camp.

11.   Transport will move with the Battalion and will meet the Battalion at
      P.36.b.90.15.
      Time will be notified later.

                                                                Captain.
                                        A/Adjt. 2nd Duke of Wellington's Regt.

                              D I S T R I B U T I O N.

           Copy No. 1 Bn.H.Q.   Copy No. 7 T.O. & QM
                   2 – 5 All Coys.   8 Details
                   6 A/R.S.M.   9-11 War Diary.
                                                    12 File.

SECRET. 　　　　　2nd Bn. Duke of Wellington's Regt.　　　　Copy No. 9.
　　　　　　　　　　(OPERATION) ORDER No. 132.
Ref: Map Sheet 51.b. & LENS 11.　　　In the Field, 4th October, 1918.

INTENTION.　1. The Battalion will move by Route March to WANQUETIN on the
　　　　　　　　5th inst.

INSTRUCTIONS. 2.(a) DRESS.
　　　　　　　　　　Battle Order, less Greatcoats & Picks & Shovels.
　　　　　　　(b) ORDER OF MARCH.
　　　　　　　　　　Bn.H.Q., D. C. B. A. Companies.
　　　　　　　(c) STARTING POINT.
　　　　　　　　　　D.Coy.H.Q. All Companies to be clear of the ARRAS-CAMBRAI
　　　　　　　　　　Road.
　　　　　　　(d) TIME. 12 Noon.
　　　　　　　(e) ROUTE.
　　　　　　　　　　TILLOY - ARRAS - DAINVILLE - WARLUS - WANQUETIN.
　　　　　　　(f) INTERVAL.
　　　　　　　　　　A distance of 100 yards will be maintained between Coys. and
　　　　　　　　　　100 yards between Transport and Rear Company.
　　　　　　　(g) BILLETING PARTY.
　　　　　　　　　　All C.Q.M.Sergts. and 1 R.S.O. for Bn.H.Q. will precede the
　　　　　　　　　　Battalion and report to Capt. E.C.COKE at the Town Major's
　　　　　　　　　　Office, WANQUETIN, at 1100.
※　　　　　　(h) STORES.
　　　　　　　　　　All Stores and Lewis Guns will be stacked as detailed in
　　　　　　　　　　Warning Order No. 1, with the exception that Tools carried
　　　　　　　　　　by the men will be stacked at the same place by 0930 for
　　　　　　　　　　conveyance by lorry.
　　　　　　　(j) DETAILS.
　　　　　　　　　　Men from Details will join Battalion in new area.
　　　　　　　　　　Men for Details will proceed as already ordered.
　　　　　　　(k) TRENCH SHELTERS.
　　　　　　　　　　All Trench Shelters, Tents, Tables, etc., in the present
　　　　　　　　　　Camp will be handed in to the Town Major's ORANGE HILL,
　　　　　　　　　　(H.35.a.2.5.) by 1030.
　　　　　　　　　　Companies will be responsible for handing in everything
　　　　　　　　　　taken over in present Area, and receipts will be forwarded
　　　　　　　　　　to Orderly Room by 1100.

TRANSPORT.　3. (a) Transport are not allowed to move WESTWARD along ARRAS -
　　　　　　　　　　CAMBRAI Road, East of H.31.a.9.1.
　　　　　　　(b) The Transport Officer will therefore arrange for Transport
　　　　　　　　　　to proceed via WANCOURT & TILLOY and join the Battalion
　　　　　　　　　　at Road Junction G.36.b.15.90. to be at this point by 1300.
　　　　　　　(c) He will arrange collection of :-
　　　　　　　　　　(a) Cookers, Water Carts, L.G.Limbers, etc.
　　　　　　　　　　(b) Officers Chargers to report at Bn.H.Q.Starting Point
　　　　　　　　　　　　at 1145.
　　　　　　　　　　(c) Mess Cart to report at Bn.H.Q. at 1145.

REPORTS.　　4.　Head of the Column.

　　　　　　　　ACKNOWLEDGE.

　　　　　　　　　　　　　　　　　　　　　　　　　　　D. McLellan
　　　　　　　　　　　　　　　　　　　　　　　　　　　　Captain.
　　　　　　　　　　　　　　　　　　　A/Adjt. 2nd Duke of Wellington's Regt.

※ INSTRUCTIONS. 2 (g) Capt. E.C.COKE will report to Lieut. T.PATERSON (10th Inf:
　　　　　　　　Bde.) at the same hour at the Town Major's Office for
　　　　　　　　Instructions re Billets.

DISTRIBUTION.

Copy No. 1 Bn.H.Q.   Copy No. 8 Details.
         2 - 5 All Coys.   9 - 11 War Diary.
         6 10th Inf: Bde.   12 File.
         7 T.O. & Q.M.

A.

Copy. No. 11

SECRET.

2nd Bn. Duke of Wellington's Regiment.
OPERATION ORDERS No. 121.

Ref. Map VALENCIENNES. 12.   In the Field. 11th October 1918.

INTENTION.	1. The Battalion will move by Bus to-day to FONTAINE and will occupy area formed by triangle of ARRAS-CAMBRAI and CAMBRAI-BAPAUME ROADS.
INSTRUCTIONS.	2. (a) <u>DRESS</u>. Full Battle Order and one Blanket. (b) <u>ORDER OF MARCH</u>. B.H.Q., A.B.C.&D. Companies. (c) <u>STARTING POINT</u>. Entrance to Camp near Orderly Room. All Companies to be on the road in Column of route facing North. (d) <u>TIME</u>. 1010. (e) <u>STORES</u>. (i) Lewis Guns will be carried on the men. (ii) All Valises, Company Mess Stores, Packs, etc. will be stacked at Q.M.stores at 0900. (f) <u>RATIONS</u>. Will be carried as detailed in Warning Order No. 1. (g) <u>DETAILS</u>. Orders re time of starting and stores of Details will be issued later. (h) <u>BILLETS</u>. All Billets Etc. <u>MUST</u> be left Scrupulously Clean.
TRANSPORT.	3. Transport and Cookers will move under Brigade arrangements at 1100.

ACKNOWLEDGE.

signature
Captain,
A/Adjt. 2nd Bn. Duke of Wellington's Regiment.

DISTRIBUTION.

Copy No. 1.	B.H.Q.	Copy No. 7.	P.O. and Q.M.
" " 2-5.	Companies.	" " 8.	Details.
" " 6.	10th Infy. Bde.	" " 9-11.	War Diary.
		" " 12.	File.

2nd Bn. Duke of Wellington's Regiment.

WARNING ORDER No. 1. Ry O.O. 121   10th October 1918.

(1) Battalion will move to aproximately Cambria Area by Bus to-morrow. Dress will be Battle Order plus one Blanket. Blanket will be rolled in Waterproof Sheet and fastened to belt. Mess Tins will be fastened to flap of Haversack.

(2) Transport will not rejoin Bn. probably for 24 hours. Arrangements will be made for Fresh Meat to be cooked to-night & carried on the men to-morrow.

(3) Companies will be prepared for an early move.

(4) All packs will be stacked at Q.M.Stores by 0830.

(5) Tailors, Shoemakers, and Surplus Pioneers will proceed with Details, and their Equipment will be left with Packs.

(6) Quarter-Master will only move with what he actually requires in the line, remainder of stores will be left with Packs at present Q.M.Stores. Details will furnish a guard consisting of one N.C.O. and three men for above stores.

(7) Details will move under separate orders by Route March to Arras. Dress, Full Marching Order.

(8) Rations for 12th will be delivered in new area.
Rations for details for 12th will be delivered in Arras.

(9) Lewis Guns and Magazines will be carried by the men.

(10) One cooker will proceed with Details and rejoin Bn. later, this cooker will have Camp Kettles for the use of Details whilst in Arras.

(11) Hat Covers and Blankets will be collected in new Area.

Capt.

A/Adjt.   2nd Bn. Duke of Wellington's Regiment.

B.

Copy. No. 10

SECRET.   2nd. Bn. Duke of Wellington's Regiment.

OPERATION ORDERS NO. 122.

Ref. Map VALENCIENNES. 1:   In the Field, 12th October 1918

INTENTION.   1. The Battalion will move by March Route to NAVES.

INSTRUCTIONS.   2. (a) Dress. Battle Order.
                   (b) Starting Point. will be road junction A.1.d.3.5. (A CoysH.Q.)
                   (c) Order of March. B.H.Q., A.C.D.B.Companies, and Transport.
                   (d) Time. 0800.
                   (e) Starting Point. All Companies to be on road running N.&.S.
                       through A.1.d. facing N.
                   (f) Transport. Will accompany the Battalion.
                   (g) Billeting Party. All C.Q.M.S. and one N.C.O. from Bn. H.Q.
                       representative for Q.M. will report to Lieut. Jackson at
                       Orderly Room at 0730.
                   (h) Water Bottles. Must be filled.

                                                          Captain,

                                   A/Adjt. 2nd Bn. Duke of Wellington's Regiment.

          DISTRIBUTION.

Copy No 1.   B.H.Q.   Copy No. 7.   T.O. and Q.M.
  "   " 2-5.   Companies.   "   " 8-10   War Diary.
  "   " 6.   10th Infy. Bde.   "   " 11   File.

SECRET.   Copy.No. 10

                    2nd Bn. Duke of Wellington's Regiment.
                    OPERATION ORDERS No. 123.
Ref. Map Sheet 51a.1/40.000.   In the Field, 17th October 1918.

INTENTION.   1. The 2nd Bn. Duke of Wellington's Regiment will relieve the
                   6th Bn. Duke of Wellington's Regiment, 147th Infantry Brigade,
                   in the Right Sub Section of the Right Brigade Front, 49th Divn.
                   on the night of the 18th/19th October 1918.

INSTRUCTIONS.   2. (a) RELIEFS.
                   C.Coy. 2nd D.of W's. relieves A.Coy 6th D.of W's as Right
                                                                    Front Company.
                   B.Coy.   -do-   -do-   D.Coy   -do-   as Left
                                                                    Front Company.
                   A.Coy.   -do-   -do-   C.Coy.   -do-   in Support
                   D.Coy   -do-   -do-   B.Coy   -do-   -do-
                   (b) Guides.
                   1.Guide per Platoon, and 1 Guide per Company H.Q. and 2 for
                   Bn.H.Q., will be at Road Junction U.10.b.5.6. at 1800 hours.
                   (c) ORDER OF MARCH.
                   C.B.A.D.Coys and Bn.H.Q., C.Coy will leave Billets at 1700.
                   Hours. Distance between Companies, 100 yards as far as IWUY-
                   RIEUX Road. East of this point, by platoons at 100 yards
                   distance.
                   (d) ROUTE.
                   Companies will follow lines of Telegraph Poles starting in
                   T.23.b. and running through T.18.c.&.B. across Sunken Road
                   at U.9.a.2:5. and thence follow along Railway to U.9.a.9.5.
                   -U.10.b.5.6.
                   (e) DRESS.
                   Fighting Order, Greatcoats.rolled Bandolier Fashion.
                   (f) TRENCH STORES.
                   All Trench Stores, Special Maps, Defence Scheme will be taken
                   over and receipts forwarded to Bn.H.Q. by 1900 Hours 19th
                   inst.,
                   In addition, one Anti-Tank Rifle and Ammunition will be
                   taken over by Support Companies.
                   B.Coy will also take over Bridging Material as under:-
                   P.26.b.2.1. 3.Long Duck-Board Bridges with one Crate.
                   P.26.d.5.8. 3.. "   "   "   "   No Crate.
                   P.26.d.1.3. 3.   "   "   "   "   "   "
                   P.26.d.9.1. 3.   "   "   "   "   "   "
                   (g) COMPLETION OF RELIEF. will be notified to B.H.Q., by
                   the usual Code.
                   (h) DISPOSITIONS.
                   Maps showing Dispositions will be forwarded to B.H.Q., by
                   0700 Hours 19th inst.
                   (i) ADVANCE PARTY.
                   1.Officer, 1.N.C.O. and 2Runners per Company, 2/Lieut.
                   H.D.Bidlake, 2 Runners, 1.Signaller, and 1.Stretcher-Bearer
                   for B.H.Q.will proceed to take over Trench Stores etc.
                   during the afternoon. These Officers will return and meet
                   their Companies at the rendezvous.for Guides at 1800 Hours.
                   All parties will report at the Bn.H.Q.of the 6th Bn.
                   Duke of Wellington's Regiment.
                   (j) LEWIS GUNS.
                   Lewis Guns will be carried by Transport to rendezvous for
                   Guides. Each Company to Detail one Gunner to look after
                   the Guns.

        (k) RATIONS.
Rations for the 19th Inst. will be carried on the men, 15 Tins of water per Company and Bn.H.Q. will be dumped at present Ration Dump. Companies will arrange to fetch these as soon as possible.

        (l) BILLETS.
Billeting Parties of the 6th Bn. Duke of Wellington's Regt. will report to Companies to-morrow morning to take over present billets.
All billets must be left perfectly clean and a Certificate to this effect obtained.

        (m) STORES.
(i) All Blankets will be stacked at Q.M. Stores by 1100 Hours.
(ii) All remaining Stores by 1430.
(iii) Lewis Gun Limbers will collect Guns at 1600.

TRANSPORT.   3. Transport and Q.M. Stores will move under separate orders during the afternoon to RIEUX. and will occupy present Transport Lines of 6th Bn. Duke of Wellington's Regt.
Transport Officer will arrange for:-
(1) Collection of Lewis Guns.
(2) Carrying of Rations and Water.
(3) Removal of Cookers, Maltese Carts, etc, at 1700 Hours.
(4) One Limber to report to Bn.H.Q. at 1645.
(5) One Limber to carry Reserve Ammunition and Reserve Lewis Gun Magazines to Bn.H.Q.
(6) To provide Transport required by Q.M.

BATTALION H.Q.   4. Battalion H.Q. will be at U.6.c.4.8.

AID POST.   5. Aid post will be at U.6.c.2.8.

       ACKNOWLEDGE.

                                                     Captain.
                A/Adjt. 2nd Bn. Duke of Wellington's Regiment.

            D I S T R I B U T I O N.

Copy No. 1.	Bn.H.Q.	Copy No. 8.	6th D. of W's. Regt.
" " 2-5.	Companies.	" " 9.	10th Infantry Brigade.
" " 6.	Q.M.	" " 10-11.	War Diary.
" " 7.	T.O.	" " 12.	File.

SECRET.

Copy No. 10.

2nd. Bn. Duke of Wellington's Regiment.

AMENDMENT TO O.O.123., Para 2. a.&.b.

---

(1) B.Coy 2nd Duke of Wellington's Regiment.
No. 5.&.6.Platoons will relieve the whole of A.Coy 6th Duke of Wellington's Regiment.
No. 7.&.8.Platoons will relieve the whole of D.Coy 6th Duke of Wellington's Regiment.
C.H.Q.at present C.H.Q.of A.Coy 6th D.of.W's. Regt.

(2) C.Coy 2nd Bn. Duke of Wellington's Regiment.
will not relieve any Coy. 6th D.of.W's. but will be dug in approximately the vicinity of Bn.H.Q. outside the Village.

(3) O.C.C.Coy. will send one Officer and guide to reconnoitre this position this afternoon, and will make arrangements for his own guides.

Captain,
A/Adjt. 2nd.Bn. Duke of Wellington's Regiment.

SECRET.   Copy No. W.D.

2nd. Bn. Duke of Wellington's Regiment.
OPERATION ORDERS No. 184.

Ref. Map Sheet 51 A.S.E.   In the Field. 19th October 1918.

INSTRUCTIONS. (1) At ZERO HOUR +50 the Battalion will be disposed on first object (BLUE LINE) as follows:-
   B.Coy. on RIGHT. P.34.a.0.7. through COPSE at P.27.d.6.8.inclusive
   From there ROAD.(Inclusive)
   C.Coy to POINT in P.27.a.7.9. thence
   D.Coy. to QUARRY in P.21.c. inclusive with flank thrown back
   across RAILWAY at P.20.d.6.4.- MILL P.20.d.3.0.
   A.Coy. will be in RAILWAY cutting P.27.a. and along line of
   RAILWAY to P.27.b.0.0.

(2) As soon as barrage lifts at ZERO + 70 D.Coy will form a defensive flank from Brigade Boundary at the MILL.P.20.c.3.5.-ROAD. P.20 b.25.25. and B.Coy will advance behind the 2nd. SEAFORTH HIGHLANDS to SUNKEN ROAD. P.27.b.8.2.-P.28.d.4.6.and will place it in a -R state of DEFENCE. Liaison Post Strength not less than 1 SECTION with 19th Division at P.28.d.7.8. by B.Coy.

(3) Protective Barrage on a line approximately 250 yards in front of First Objective will commence at ZERO +50 and will lift at ZERO + 70 advancing at rate of 100 yards every four minutes.

(4) D.Coy. will wear White Arm Bands above the elbow on the LEFT ARM and the right Bn. of the 11th Brigade on the left will wear WHITE BANDS on the RIGHT arm.

(5) All reports by runner will be sent to B.Coy old H.Q. in P.32.c. Each Coy. will send one Runner to this point at 0145.

(6) ZERO will be 0200.

(7) Bn. H.Q.will not move at present.

                                                        Captain.

            A/Adjt. 2nd Bn. Duke of Wellington's Regiment.

ACKNOWLEDGE.

2nd Bn. Duke of Wellington's Regiment.
OPERATION ORDER No. ...

Ref. Map Sheet 1/20,000, 51.A.S.E.   In the Field October 21st 1918.

INSTRUCTIONS.

(a) B. and D.Coys will be distributed over the Brigade front on the Battalion's present (BLUE) Line from P.21.b.25.25.- P.21.d. 0.00.-Road Junction P.27.b.65.15. Along Sunken Road to P.28.1.4.7.

(b) Dividing line between B.(Right) and C (Left) P.21.d.00.00.

(c) A. and B. Coy. will be in support in rear of Railway Line.

(d) C.Coy. will take over post in Mill at P.20.c.3.5.

(e) Relief to take place immediatley and to be arranged between the Company Commanders Concerned.

(f) Battn H.Q.will be notified when relief is complete and accompanied by sketch of new dispositions.

(g) Touch will be established with right and left, but defensive flank at present maintained by D.Coy. will not be re-established by C.Coy.

(h) A. and D.Coys when relieved will retire to position located in accordance with G.706.

                (Signed) D.G.R.Bilham. Captain,
A/Adjt. 2nd Bn. Duke of Wellington's Regiment.

Issued at 1225 Hours.

Copies to:-   All Coys.
               B.H.Q.
               War Diary.

SECRET.   F   Copy No. W.D.

2nd Bn. Duke of Wellington's Regiment.
OPERATION ORDERS No. 126.

Ref Map. 51a S.E. 51a N.E.   In the Field, 23rd October 1918.

INTENTION.   1. The 2nd Bn. Duke of Wellington's Regiment will attack and capture the high ground W. and S.W. of QUERENAING on the 24th October 1918.

INSTRUCTIONS. 2. (a) The attack will be carried out in accordance with 2nd. Bn. Duke of Wellington's Regiment's "Instruction for offen No.3" of to-day's date.

(b) INTER-COMPANY BOUNDARY.
P.17.d.50.70.- across Railway at P.12.d.10.05. (Station Inclusive to C.Coy.)- Road Junction P.12.c.70.8.8.- thence along Road (Inclusive to Right Company to P.12.b.25.40.)- N.W.corner of MUR COPSE (Q.1.c.3.9.)-Q.2.a.5.5.- Junction of Hedges at Q.2.b.95.95.

(c) FORMING UP LINE.
A tape will be laid to Forming up Line as detailed in instructions.

(d) DISPOSITION OF BATTALION.
On the Forming Up Line the Battn. will be disposed as follows:- (i) Front Wave, C.Coy Left B.Coy Right, each on 2 Platoon Frontage, (ii) Supports, A.Coy Left, D.Coy Right. Artillery Formation, Distance between Coys. 200 Yds

(e) MOPPERS UP.
The 2nd SEAFORTH HIGHLANDERS will attach one platoon to C.Coy. and one Platoon to B.Coy., for Mopping Up the HERMANN STELLING LINE. These will report to representative of the above Companies at P.17.d.20. at 0200 Hours and be guided to their positions, in rear of the Companies.

(f) METHOD OF ADVANCE.
B.and C.Coys. will advance in open order behind Barrage and capture the first Objective or Blue Line, with A.and D.Coys. in support. At Zero plus 100 the advance will be continued by A.and D.Coys. passing through C.and B.who will reorganise as follows in Support of A.and D.
A.&.D. will capture the Yellow and Green Line with the two leading Platoons of each Company, these four platoons consolidating on this line. At Zero plus 180 the four rear platoons of A.and D.Coys. will pass over their consolidated front platoons, and capture the Red Line, supported by C.and B.Companies.

(g) ACTION WHEN FINAL OBJECTIVE IS GAINED.
O.C. "D" Coy. will take command of two platoons A.Coy, and two platoons D.Coy. which attack the final objective and consolidate thereon. He will send forward patrols to ascertain if the village of QUERENAING is occupied by the enemy, but patrols will not proceed further than Road running from Road Junction K.26.d.8.0. to the junction of final objective and Right Brigade Boundary passing through K.32.b.9.0.

(h) BRIDGES.
Four bridges are provided in the event of the River Ecall being in flood. These will be carried by C.& B. Coys.(2 each) 8 men per bridge being detailed. Special Bridging parties detailed by these two Coys. will fetch Bridges from P.17.c.4.4. when the Battn is forming up.

(i) All officers taking part in the attack will know the Compass Bearing of their objective.
(j) Contact Patrols will call for flares at Zero plus 3½, 5½ and 7½ hours, flares and flappers will be used.
(k) COUNTER ATTACK MACHINES
will be in the air from daylight to dark and fire Red Flares in any direction the enemy may be massing.
(l) ARTILLERY.
First two rounds from every gun fired in a protective Barrage will be smoke which will indicate when the objectives have been gained.
(m) COMMUNICATION.
On the capture of the First objective visual to Bn. H.Q. will be established on Cross Roads I.12.a.4.9. which will afterwards become Report Centre. All runners proceeding to H.Q. after the Battn is past the first objective will call at Report Centre for Instructions.
(n) AMMUNITION at Bn. H.Q.
(o) BATTALION H.Q. will be First Place, P.17.d.2.2. Second place Report Centre, P.12.a.4.9. when first Objective taken.
(p) REGIMENTAL AID POST. P.22.c.8.4. and will move into VERCHAIN
(q) Battn. will be relieved in the line Night of the 24th/25th October 1918. and preparations for Guides to be sent to Bn H.Q. will be made.
(r) ZERO HOUR. will be at 0400.

                     (Signed) D.G.R.Bilham. Capt.
A/Adjt 2nd Bn. Duke of Wellington's Regiment.

ACKNOWLEDGE.

Identification Trace for use with Artillery Maps.

Monchaux

34   35   36   32

J K
P Q

3   4   5   6   2

11TH BDE 9   10   11   12

10TH BDE

51ª N.E
51ª S.E.

Tracing taken from Sheets 51ª N.E. & S.E.

of the 1:20,000 map of FRANCE.

G.S.G.S. 3095.

Date 25/10/16

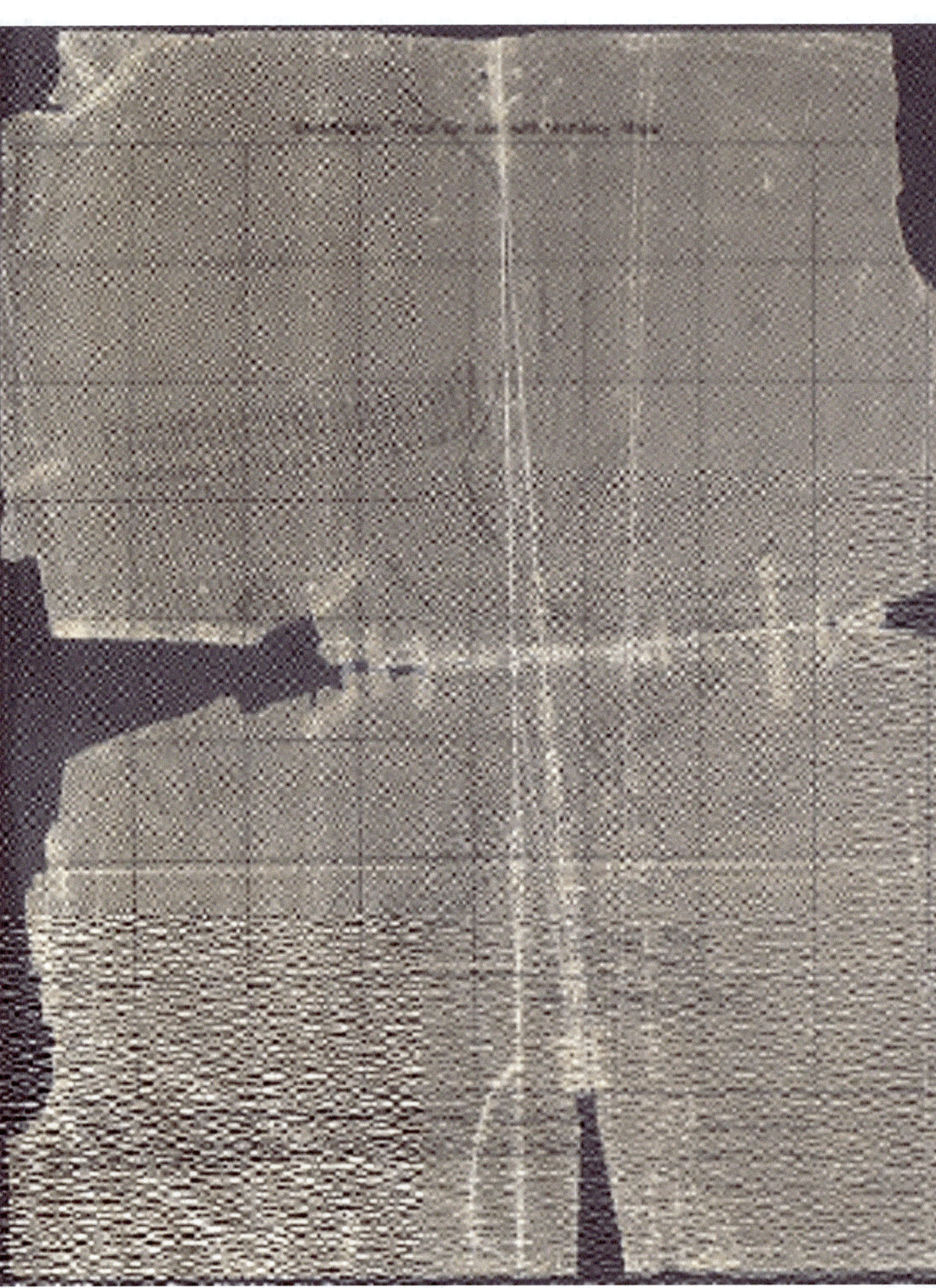

SECRET.

WAR DIARY.

of

2nd Bn. Duke of Wellington's Regt.

From 1st Nov. 1918
To 30th Nov. 1918

VOLUME.

S. Lawler
Lieut. Colonel.
Commanding 2nd Bn. Duke of Wellington's Regt.

Dec. 1. 1918.

Army Form C. 2118.

WAR DIARY
or
INTELLIGENCE SUMMARY.
(Erase heading not required.)

Instructions regarding War Diaries and Intelligence Summaries are contained in F.S. Regs., Part II. and the Staff Manual respectively. Title pages will be prepared in manuscript.

Place	Date	Hour	Summary of Events and Information	Remarks and references to Appendices
	NOVEMBER 1918			
VERCHAIN	1.	at 14.30 hours	the Battⁿ moved forward and were placed at the disposal of the 11th Bde. A. Coy at K.31.a. B. Coy at K.31.c. and C+D Coys in K.31.B at 19.00 the Battⁿ again came under the command of the 10th Bde. 1 O.R. Killed. 1 O.R. Wounded.	A.1. A.2. A.3.
"	2.		The Battⁿ was relieved during the afternoon by the 7th South Staffordshire Regt (11th Div) and moved back into billets at VERCHAIN. 2nd LT L.R. RANDOLPH to Hospital from Small Course.	B.
SAULZOIR	3.		The Battⁿ marched to SAULZOIR and went into billets there. 6 O.R. joined the details from the Base.	C.
"	4.		The day spent in cleaning up. Scrubbing equipment and resting.	
"	5.		Battⁿ in training. Platoon and sections in the attack. S.O.R. to C.C.S.	
"	6.		Battⁿ in training. Platoon and sections in the attack.	
PRESEAU	7.		The Battⁿ marched to PRESEAU and moved into billets there.	D.

WAR DIARY
or
INTELLIGENCE SUMMARY.
(Erase heading not required.)

Army Form C. 2118.

Place	Date	Hour	Summary of Events and Information	Remarks and references to Appendices
			NOVEMBER. 1918.	
PRESEAU	8.		Batt'n in Training. P.T. & B.F. Pelaton Drill and Arms Drill under the R.S.M.	
"	9.		Batt'n in Training. Pelaton in the attack. Extended order drill.	
"	10.		G.O.R. joined the Batt'n from the Base. Church of England Parade, and Non-Conformist Parade.	
"	11.		Batt'n in Training. Close order drill and Coy in the attack scheme.	
"	12.		" P.T & B.F. Batt'n arms drill parade under R.S.M. LT GLOVER joined the Batt'n. 10 R joined from the Base.	
"	13.		Batt'n in Training. Coy. Drill. Batt'n Ceremonial Parade. CAPT KNOCKER joined the Batt'n. G.O.R. from the Base.	
"	14.		Batt'n in Training. Coy drill and salvage work. G.O.C. Division congratulated the C.O. on the smart guard furnished by the Batt'n for Divisional H.Q.	
"	15.		Batt'n in Training. Batt'n short route march.	

BAR TO MILITARY MEDAL: No 203594 Pte BATES M.M.
No 11165 L/Cpl HAINSWORTH M.M.
MILITARY MEDAL No 305546 Cpl WALKER.E. No 16597 Pte HILLS.
No 12516 Sgt COOPER.T.

Army Form C. 2118.

WAR DIARY
or
INTELLIGENCE SUMMARY.
(Erase heading not required.)

Place	Date	Hour	Summary of Events and Information	Remarks and references to Appendices
PRESEAU	NOVEMBER, 1918			
	15 (continued).		No 49800 Pte KIRBY. W. No 35319 Pte BROOK C.G. No 12492. Pte (L/c) CARROL. J.	
			No 32329. Pte BATES .D. No 329718. Pte. DOYLE. H.	
	16		Battⁿ in Training. Battⁿ Ceremonial Drill and Educational Training.	
			4.O.R. joined from Base. 10.O.R. to Base struck off the strength	
	17.		Divisional Church of England Service. 10R to C.E.S. 10.O.R. joined	E.
			from the Base.	
	18.		Battⁿ in Training Brigade Ceremonial Parade. 6.O.R. from Base.	F.
VALENCIENNES	19.		The Battⁿ marched to VALENCIENNES and moved into billets	
			there.	
	20.		Battⁿ in Training. Divisional Ceremonial Parade. 10R C.E.S. 12. O.R.	
			joined from the Base.	
"	21.		Battⁿ in Training. Platoon and Coy Drill.	
			Bar to MILITARY MEDAL.	
			12263. Pte. J. SPELLMAN.	
			MILITARY MEDAL.	
			No 201934. L/Cpl H. CUNNINGHAM. No 200447 Pte A. CORDINGLEY. No 10930. Cpl. H. PRIOR.	
			No 204113 Pte. W. BOWERS. No 20364 Pte .C. BATES No 29674 Cpl. S. COCKROFT.	
			No 25520. Cpl. A. BALL. No 16676. Pte. J. COSTELLO.	
			No 202900 L/Cpl. G.W. WORMALD.	

Army Form C. 2118.

WAR DIARY
or
INTELLIGENCE SUMMARY.

(Erase heading not required.)

Place	Date	Hour	Summary of Events and Information	Remarks and references to Appendices
			NOVEMBER 1918.	
VALENCIENNES	22.		Battn in training. Platoon Drill and Coy Ceremonial Drill. 1. O.R. to CCS 6 O.R. from Base.	
"	23.		Battn in training. Scrubbing equipment. Educational Parade. Capt KNOCKER to England. 2/Lts BEST and HASTIE joined the Battn 5 O.R. joined from the Base.	
"	24.		Battn Church Parade. 2/LT LISTER joined the Battn 2/LT C.M.YOUNG joined the Battn MAJOR WILLIS M.C. to the 1st R.WARWICKSHIRE REGT 30 O.R. joined from the Base.	
"	25.		Battn in training. Musketry and Coy Drill. 2/LT OLLEY D.C.M. joined the Battn 30.R. joined from the base.	
"	26.		Battn in training. Platoons in the attack. Educational Parade.	
"	27.		Battn in training. Demonstration parade (Guard mounting etc). Educational Parade. 12. O.R. joined from the base.	
"	28.		Battn in training. Divisional Ceremonial Parade before the 1st ARMY COMMANDER.	
"	29.		Battn in training. Pte R.F. Coy Drill. Educational Parade.	
"	30.		Battn " " Scrubbing equipment. Educational Parade.	

Comdg. 2nd Battn. the Duke of Wellington's Regt.

SECRET.   Copy No. WD

2nd Bn. Duke of Wellington's Regiment.
(PROVISIONAL) ORDER No. 1.
In the Field, 1st November, 1918.

Provisional Orders in case Battalion have to move forward to occupy Defensive Positions.

1. Latest report show that the enemy have counter-attacked along the whole of our front. Situation not yet known.

2. In case of the Brigade in front using up all their Reserves in counter-attack, the Battalion will be moved forward to man a rear line of resistance.

3. Probable line will be Line of Railway from K.34.a.5.9. to K.20.d.8.0.

4. Companies will be disposed as follows :-
   RIGHT FRONT.   A. Company disposed in depth along Line of Railway from Right Boundary to K.27.c.9.9.
   LEFT FRONT.   B. Company in depth from K.27.c.9.9. to Left Boundary.
   RIGHT SUPPORT COMPANY. C. Company.
   LEFT SUPPORT COMPANY.   D. Company.

5. BOUNDARIES.   Battn. RIGHT BOUNDARY.
   K.34.a.5.9. straight line through K.34.a.0.0.

   Battn. LEFT BOUNDARY.
   HALT(K.20.d.8.0.) thence straight line through K.25.d.0.0.

   Inter-Company BOUNDARY.
   K.27.central. and straight line through K.27.c.0.0.

6. SUPPORT COMPANIES.
   Will be disposed on high ground on a line from K.33.central to K.36.central.

7. ORDER OF MARCH.
   "A" "B" "C" "D" Companies, Battn. Headquarters.

8. Each Company will move at 100 yards between Platoons, and usual Battle Precautions will be taken.

9. Battn. Headquarters will be at K.32.d.central.

10. R.A.P. will be notified later.

11. Unless dispositions are altered Companies will move off on receipt of Code "MAN BATTLE POSITIONS", reporting their departure.

12. ACKNOWLEDGE.

Captain.
A/Adjt. 2nd Bn. Duke of Wellington's Regt.

SECRET.   E.   Copy No. 11

                    2nd Bn. Duke of Wellington's Regiment.
                           (WARNING) ORDER No. 1.
Map Ref: 51A.
                                        In the Field, 18th November, 1918.
_____

INTENTION.   1. The Battalion will move to VALENCIENNES tomorrow, 19th inst.

INFORMATION. 2. (a) Probable time of Start will be 10.30 hours.
                 (b) Dress - Full Marching Order.

                                                    [signature]
                                                           Captain.
                            A/Adjt, 2nd Duke of Wellington's Regt.

                            D I S T R I B U T I O N.
                            _____

        Copy No. 1 Bn.H.Q.   Copy No. 8 T.O.
                 2 Adjt.   9 10th Inf: Bde.
                 3 - 6 All Coys.   10 - 11 War Diary.
                 7 Q.M.   12 File.

SECRET.   A.2.   Copy No. 9

2nd Bn. Duke of Wellington's Regiment.
(WARNING) ORDER No. 1.

Ref. Map 51A. S.E. & N.E.   In the Field, 1st November, 1918.

---

1. The Battalion will relieve the 1st SOMERSET L.I. tonight in SUPPORT on the Divisional Front.

2. Owing to situation in front being at present obscure, it is not possible to give Dispositions or Order of Relief yet.

3. DRESS. will be Battle Order with Leather Jerkins.

4. Lewis Guns will be carried up by the men.

5. Rations will be issued before departure and carried up on the man.

6. Water for Companies will be carried up by Limber to Bn.H.Q.

7. All Stores, Valises, Greatcoats, etc., will be stacked at Coy.H.Q. by 15.00 hours.

8. All surplus Lewis Guns and Magazines will be stacked at Bn.H.Q. at 15.00 hrs also. Transport Officer will arrange collection of these.

10. 9. Teas will be served at 16.00 hours, after which cookers will return to the Transport Lines.

10. ACKNOWLEDGE.

Captain.
A/Adjt. 2nd Duke of Wellington's Regt.

DISTRIBUTION.

Copy No. 1 Bn.H.Q.	Copy No. 7 T.O.
2 – 5 All Coys.	8 – 9 War Diary.
6 Q.M.	10 File.

SECRET.
                    A.3.   2nd Bn. Duke of Wellington's Regt. K.437.

1. The Battalion will move at once and occupy the trenches in K.31.a.&.c.

2. Companies will be disposed :-
   LEFT FRONT - A. Company in trenches in K.31.a.
   RIGHT FRONT - B. Company in trenches in K.31.c.

   LEFT SUPPORT - C. Company.
   RIGHT SUPPORT - D. Company.

   Support Companies will dig themselves in in depth about 200 yards in rear of the Front Companies.

3. Battalion Headquarters and Regtl. Aid Post will be at approx: P.6.b.4.2. till further notice.

4. Companies will report departure from billets and notify when they are in position.

5. Rations will be issued later.

                                            (Sgd) D.G.R.BILHAM, Captain.
                                          A/Adjt. 2nd Duke of Wellington's Regt.

4/11/18

SECRET.   B,   Copy. No. 9
                    2nd Bn. Duke of Wellington's Regiment.
                         (OPERATION) ORDER No. 128.
Ref.Map 51A.S.E.&.N.E. 1/20.000   In the Field, 2nd November, 1918.

INTENTION.   1.   The Battalion will be relieved this afternoon by the 7th
                    SOUTH STAFFORDSHIRE Regt. during the afternoon of the 2nd November

INSTRUCTIONS. 2.(a) Billeting Parties from relieving Companies will report to
                    Companies during the afternoon.
                    These parties will provide guides for in-coming unit.

              (b)   On completion of relief Battalion will proceed to Billets in
                    VERCHAIN. Guides will meet Companies on arrival.

              (c)   Completion of Relief will be notified to Bn.H.Q. in usual
                    Code.

              (d)   All lewis guns, empty water tins, etc., will be carried
                    with Companies to Billets.

                                              (Sgd) D.G.R.BILHAM. Captain
                                        A/Adjt. 2nd Duke of Wellington's Regt.

              DISTRIBUTION.

        Copy No. 1 Bn.H.Q.   Copy No. 7 T.O.&.Q.M.
                 2 Adjt.   8 - 9 War Diary.
                 3 - 6 All Coys.   10 File.

SECRET.   C.   Copy No. 9.
                              2nd Bn. Duke of Wellington's Regiment.
                                  (OPERATION) ORDER No. 129
Ref. Map 51A. 1/40.000.   In the Field, 2nd November, 1918.

INTENTION.   1. The Battalion will move by Route March to SAULZOIR on the 3rd inst.

INSTRUCTIONS.   2. (a) DRESS.
                       Battle Order with Greatcoats. Leather Jerkins to be rolled
                       inside the Ground Sheet.
                    (b) ORDER OF MARCH.
                       Bn.H.Q., Drums., A. B. C. & D. Companies.
                    (c) STARTING POINT.
                       Road Junction P.6.c.75.05.
                    (d) TIME.
                       Will be notified later. (approx: time 12.40 hours.)
                    (e) ROUTE.
                       P.6.c.75.05. – TRESTLE BRIDGE P.11.a.0.5. thence across
                       country to STATION (at SAULZOIR) but to follow general.
                       direction of Road running through P.16.1.& P.21.
                    (f) INTERVAL.
                       100 yards will be maintained between Companies.
                    (g) MARCH DISCIPLINE.
                       The strictest March Discipline is to be maintained on the
                       march.
                       All movement on roads will be in file.
                    (h) BILLETING PARTIES.
                       (1) All C.Q.M.Sergts. and one N.C.O. of Bn.H.Q. will report
                           to Capt. E.C.COKE at Area Commandants Office SAULZOIR at
                           09.15 hours.
                       (2) Capt. E.C.COKE will report to the Staff Captain at the
                           above rendezvous at 09.30 hours.
                       (3) C.Q.M.Sergts. will meet Companies at the STATION SAULZOIR.
                       (4) Present Billets will be taken over by the 11th
                           MANCHESTER Regt. Each Company will detail one N.C.O.
                           to meet billeting party of in-coming unit at VERCHAIN
                           CHURCH at 10.00 hours.
                    (j) DINNERS.
                       Dinners will be served at 11.30 hours.
                    (k) STORES.
                       All Officers Valises, Company Stores and Lewis Guns will be
                       stacked at Coy.H.Qrs. by 10.00 hours.

TRANSPORT.   3.   Transport Officer will arrange :-
                    (a) Collection of Stores mentioned in para. 2.(k).
                    (b) Collection of Water Carts, Maltexe Cart and Cookers.
                    (c) Officers Chargers to report to their riders at 12.00 hours.
                    (d) Mess Cart to report to Bn.H.Q. at 12.30 hours.

REPORTS.   4.   Head of Column.

                 5.   ACKNOWLEDGE.

                                                              Captain.
                                              A/Adjt. 2nd Duke of Wellington's Regt.

                              D I S T R I B U T I O N.

                    Copy No. 1 Bn.H.Q.   Copy No. 8 T.O.& Q.M.
                            2   Adjt.   9 – 10 War Diary.
                            3 – 6 All Coys.   11   File.
                            7   10th Inf: Bde.

SECRET.   Copy No. 4

                    2nd Bn. Duke of Wellington's Regiment.
                      (OPERATION) ORDER No. 130.
Ref:Map 51A.1/40.000   In the Field, 6th November, 1918.

INTENTION.   1. The Battalion will move by Route March to PRESEAU on the 6th inst.

INSTRUCTIONS.   2. (a) DRESS.
                       Full Marching Order. Leather Jerkins to be rolled on top of
                       the Pack and wrapped in the Ground Sheet.
                   (b) ORDER OF MARCH.
                       Bn.H.Q., Drums, B. C. D. A. Companies.
                   (c) STARTING POINT.
                       Road Junction Q.28.a.1.1. Companies to be clear of and on
                       North side of SAULZOIR - VERCHAIN Road.
                   (d) TIME.
                       08.45 hours.
                   (e) ROUTE.
                       Across country, but to follow general line South of the
                       SAULZOIR - VERCHAIN - QUEREMAING - ARTRES - PRESEAU Road.
                   (f) INTERVAL.
                       A distance of 100 yards will be maintained between Companies.
                   (g) BILLETING PARTY.
                       All C.Q.M.Sergts. & 1 Other Rank per Company & 1 N.C.O. &
                       1 Other Rank for BN.H.Q., & 1 representative for Q.M. will
                       report to 2Lieut. F.P.GLEADOW,M.C.M.M. at Orderly Room at
                       08.00 hours.
                   (h) STORES.
                       (1) Officers Valises, Mess Stores, &Coy. Boxes will be stacked
                           at the CHATEAU by 07.30 hours.
                       (2) Lewis Guns will be stacked at Coy.H.Q. by 07.30 hours.
                       (3) All Blankets and surplus Officers Kits & all other Stores
                           will be stacked in the Present Bn. Guard Room by 07.15 hours.
                       (4) Q.M. will arrange dump for all surplus stores that he is
                           unable to move, and will arrange a guard for this.

TRANSPORT.   3. (a) No extra Transport is available at present, but surplus
                       stores mentioned in para.2.(h)(3 & 4) will be moved as
                       soon as Transport is available.
                   (b) Transport will move under Orders of the Transport Officer,
                       but must be clear of Railway Crossing P.27.d.4.8. by 08.40 hrs
                   (c) Transport Officer will arrange :-
                       (1) Collection of Stores mentioned in para.2.(h)(1).
                       (2) Collection of Lewis Guns, Water Carts, Maltese Cart &
                           Cookers.
                       (3) Officers Chargers to report to their riders at 08.00 hrs.
                       (4) Mess Cart to report to Bn.H.Q. at 08.00 hours.

REPORTS.   4. Head of Column.

                5. ACKNOWLEDGE.

                                                           Captain.
                                                A/Adjt. 2nd Duke of Wellington's Regt.

DISTRIBUTION.

```
Copy No. 1  Bn.H.Q.          Copy No. 8   Q.M.
         2  Adjt.                     9   10th Inf: Bde.
         3 - 6 All Coys.              10 - 11 War Diary.
         7  T.O.                      12  File.
```

SECRET.   Copy No. 11

2nd Bn. Duke of Wellington's Regiment.
(OPERATION) ORDER No.131

Ref: Map 51A. 1/40.000   In the Field, 12th November, 1918.

__INTENTION.__ 1. The Battalion will move by Route March to VALENCIENNES on the 13th inst.

__INSTRUCTIONS.__ 2. (a) DRESS. Full Marching Order, S.D.Caps. Steel Helmets to be fastened on the back of the pack.
  (b) ORDER OF MARCH.
      Battalion Headquarters, Drums, C. D. A. & B. Companies.
  (c) STARTING POINT.
      Road Junction opposite 10th Field Ambulance.
  (d) TIME.
      10.10 Hours.
  (e) ROUTE.
      Cross Roads S.30.a.15.10 - MARLY.
  (f) INTERVAL.
      Will be as laid down in Infantry Training.
  (g) ADVANCE PARTIES.
      1. 3 Q.M.Sergts. and 2 O.R. per Coy., and 1 L.C.S. and 2 O.R. for Bn.H.Q., who will leave billets at 07.30 Hours and proceed in advance to arrange rooms and clean up the new Z.billets.
      2. 6 Regtl. Pioneers & Pte. J.NURN (Bn.H.Q.) will report to the Q.M. at 9.00 hours to proceed in advance of the Battn.
      3. 1 Officer & 1 Runner per Coy. will report to the Q.M. at the BARRACKS in VALENCIENNES at 11.00 hours.
  (h) STORES.
      1. Blankets will be stacked at Q.M.Stores by 08.30 hours.
      2. Officers Valises and Mess Stores ———— 09.00 hours.
  (j) BILLETS.
      1. All Billets must be absolutely clean by 09.30 hours. Each Coy. & Bn.H.Q. will detail 2 men & Coy. one full man in addition to be left behind as Cleaning up Party. These parties will report to 2Lieut. E.L.WOOLFORD at Orderly Room at 09.30 hours.
      2. No furniture or fittings are to be moved from one room to another in the new billets until permission has been obtained from the Q.M.

__TRANSPORT.__ 3. Transport will move with the Battalion.

__REPORTS.__ 4. Head of Column.

5. ACKNOWLEDGE.

                                            Captain.
                                A/Adjt. 2nd Duke of Wellington's Regt.

        D I S T R I B U T I O N.

Copy No. 1 Bn.H.Q.   Copy No. 8 18th Inf: Bde.
        2 Adjt.   9 R.S.M.
        3 - 6 All Coys.   10 - 11 War Diary.
        7 T.O. & Q.M.   12 File

Original

W A R   D I A R Y

of

2nd Bn. Duke of Wellington's Regt.

From December 1st 1918
To December 31st 1918

VOLUME

M'L Toole Capt.
Commanding 2nd Bn. Duke of Wellington's Regt.

Army Form C. 2118.

WAR DIARY
or
INTELLIGENCE SUMMARY.
(Erase heading not required.)

Place: VALENCIENNES

DECEMBER 1918

Date	Hour	Summary of Events and Information	Remarks and references to Appendices
1.		The Battn. in training. Company & Platoon drill. Parade Ground VINCENT BARRACKS. 2/Lt. E. BRIGGS joined the Battn.	COLOUR PARTY. Lt. LENNON DSO MC
2.		The Battn. in training. 2/Lt. G.E. WEBSTER joined the Battn.	L. COLSON MM
3.		The Battn. in training. Rifle Range allotted to Battn. Team also in for training. Divisional Competition. Education.	Y. BANHAM M.C. R. GLEADOW MC MM RSM. TEARCE M.C.
4.		The Battn. in training. Ceremonial Parade for inspection by the King. The Commanding Officer was honoured by being presented to His Majesty. The Regimental Team v. the 4. Battn. M.G.C. at association football	CQMS. HARVEY DCM MM Sgt/GILGALLEN MM Sgt. SHORT MM Cpl. STOPS MM Pte. BENNET MM
5.		The Battn. in training. Company & Platoon drill. A Battn. Boxing Tournament took place at the "DUKES" BOXING HALL. The show was a most successful one. General Sir HENRY HORNE was present & expressed his appreciation of the excellent entertainment provided. The Divisional Commander was also present.	
6.		The Battn. in training. Interior Economy. Kit Inspection. Cleaning Kit etc. The Battn. Orchestra under Cpl. CLAPHAM was commanded to play before HIS MAJESTY THE KING. The "Colour Party" left for ENGLAND to fetch the COLOURS.	
7.		The Battn. in training.	

Army Form C. 2118.

WAR DIARY
or
INTELLIGENCE SUMMARY.
(Erase heading not required.)

Instructions regarding War Diaries and Intelligence Summaries are contained in F. S. Regs., Part II. and the Staff Manual respectively. Title pages will be prepared in manuscript.

Place	Date	Hour	Summary of Events and Information	Remarks and references to Appendices
VALENCIENNES	DECEMBER 1918			
	8		Batn. Church Parade at 10.00 hours -	
	9		The Battn. in Training - A + B Coys Range. Also Battn. Teams in musketry - Capt. M.C. HOOLE, M.C. reported as 2nd in command of the Battn. - Lieut. L. SHAW M.C. " " O/C A. Coy.	
	10		The Battn. in training - Company + Platoon drill - Education -	
	11		The Battn. in training. Company + Platoon drill. 2. O.R. demobilised -	
	12		The Battn. in training. Company + Platoon drill - Education. 8. O.R. demobilised -	
	13		The Battn. in training - do -	
			Lieut. J.A. LENNON. M.C. promoted Captain. Whilst commanding a Company - THE DISTINGUISHED SERVICE ORDER. BAR to THE MILITARY CROSS	
			2Lt. (A/Capt.) J. COOKE M.C. Temp. Capt. G.D. WATKINS D.S.O. M.C. R.A.M.C.	
			THE MILITARY CROSS THE DISTINGUISHED CONDUCT MEDAL	
			2Lt. W. STARKEY. Sergt. A.W. HARRISON M.M. Sergt. A. FREAR.	
	14		The Battn. in training - Commanding Officers Inspection - Colour Party Returned.	
	15		Battn. Church Parade - Continuing a ceremonial service for the formal handing over of the colours to the Commanding Officer -	
	16		The Battn. in Training - Company + Platoon Drill -	

Army Form C. 2118.

WAR DIARY
or
INTELLIGENCE SUMMARY.
(Erase heading not required.)

Instructions regarding War Diaries and Intelligence Summaries are contained in F. S. Regs., Part II. and the Staff Manual respectively. Title pages will be prepared in manuscript.

Place	Date	Hour	Summary of Events and Information	Remarks and references to Appendices
VALENCIENNES	DECEMBER 1918.			
	17.		The Battn in training. Company & Platoon drill. Education. FOOTBALL. C. Company, 2d R. W's Regt. v. C Company, 1st R. Warwick Regt. Lost 2 goals to 1. 12. O.R. demobilised. 63. O.R. demobilised.	
	18.		The Battn in Training. VICTORIA CROSS. 2/Lieut. J. P. HUFFAM. DISTINGUISHED SERVICE ORDER. Capt. J. A. LENNON. M.C. A dinner was given at H.Q. Mess in honor of the above awards. The recipients being chief guests.	
	19.		The Battn in training. Lt. R. SHEPHERD. D.C.M. } Sent to Hospital in England. Capt. COKE } FOOTBALL. 11th Battn Team v. DIVISIONAL H.Q. Divisional H.Q. won by two goals. Having after a very strenuous game the Battn had to play 15 min extra each way.	

Army Form C. 2118.

WAR DIARY
or
INTELLIGENCE SUMMARY.
(Erase heading not required.)

Place	Date	Summary of Events and Information	Remarks and references to Appendices

DECEMBER 1918

20. The Battn in training – Company & Platoon drill –
21. The Battn in training – Commanding Officer's inspection – 9 - O.R. demobilised.
22. Battn Church Parade –
Rugby Football Battalion Team v 2d SEAFORTH HIGHLANDERS.

RESULT Won by the Dukes. 10 points to nil –

23. The Battn in training: 4 - O.R Demobilised –
TUG OF WAR. Divisional Competition. Heavy & light teams both Lost –
BOXING Brigade Boxing Tournament at the DUKE'S BOXING HALL.

24. The Battn in training – Company & Platoon in the attack –

VALENCIENNES

25. Christmas Day Battalion Church Parade at 10.45 –
at 1330 hours all O.R. with the exception of members of the Sergeants Mess, had their Christmas dinner – Companies in their respective dining rooms 4Bn.H.Q in the Recreation Room which was very well decorated with HOLLY – EVERGREENS & various LANTERNS etc. – The General opinion was that it was the best Christmas Dinner that could be remembered –

WAR DIARY or INTELLIGENCE SUMMARY

Army Form C. 2118.

Comdg. 2nd Battn. the Duke of Wellington's Regt.

Withers Lieut.

Place	Date	Hour	Summary of Events and Information	Remarks
VALENCIENNES	DECEMBER 1918			
	25.		In the evening the Sergeants had their dinner which was a great success — BRIGADIER-GENERAL GREENE D.S.O. went round & visited all Companies & the Sergeants Mess. The Officers dined in their own Messes — & C. mess & B.H.Q. Altogether the day was a most successful one — 10. O.R. Demobilised —	
	26.		BOXING DAY. A holiday fall. A letter of good wishes & congratulations was received from Sir. H.E. BELFIELD K.C.B., K.C.M.G., D.S.O. — The Battn. in training — Commanding Officers Inspection — In the evening there was a dance at B.H.Q.	
	27.		The Battn. in training. 10. O.R. Demobilised — Battn. Church Parade — 1. O.R. Demobilised	
	28. 29.			
	30.		The Battn. in training — Platoon & Company in the attack — 4. O.R. Demobilised	
	31.		The Battn. in training — The Sergeants of the Battn. held a dinner in honour of Lt. HUFFAM V.C. The dance was a great success. NVL NEW YEAR was seen in —	

Army Form C. 2118.

2nd Bn. Duke of Wellington Regt.
Jan - June 1919

WAR DIARY
or
INTELLIGENCE SUMMARY.
(Erase heading not required.)

55 F
6 sheets

Place	Date	Hour	Summary of Events and Information	Remarks and references to Appendices
	JANUARY 1919.			
VALENCIENNES	1.		New Year's Day. Holiday for all –	
	2.		9. O.R. to WATFORD DETAILS – 3 O.R. demobilised –	
	3.		1. O.R. joined from C.C.S. 1. O.R. to hospital – England –	
			Football – The Battn. met the R.A.M.C. in the re-play of the 3rd Round of the LUCAS CUP. After again being beaten extra time the Battn. won by 2 gr. als.	
			1 O.R. to C.C.S. – 1 O.R. & person –	
	4.		Rugby. A friendly match was played against the WARWICKS. resulting	
			in a win by one try to the W.R. – unfortunately 3 gunners had	
			to leave the field, badly hurt –	
			Battalion Church Parade in the Recreation Room –	
	5.		New Year's Honours – Member of the British Empire. Lt./Qm. C. SHEPHERDSON.	A
BINCHE	6.		L/Sgt. ROBERTSHAW to England – (sick)	
			The 10th Brigade march to BINCHE on this to Longuin – The Battn. proceed	
			at 8.30 hours & arrived at BINCHE at 12.00 hrs.	
	7.		Re-arrangement of Billets under Company arrangements.	
			5. O.R. to C.C.S. 1. O.R. to hospital to England – 1. O.R. from C.C.S.	

Army Form C. 2118.

WAR DIARY
or
INTELLIGENCE SUMMARY.
(Erase heading not required.)

Instructions regarding War Diaries and Intelligence Summaries are contained in F. S. Regs., Part II. and the Staff Manual respectively. Title pages will be prepared in manuscript.

Place	Date	Hour	Summary of Events and Information	Remarks and references to Appendices
	JANUARY 1919			
{ BINCHE	8.		Lecture on "Reconstruction Problems" -	
	9.		1. O. R. to C.C.S. 9. O. R. from base -	
			1. O. R. from C.C.S. The Regt. new kit band arrived from England -	
	10.		11. O. R. demobilised -	
	11.		Commanding Officer's Inspection of Billets -	
			39. O. R. demobilised - 3. O. R. C.C.S.	
	12.		Battn. Church Parade - 3. O. R. from Base -	
			15. O. R. demobilised - 3. O. R. from Base -	
	13.		Major WELLESLEY joined the Battn. -	
			Major WELLESLEY took over command of the Battn. from Capt. M. J. FOOLE. M.C.	
	14.		15. O. R. demobilised -	
			The Divisional Baths were allotted to the Battn. -	
			1. O. R. from C.C.S.	
	15.		Football Right half Battn. V. Left half Battn. — Right half won by 2 goals	
	16.		2. O. R. joined from the Base. -	

Army Form C. 2118.

WAR DIARY
or
INTELLIGENCE SUMMARY.
(Erase heading not required.)

Place	Date	Hour	Summary of Events and Information	Remarks and references to Appendices
	JANUARY 1919			
	17.		Bath. Route march – Battn. Cross Country run – Won by 'D' Coy. First three individual runners – (1) Sergt. GARSIDE. (2) Capt. COOKE. D.S.O. M.C. (3) 2/Lt. CROFT.	
	18.		Football DUKES Rt. Rly v WARWICKS Left Half – Lost. do Left Half v Rt. Rly, Draw – 1.0.R. L.C.C.S. 1.0.R. 8 hospital in England 1.0.R. 8 from Base – 1.0.R demobilised. 10. O.R demobilised.	
	19.		Lt. HORSLEY demobilised.	
	20.		Brigade Ceremonial parade – The Brigade paraded in the GRAND PLACE & was inspected by the Divisional Commander – the Burgomaster – In the afternoon the Brigade furnished an Escort to the Burgomaster & Capt. M.C. HOOLE M.C. In the evening the Inhabitants gave a concert & dance to which all Officers were invited – 9. O.R Demobilised. by 1 Tony –	
	21.		Rugby. The Battn. beat the 2nd WEST YORKS by 1 Try – Q.O.R Demobilised 1.O.R L.C.C.S. 1.O.R 8 hospital in England.	

WAR DIARY or INTELLIGENCE SUMMARY

Army Form C. 2118.

Place	Date	Hour	Summary of Events and Information	Remarks and references to Appendices
	JANUARY 1919			
	22.		Football. DUKES Rt. Half v. 10th Infy. Bde. - Draw.	
	23.		1. O.R. K.C.C.S.	
	24.		Battalion Route March -	
			Football. DUKES Left Half v SEAFORTH'S Rt. Half - Lost by one goal.	
			Mentions in Service Medal.	
			C.Q.M.S. A.J. BROWN. Sgt A. HALFACRE Sgt E. PEGSON D.CM	
			12. O.R. Demobilised -	
	25.		Football. 1st & 2nd Bn. Devl. Wilts Yorks Reg. v 1st R'gal Warwicks Lost 1 goal.	
			15 O.R. Reenlisted -	
	26.		Battalion Church Parade. 2Lt. YOUNG t/a o.c. Demobilisation	
	27.		Divisional Cross Country Run. - Won by the Battalion by 43 points.	
			The Battalion thus becomes the representative for the Division in	
			the XXII Corp serins. 1. O.R. & C.C.S.	
			Lt. I.C.K RINGILL + 10. O.R. Demobilised.	
	28.		P.O.R. Demobilised -	
	29.		Football Cancelled owing to the ground being frozen	
	30.		hard - Major R.C.A.R.E. M.C. Demobilised.	
	31.		24 J. SCROFT. Demobilised	

BINCHE

SECRET.   Copy No. 11

                          2nd Bn. Duke of Wellington's Regiment.
                               (OPERATION) ORDER No. 1
Map. Ref: VALENCIENNES & NAMUR.
                                                In the Field, 4th January, 1919.
_____

INTENTION.   1.   The Battalion will move by Bus to BINCHE on the 5th inst.

ADMINISTRATION.
INSTRUCTIONS. 2.   (a) DRESS.
                         Full Marching Order with one blanket.
                     (b) ORDER OF MARCH.
                         Bn.H.Q., Drums., A. B. C. & D. Companies.
                     (c) PARADE.
                         Battalion will parade in the Big SQUARE at 08.30 hours.
                         Markers will report to R.S.M. at 08.20 hours.
                     (d) ROUTE.
                         Route will be VALENCIENNES – MONS Road.
                     (e) BILLETS.
                         (1) 1 Senior N.C.O. per Company will report to 2Lieut. H.D.
                         Didlake at Orderly Room at 07.45 hours on the 5th inst. to
                         proceed in advance of the Battalion.
                         2Lieut. H.D.BIDLAKE will report on arrival to the Area
                         Commandant.
                         Two days rations will be carried by this party.
                         (2) Billets for A. Company, Bn.H.Q. & Transport will be
                         arranged by Sergt. WEST & Sergt. SPRIGGS respectively.
                         (3) All Billets at present occupied by the Battalion must be
                         left scrupulously clean and certificates rendered to Orderly
                         Room by 08.15 hours to this effect.
                         (4) Capt. R.T. EDWARDS will inspect all Billets at 08.15 hours.
                         Each Company will leave one representative to go round their
                         Company Billets with him.
                     (f) KITS.
                         All Officers Valises, Company Stores, etc., will be stacked
                         at the Q.M.Stores by 20.00 hours.
                     (g) LEWIS GUNS.
                         Lewis Guns will be stacked in their L.G.Limbers by 18.00 hours
                         on the 4th inst.
                     (h) RATIONS.
                         Rations for the 5th will be carried on the man.

TRANSPORT.   3.   (a) All 1st Line Transport (less Officers Chargers) will move
                         under orders of the Transport Officer on the 5th inst.
                     (b) Officers Chargers will move on the 5th inst.
                         Transport Officer will arrange for a N.C.O. or Senior Private
                         to be in charge of this party.

RS CATS.   4.   Head of the Column.

               5.   ACKNOWLEDGE.

                                                          R.J.A.Silke
                                                          Captain.
                                                A/Adjt. 2nd Bn. Duke of Wellington's Regt.

                                   D I S T R I B U T I O N

        Copy No. 1 Bn.H.Q.   Copy No. 8 Q.M.
                2 – 5 All Coys.   9 T.O.
                6 Adjt.   10 – 11 War Diary.
                7 10th Inf.Bde.   12 File.

SECRET.

WAR DIARY.

of

2nd Bn. Duke of Wellington's Regt.

From February 1st 1919
To February 28th 1919

VOLUME.

4th February 1919.

D. McWilliam Capt
for Lieut. Colonel,
Commanding 2nd Bn. Duke of Wellington's Regt.

Army Form C. 2118.

WAR DIARY
or
INTELLIGENCE SUMMARY.
(Erase heading not required.)

WO 53

Place	Date	Hour	Summary of Events and Information	Remarks and references to Appendices
FEBRUARY 1919				
BINCHE	1.		2/Lt. GLEADOW M.C.M.M. & 9.O.R. demobilised —	
	2.		Batt. Church Parade.	
	3.		1. O.R. rejoined from C.C.S.	
	4.		Conference in attack on manoeuvre areas.	
	5.		F/Lt G.W. SMITHAM & 6 O.R. demobilised. 1. O.R. to C.C.S.	
	6.		L/M BANHAM M.C. & 9.O.R. to —	
			The Battalion Band played in the KURSAL at 5.30 p.m.	
	7.		Commanding Officers Inspection & Billets — 4 O.R. demobilised — 1 or & C.C.S.	
	8.		2/Lt. H. RAWNSLEY & 9.O.R. demobilised —	
	9.		Batt. Church Parade. Lt. T WORSICK 2/Lt. C.E. TEALE. 2/Lt B. HOUGHTON & 6 O.R. demobilised — 2 O.R. from home.	
	10.		11. O.R. demobilised —	
	11.		Battalion attack on Brigade Manoeuvre area	
	12.		2/Lt. T. BEST & 10. O.R. demobilised —	
	13.		2/Lt. H.W. LISTER M.C. to U.K. for 2 months leave prior to joining 1st Batt. in INDIA.	

56 F
5 sheets

Army Form C. 2118.

WAR DIARY
or
INTELLIGENCE SUMMARY.
(Erase heading not required.)

Place	Date	Hour	Summary of Events and Information	Remarks and references to Appendices
BINCHE	FEBRUARY 1919. 14.		Commanding Officer Inspected 1/5 Battn. Amalgamation of Companies. Owing to the depleted numbers of the Battalion it was found necessary to re-arrange as 2 Companies. A'o'C' to be known as 'A' Coy. B'oD' to be known as 'B' Coy. Company Commanders. A Coy. Capt. J.H. LENNON B.Sc. M.C. B Coy. Capt. R.E. EDWARDS. Education Capt. M.C. HOODLE M.C. Assumed duties of Battn. Educational Officer. 2Lt. FILLINGHAM & 8.D.R. Chamberland 2 O.R. & C.E.S. Lt. G. HARNETT - 2d LAW & 14. O.R. Mayes ex from T.M.B. Lt. HUTTON joined the Battalion.	
	15.		The Battn. represented the Division at the XXII Corps Cross Country Run - held at THULIN near MONS. The team, the majority of the Battalion went well on Lorries. Result of Run. 52d Div 1st. 4 Div. 2d. These two teams to represent the Corps in the 1st Army run.	

Army Form C. 2118.

WAR DIARY
or
INTELLIGENCE SUMMARY.
(Erase heading not required.)

Place	Date	Hour	Summary of Events and Information	Remarks and references to Appendices
BINCHE	FEBRUARY 1919.			
	16.		Battalion Church Parade.	
	17.		The Battalion Band played at the KURSAL in the afternoon.	
			16. O.R. demobilised.	
			1 O.R. proceeded on leave U.K.	
	18.		Nil.	
	19.		Nil.	
			14. O.R. demobilised.	
	20.		do.	
			18. O.R. do.	
	21.		The Battalion met the 1st Battn. Somersets in the final of the Divisional Rugby Competition. The Battalion won by 12 points to Nil after a very fine game.	
	22.		5. O.R. demobilised.	
			3. O.R. demobilised.	
	23.		2. O.R. demobilised.	
	24.		Lt. T. HUTSON C. to U.K. prior to going 1st Battn. to INDIA.	
	25.		1. O.R. on leave.	

Army Form C. 2118.

WAR DIARY
or
INTELLIGENCE SUMMARY.
(Erase heading not required.)

Place	Date	Hour	Summary of Events and Information	Remarks and references to Appendices
FEBRUARY 1919	26		I.O.R. No. C.C.S.	
	27		The Cross Country team went to VALENCIENNES to the 1st Army races.	
	28		The Battalion representing the XXII Corps won the 1st Army Championship Cross C.C. Runners. 5 of the Batt. team ran in the first ten. Sergt. GARSIDE + Pte BASTOW of the Batt. finishing first + second.	
BINCHE				

SECRET

O off i/c No 2 Sub Sect.
    RECORD OFFICE.
    British Troops in France & Flanders
    WIMEREUX.

Off i/c No 2 Section
    RECORDS
    YORK.

Herewith War Diary of Bn from

1st June — 8th JUNE 1919.

being date Bn left for ENGLAND

Please acknowledge to
    c/o Depot
    The Barracks
    HALIFAX

D.G. Wilkinson Capt
    & a/Adjt
    for Major
2nd Bn DUKE OF WELLINGTON Rgt

16/6/19

2 W Riding 94
57

WAR DIARY   2nd Bn DUKE OF WELLINGTON'S Regt

Place	Date	Time	
BINCHE (Belgium)	June 1st	1000 Hours	The Bn sent a presentation party of 1 NCO & 6 men to a presentation parade on the occasion of the 4th Bn presenting a Union Jack to the town of BINCHE. The presentation was made by Lt. Col. PAWLETT. D.S.O. 6m d.g. 4 D.w. at this time.
	2nd		Orders received that the Div would leave for ENGLAND between the 6th & 13th of the month
	4th		Orders received that the Bn CADRE would entrain on the 6th inst
	5th		Day was spent in packing equipment & stores ready for entrainment
	6th	2200 hrs	Bn left BINCHE. Transport loaded at 1630 hours & Bn entrained at 2100 hours. train departed at 2200 hours. Entraining Strength 5 offs & 60 O.R's (Officers entraining were Major F.H.B. WELLESLEY (in command) Capt. D.G.R. BIGHAM M.B.E (Adjt) Lt & Q.M.C. SHEPHERD. M.B.E. D.C.M. (Q.M) Capt. T. COOKE D.S.O. M.C. Capt. J.R. COLSON M.C. M.M.
ANTWERP	7th	10:15	Bn arrived at ANTWERP & unloaded vechile, & proceeded to Embarkation camp. Orders were received Bn would embark next day.
	8th	1630	Bn CADRE sailed from ANTWERP for TILBURY leaving the advance party on entrained on the 6th inst.

www.ingramcontent.com/pod-product-compliance
Lightning Source LLC
Chambersburg PA
CBHW082008220426
43670CB00014B/2577